Dilemmas of Trust

Every human relationship, whether between lovers, friends, family members, or colleagues, raises questions about trust. When we trust, we take for granted that others are not out to harm us; we relax and feel safe. When we distrust, we are fearful; we withdraw and try to protect ourselves. In *Dilemmas of Trust* Trudy Govier explores the profound effect trust and distrust have, not only on our relationships but on our outlook on the world and our sense of self.

Trust facilitates communication, love, friendship, and cooperation and is fundamentally important to human relationships and personal development. Using examples from daily life, interviews, literature, and film, Govier describes the role of trust in friendship and in family relationships as well as the connection between self-trust, self-respect, and self-esteem. She examines the reasons we trust or distrust others and ourselves, and the expectations and vulnerabilities that accompany those attitudes.

But trust should not be blind. Acknowledging that distrust is often warranted, Govier describes strategies for coping with distrust and designing workable relationships despite it. She also examines situations in which the integrity of interpersonal relationships has been violated by serious breaches of trust and explores themes of forgiveness, reconciliation, and the restoration of trust.

By encouraging reflection on our own attitudes of trust and distrust, this fascinating book points the way to a better understanding of our relationships and ourselves.

TRUDY GOVIER is an independent philosopher who lives and works in Calgary, Alberta. Her other books include *Social Trust and Human Communities* (McGill-Queen's), *God, the Devil, and the Perfect Pizza*, and *A Practical Study of Argument*.

DILEMMAS OF TRUST

TRUDY GOVIER

McGill-Queen's University Press
Montreal & Kingston · London · Ithaca

© McGill-Queen's University Press 1998
ISBN 0-7735-1797-9 (cloth)

Legal deposit fourth quarter 1998
Bibliothèque nationale du Québec

Printed in Canada on acid-free paper

This book has been published with the help of a
grant from the Humanities and Social Sciences
Federation of Canada, using funds provided by
the Social Sciences and Humanities Research
Council of Canada.

McGill-Queen's University Press acknowledges
the financial support of the Government of
Canada through the Book Publishing Industry
Development Program for its publishing
activities. We also acknowledge the support of
the Canada Council for the Arts for our
publishing program.

Canadian Cataloguing in Publication Data

Govier, Trudy
Dilemmas of trust

Includes bibliographical references and index.
ISBN 0-7735-1797-9

1. Trust. 2. Interpersonal relations. I. Title.

BF575.T7G76 1998   177   C98-900800-2

This book was typeset by Typo Litho
Composition Inc. in 10/12 Palatino.

Contents

Preface

When I began to explore the topic of trust in 1989, I found that there were few comprehensive works on the subject. After several years of study, I started to write a large book intended to explore issues of trust and distrust in personal, social, and political contexts. This combination of themes proved to be unmanageable, and as a result, I divided my material. My reflections on social and political trust may be found in *Social Trust and Human Communities* (McGill-Queen's 1997); those on self-trust and trust in personal relationships constitute the present work. Both books are secular in orientation.

In this book I offer an account of interpersonal trust and distrust, seeking to describe and explain how and why these attitudes so profoundly affect our personal relationships. Because they underlie our interpretations of what we and others say and do, trust and distrust do much to determine our conceptions of ourselves and others. The book also includes an account of self-trust. I argue that there are close logical parallels between self-trust and interpersonal trust, and that self-trust is essential for personal autonomy. Broadly descriptive considerations about family, friendships, and self-trust occupy the greater part of chapters 1 through 6. In these chapters I make no claim to offer an original account of friendship, family, or the self. Rather, I have used the work of others to state a plausible contemporary view and have then tried to show, against the background of that position, the important roles played by trust and distrust.

Friends and acquaintances who heard about my work on trust urged me to treat the topic of "values." When is trust reasonable and appropriate? When not? When do we trust too much or too little? When we judge – as we often do in ordinary life – that someone is too trusting or too suspicious, what is the basis for such a judgment? These issues are treated in chapter 7, where I explore the kinds of evidence we appeal to when we judge people to be more or less trustworthy and the reasons we may have for deeming people to be "paranoid" or "gullible" or "too suspicious." Philosophical interviews about sensitive particular cases formed part of the basis for this work.

Although I remain impressed by the significance of trust in our relationships and its largely unremarked centrality in our lives, I do not argue that trust is always good or that distrust is always baneful. Whether trust or distrust is the more appropriate attitude, morally and epistemically, depends on evidence and circumstances.

Distrust is sometimes warranted. Yet it can become a practical problem in any relationship that we cannot sever at will. In chapters 8 and 9 I examine some phenomena of distrust and consider strategies for coping with it or trying to restore trust. Several of the approaches discussed are drawn from current work in the area of conflict resolution (sometimes known as "alternate dispute resolution"), which I have explored over some years through workshops, conferences, background reading, and my own experience as a volunteer mediator. Chapter 10 treats themes of forgiveness and reconciliation, raising the question of the relationship between trust and forgiveness. Some modest conclusions are stated in chapter 11.

In addition to appreciating the trust that we take for granted and the trustworthiness that makes it possible, we can usefully reflect on many absorbing and important dilemmas of trust. In such dilemmas we do not know whether to trust or not; neither trust nor distrust seems to be the appropriate attitude, and we know too much to be agnostic. I make no pretence here to solve such dilemmas, but I do attempt to describe them clearly and to understand their implications. Because of my conviction that attitudes of trust and distrust should be of interest to a broad audience, I have tried to write in an accessible way, seeking to keep scholarly notation and intricacies of back-and-forth argumentation within reasonable limits. Most examples are drawn from everyday life, politics, literature, or contemporary films.

I am grateful to the Social Sciences and Humanities Research Council of Canada for a generous grant (#410–89–0199), which supported my work on this topic between 1989 and 1994. It was because of this grant that I was able to employ James D.D. Smith and Donald Conrad, who gave able assistance with research in 1989–90. I want to thank them both for their enthusiasm and hard work. In addition, I am grateful to Helen Colijn, Janet Keeping, Bev Delong, Hank Stam, Janet Sisson, Doreen Barrie, Martha McManus, Beverley Kent, Bela Szabados, and Risa Kawchuk for moral support and helpful comments about various phases of this research. Members of Calgary's "public philosophy" group, the Apeiron Society for the Practice of Philosophy, provided a stimulating audience at several stages, and I would like to thank Petra von Morstein for her role in sustaining that group and inviting me to speak to it. On occasions when portions of this study have been presented in Vancouver, Victoria, Amsterdam, Warsaw, Regina, and St Cloud, Minnesota, questions and comments from members of the audience helped me to develop my ideas. Those of David Boyer at St Cloud State University were especially memorable and insightful. I have also benefited greatly from published works, especially those of Annette Baier, Sissela Bok, H.J.N. Horsburgh, Diana Meyers, Doris Brothers, C.A.J. Coady, Primo Levi, Roger Fisher, Francis Fukuyama, Steven Shapin, Robert Putnam, Niklas Luhmann, and Mark Snyder.

Parts of this book have been published previously in *Cogito, Hypatia*, the *Journal of Social Philosophy*, and the *International Journal of Moral and Social Studies*. I would like to thank the editors of these journals for permission to use some of that material here.

Most of all, I am grateful to my husband, Anton Colijn, for his prolonged moral support. He has almost certainly heard more than he would have wished about trust and distrust and the vicissitudes of my prolonged saga of reading, interviewing, reflection, writing, and editing on these subjects. At one point, he had heard so much about my pet project that he dreamed he was reading a newspaper article about trust. In his dream the newspaper reported that scientists had discovered that there was far more trust in the world than people had previously thought. It was as though, unexpectedly, there had turned out to exist an additional reserve of a treasured substance. The discovery of "more trust" was like finding gold. This dream could be interpreted as a metaphysical parody of my ideas. I do think that there is more trust in the world than we often suppose, although I do not, of course, believe that it is a commodity like gold. I would indeed argue that there is more trust – and more trustworthiness – than we commonly suppose; not because trust has been buried in a previously unknown location, but because we tend not to notice when things go right.

It would be rash to put forward as definitive any analysis of a topic as broad and fundamental as that of trust and distrust, and I make no such claim here. If my work interests others and helps to inspire further reflections on the subject, I will consider my energy well spent.

Dilemmas of Trust

CHAPTER ONE

Why Trust?

Whether it is between lovers, friends, family members, or colleagues, every human relationship features some degree of trust or distrust. And attitudes of trust and distrust have a profound effect on our relationships, influencing almost every dimension of them. When we trust, we take for granted that others are not out to harm us, that they are basically well intentioned, that we have nothing to fear from them; we can relax and be safe, enjoy each other, or work towards common goals. If we distrust, we are not at ease. We are fearful and suspicious and feel a need to close off, try to protect ourselves, or control the relationship.

For all this, there are not many books on themes of trust and distrust.[1] One reason may be that these attitudes are rather elusive and hard to define. Trust seems warm and fuzzy, somehow good, perhaps a little Pollyannaish; it is nice to be a trusting soul, but risky. People who are trusting may be nicer in many ways than suspicious and cynical ones. But one may suspect that they are rather simplistic in their thinking, that they are gullible and naive and too accepting of others. It is difficult to generalize sensibly about trust. We trust this person; we do not trust that one. We trust a friend; we want a doctor whom we can trust; we do not trust politicians. But what more can be said? Why think further about trust and distrust?

For me, at least part of the answer is that trust and distrust are endlessly fascinating. So, at any rate, I have found them to be, and my hope is to inspire others to share my fascination. Because trust and distrust so strongly affect our responses and attitudes to other people, thinking about them sheds a useful light on many relationships. Trust and distrust affect what we come to believe about other people and how we interpret their actions and intentions. Those other people affect us through the ways we think about them and respond to them.

We have feelings and beliefs about another person, we have a sense of who that person is and what sort of person he or she is, and it is on the basis of this construction of another person that we engage with him or her. Our attitudes of trust and distrust affect our outlook on the world and our sense of ourselves and others. They are centrally important in personal and collegial relationships, affecting the people we live and work with, the quality of our interactions with them, and our broad sense of human nature and the social world. We judge and allocate trust differently. Some people are more trusting, others less so; some people trust mostly themselves and their immediate family, whereas others quite readily trust acquaintances and strangers. For all of us, however, it is impossible to cope in this world without trust.

With trust, we have, and continue to build, a positive picture of another person. Small omissions such as lateness, missed appointments, forgotten birthdays, and occasional tactless remarks we will write off as just that – minor matters not implying that the other is unfeeling or does not care about the relationship. When there is trust in another person, a basically positive picture continues to strengthen itself, and a significant rupture or departure will be required to undermine that picture. With distrust, just the opposite occurs. We look at a person with some suspicion, feel nervous, and tend to see every omission and possible insult as evidence that the other is a bad type who does not care whether he or she hurts us or not. We construct a negative image, and that image has a strong tendency to perpetuate itself. Understanding our own attitudes of trust and distrust – where they come from and how they affect our responses to other people – helps us understand our relationships and, through them, the other people who are our lovers, friends, and colleagues.

Self-trust also merits attention. Just as we construct a picture or image of another person, we form one of ourselves. If we trust ourselves, we have positive beliefs and expectations about what we can do – about ourselves and our competence – and a sense that we can rely on our own judgment. This self-trust is a fundamental aspect of our persons and personalities. It is essential for our self-esteem, self-respect, and personal autonomy. Like trust in others, self-trust should have a foundation in reality. It should be based on evidence, on our own experience of what we can do and who we are. Self-trust is an essential aspect of functioning as a person. To lead an autonomous and meaningful life, we need to reflect on ourselves – on our experiences, our memories, our talents, goals, and desires. To do so, we must be able to trust our own sense of who we are, where we are in the world, and what is happening around us. We need a basic, implicit confidence that we are worthy and competent creatures with a capacity to make sensible, independent judgments. Thus self-trust is fundamental to our attitude to ourselves, and understanding it offers fresh insights into our attitudes to ourselves and others.

We tend to take trust for granted: when the people whom we trust do as we expect, we barely notice the fact. To understand the nature and importance of trust, we have to make explicit what is characteristically implicit. In reflecting on trust, we make ourselves aware of tacit feelings and expectations – vulnerabilities that we have always had, but never much noticed before. One reason that we underrate the significance of trust is our strong tendency not to notice it until it breaks down. The "normal" situation, we assume, is the one where things go as we expect – where people act reliably, institutions function as anticipated, and our trust is not betrayed. In such situations, husbands and wives are supportive and loyal, children go off to school to encounter reasonably good teachers and return home at the expected time, cars stop at the red light, dentists do honest, competent work, and so forth. When these things happen as we assume they will, we do not think much about that fact. We take it for granted. The husband was not a betrayer; the child was not abducted; the teacher gave a good and appropriate lesson; the friend was not a spy; the visitor did not steal the silver forks; the policeman was helpful; the restaurant food was safe and delicious; the garbage was picked up at the right time; and so on. Here the words "and so on" may be the most revealing of all: the range of our trust is wide, and indefinitely so.

We do not normally notice how many people have to be well intentioned and competent, have to care about each other and function as they should, for things to go right. Ordinary people notice, and remember, when something goes wrong, upsetting their characteristically unconscious expectation that things will usually go right. There are exceptions, of course. Hobbes argued that competition, greed, animosity, and suspicion were the most significant factors in human relationships, and these were the aspects he expected to find in the social world. His observations lived up to his expectations; in this area, as in so many others, observations turn out to be affected by organizing concepts. Freud regarded apparently benign relationships as underlaid by a lustful unconscious, and he expected in personal and social life the acting out of furious hidden desires. Relatively few people are wholeheartedly Hobbesian or Freudian. In everyday life we tend to trust other people much of the time, and we generally expect smooth functioning, reliability, and loyalty as routine aspects of our social world. Ironically, however, these very assumptions – that people should, for the most part, be trustworthy and that institutions should, for the most part, work appropriately – mean that we are especially shocked when things go wrong. We tend to focus on the striking and disturbing cases where distrust is deserved, where things do not go as we expect. And then this focus works to suggest a negatively biased picture of human nature and human life, one in which at the conscious level we tend to downplay and underestimate the competent functioning and good intentions of other people. Reflecting on the grounds for trust and distrust can help to sort out this tangle of positive expectations and highlighted disappointments.

In so many ways, we depend on other people and are vulnerable to them. And in so many ways, they do not let us down. In complex modern societies, nearly everyone nearly every day implicitly places his or her trust in dozens – even hundreds – of other people when speaking, listening, reading, shopping, banking, driving, cooking, and performing numerous other mundane activities. Trust, sociologists have said, is the "glue of society." We are in this world together. We trust; to a very large extent, when we interact, we are implicitly trusting. To be sure, things often go wrong, and people can act carelessly and maliciously towards each other. As anyone who reads a newspaper or watches television news is bitterly aware, things go horribly wrong sometimes. But in tolerably well run societies, many things go perfectly right. To understand this fact is illuminating, even inspiring. It helps to set the horror of the television news in perspective, giving us a more positive picture of human nature and the social world.

WHAT IS TRUST?

Trust and distrust are attitudes that affect the way we think, the way we feel, and the way we act. Trusting, we are more likely to let ourselves be vulnerable to others, to allow ourselves to depend on others, to cooperate, to confide. We feel relaxed, comfortable, safe, and at ease. Trust also affects our understanding of other people, our sense of who they are and what they are doing. In fact, it affects our basic conception of human nature and our general sense of what sort of world we live in. Trust is in essence an attitude of positive expectation about other people, a sense that they are basically well intentioned and unlikely to harm us. To trust people is to expect that they will act well, that they will take our interests into account and not harm us. A trustworthy person is one who has both good intentions and reasonable competence. Trust is a relational attitude: one person trusts another, or several others, or a group. When we trust, our positive expectations have two basic dimensions: *motivation* (the other intends to act well and does not intend to do harm) and *competence* (the other knows enough to be capable of doing as required). A trustworthy person is one who has both good intentions and reasonable competence.

Consider, for example, the matter of hiring a babysitter for a young baby, a situation where trustworthiness is of paramount importance. To hire someone as a babysitter is, implicitly or explicitly, to trust that person. She must be of good character – not an abuser, not cruel, not careless or neglectful, dishonest, or mentally unstable. She must be well disposed towards the baby and towards us. If she is willing to babysit, she must want to keep the baby comfortable and happy and to take good care of him. If we trust her to care for the baby, we assume implicitly that that is the sort of person she is – a good type, not someone who would neglect or wilfully harm him. But good character is not enough. Competence matters too: the babysitter has to know how to change a diaper, heat up a bottle, burp the baby, support his head when holding him, lock the doors, call 911 in an emergency, handle telephone messages, and so on. In this explanation, the "and so on" is again highly significant. Our expectations, when we trust, have an open-ended quality; we expect the trusted person to do the appropriate thing, whatever that is in the circumstances. In hiring someone to babysit, we are trusting her – entrusting to her the care of a small and helpless creature whom we dearly cherish. For this entrusting, both character and competence are essential.

Our trust is based on our beliefs, and our beliefs are grounded on evidence from experience. Trust is not pure faith; we need not trust blindly. We may trust a babysitter because we have evidence, based on past experience, about her character and competence. We may trust her because friends or colleagues, whom we also trust, have told us that she is honest and reliable. Or we may depend on a kind of instinctive sense of her character and competence, based on the way she strikes us when we meet her or talk with her. Often we have an intuitive sense of whom we can trust and whom not, relying on a lifetime of experience of human expressions, gestures, and character. One might say, "Her face lit up the minute she came in and saw the baby. I knew she'd be good." Or, "The moment I saw him, I knew I could trust him." Or, "There was something fishy about him right from the start."

Such intuitions are obviously fallible, but we use them anyway. Lacking particular evidence or intuitions, we base our trust on generalizations about what sorts of people tend to be reliable and honest; we may rely on almost stereotypical beliefs – a neatly dressed person is seen as more reliably than a sloppily dressed one, a middle-aged women as more trustworthy than a young man.[2] Some people are more trusting, others less so. Whatever the grounds for our attitudes, they are based upon underlying beliefs about what other people are like and what they are likely to do. When we trust others, we expect them to act well towards us. When we distrust them, we fear that they will act badly.

Trust is a risky business because the people whom we trust can let us down, and we are vulnerable to harm when they do so. It is important to attend to the risks of trust and not to take the simplistic view that trust is always good. Sometimes we trust too easily and risk a great deal in doing so. Our trust is generally based on experience with other people; on the basis of that experience, we construct a characterization or picture of them. But other people are free agents, with dimensions and depths that go beyond our beliefs about them. We never fully or completely know another human being. Nevertheless, when we trust, we feel confident that another's words and gestures represent that person as he or she is; we do not feel that we have to probe a superficial appearance to make estimations as to what the real person is like.

Trust is a presumption of meaningful communication: we must believe that the other says what he means and means what he says. Listening to another is usually worthwhile because we assume that we can believe much of what he says; speaking to another is worthwhile because we credit her with the capacity and desire to hear what we are saying and to understand it. Given this centrality of trust in communication, we may also expect it to be pivotally important in education. To learn, a student must believe (most of) what the teacher tells him or her and must have some confidence in the teacher's values. That is to say, a workable student-teacher relationship presumes a considerably degree of trust. In developing our self-trust, we are dependent on responses from other people. And for those responses to confirm us, we must trust that they are genuine.[3]

For all this, trust remains risky. There are always surprises, some of them nasty. The other person may do something we did not expect or fail to do something we did expect. He or she may fail to cope in difficult circumstances, let us down, hurt us, or betray us. When we trust, we are vulnerable to those possibilities: we take a chance. Sometimes we are unaware of these risks, comfortable and even complacent in our assumption that things will be all right. When we trust – even though we know, at some level, that things could go wrong – we confidently assume that they will not. If we trust, we believe the risk is small, and we are prepared to accept it.

Trust, then, is an attitude that affects our emotions, beliefs, actions, and interpretations. When one person trusts another, he or she has a positive feelings towards that other person and positive expectations about what the other is likely to do. Trust is based on the belief that the trusted person is competent and well motivated and therefore likely to live up to these positive expectations. Consider the case of Juan, who trusts his wife, Elena, but has been told by a friend that she has been seen leaving a fancy restaurant with another man. Because he trusts her, he does not leap to the conclusion that she must be having an affair; he does not immediately assume the worst. Instead, Juan gives an innocent meaning to the event. Perhaps Elena had a business appointment; perhaps she was visiting with a relative or an old friend who had arrived from out of town. It is even possible that she was not lunching out at all, and the story was based on a mistake. If Juan were suspicious of Elena, he would react differently, crediting the story immediately, leaping to the conclusion that she was having an affair, and beginning to wonder how long this had been going on and what he should do about it.

As this example illustrates, trust involves vulnerability to harm. Clearly, a trusting husband, like any other trusting person, could be wrong. If the lunch date was not so innocent, if he later discovered that his wife was indeed having an affair, Juan might someday come to regret his trusting attitude and assumption that the lunchtime tête-à-tête meant nothing. Trust brings risks which the trusting person accepts. However, the fact that trust is risky should not be taken as a reason for generalized or systematic distrust. There are many arguments against a stance of systematic distrust, which has risks and costs of its own.[4]

ETHICS, TRUST, AND EVIDENCE

Trust facilitates many good things – communication, love, friendship, partnership, cooperation, knowledge, and economic development, to name just a few. For this reason, we have a tendency to think that it is good. Should we "moralize" trust, assuming that it is always something good? Is trust always *better* than distrust?[5] At one level, this question can be answered simply with a firm no. We may trust too easily, on the basis of weak evidence, with no evidence at all, or in the face of all evidence. And we may bring harm to ourselves and others by doing so. In such cases, trust is not the best attitude to have; distrust or neutrality would clearly be better. When much is at stake, the fact that things "seem all right" or that we "have a good feeling about that person" is simply not an adequate basis for trust.

Consider, for instance, the case of Betty and Alfred, middle-aged parents whose son Bob was killed in a skiing accident. They were still grieving for him when Carol arrived at the door of their suburban home with a small child, Nicholas, in tow. She said that she had been Bob's girlfriend and this child was their grandson. The parents had never heard of Carol or Nicholas, although the boy was old enough to have been born before Bob's death. Nevertheless, they accepted the story without question and welcomed them into their family. They gave Carol ample financial support and came to prefer Nicholas over their two other grandchildren. Betty and Alfred trusted Carol completely, on no evidence at all, in quite peculiar circumstances. They did so at a time when they were emotionally vulnerable and much was at stake. Was their trust "good"? Did they employ sound judgment when they trusted in these circumstances? I think that, without rejecting Carol and Nicholas outright, Betty and Alfred would have been more responsible to investigate the connection and ask some questions before taking them into the family. Why had they never heard of Carol before? Did any of Bob's friends know her? Could any friends vouch for the relationship? Where was Nicholas born? Was Bob's name on his birth certificate? If Carol had been Bob's girlfriend, how long had he been involved with her before Nicholas was born? Was there any evidence that Bob had believed Nicholas was his child? In this case, unquestioning trust seems naive and unwise to the point of being irresponsible, especially given the emotional impact of Nicholas on them and their other grandchildren. An initial suspension of judgment and a process of seeking further information would seem more appropriate.[6]

There are many ways, small and large, in which we naturally trust strangers. In many contexts, if we did not do so, life would be difficult indeed.[7] But there are also, quite rightly, ways and contexts in which we are taught not to trust strangers. Children learn not to accept candy or rides from strangers and not to go into homes or rooms with adults whom they do not know. They are at risk of assault and abduction, and they have to be taught not to trust. Most women retain such lessons for a lifetime: feeling nervous if they accept rides from men they do not know and refraining from walking alone after dark because they fear that some man might attack them. If a young woman accepts a ride from a man late at night and accompanies him to his apartment, though she has never met him before, she is trusting a stranger. She may or may not be assaulted as a result, but she is taking great risks. Such trust is careless and foolish, not virtuous. To say this is not to fall into the trap of blaming the victim. Obviously, any assault is the responsibility of the assailant, and he is properly blamed for it. If a young woman is assaulted after accepting a ride unwisely, it remains that case that she is the victim; she did not wrong the other, and she is not blameworthy for the assault itself. Nevertheless, her trust was careless and ill-founded, and she trusted foolishly.

Trust is necessary for relationships and society to work smoothly. We need it to cooperate, and only through trust can we rely on each other for knowledge. Trust has been called "social capital," a social good that facilitates economic growth and development. Trusting, we see the best in other people. The fact that trust is in so many ways presupposed by other goods makes it natural to think that trust itself is good. And talk of the benefits of trust in society, which are necessarily couched in general terms, may seem to imply that it is always good.[8] Another factor which may make this assumption seem plausible is that, from an internal point of view, the position of one who trusts, trust cannot be separated from value judgments. When we trust others, we expect them to do what we regard as good or beneficial and not to do what we consider evil or harmful.. Thus we trust our friends to be sympathetic and responsive, to keep us company, to be dependable about arrangements; these are things we regard as necessary and good. We trust our friends not to betray confidences or gossip about us behind our backs; these are things we consider harmful and bad. Each person makes judgments of trust and distrust with reference to his or her own values. When we distrust people, we suspect or fear that they will do things harmful to us, things we regard as wrong. A woman who distrusts her babysitter enough to set up a surveillance mechanism fears that the babysitter is neglecting or abusing the child.

Remarks such as "You can trust that treasurer to confuse the accounting every time" or "You can trust a specialist to leave out everything important" are ironical. Needless to say, we do not want treasurers to confuse the accounting or specialists to omit important matters; in such comments we express our belief that they will nevertheless do so. What is meant is that we can expect these people to make mistakes; we can (also ironically) "count on" them to do something unwanted.

Trust is a necessary condition of many other good things, and each of us, from his or her own point of view, makes judgments of trust from the perspective of expectations of benefit and harm, based on personal values. These phenomena suggest that trust is a "good thing." And indeed, it often *is* good, being in many cases based on understanding and a reasonable and flexible open-mindedness, and generally expressing a positive attitude towards other people. Other things being equal, trust is a good; other things being equal, an attitude of trust is preferable to one of distrust. But other things are not always equal. In some contexts, and with some people, it is necessary and right to be suspicious.

In a trusting relationship there are two sides: the one who trusts and the one who is trusted. Ideally, each person trusts *and* is trusted in turn. Within a relationship, trust is less risky when the trusted person is *trustworthy*. A trustworthy person is one who can be counted on to be reliable, consistent, loyal, and dependable. When we count on someone trustworthy, that person does not let us down. Suppose that John and Michel are friends; each trusts the other, and both are trustworthy within the relationship. From the point of view of trust, their relationship would seem ideal: each trusts the other, and each is trustworthy so far as his actions towards the other are concerned. Neither puts the other at risk; each can count on the other; neither is likely to betray the other. John and Michel can be open to each other, talk easily together, readily understand each other, make and keep arrangements, and work and play together. When small things go wrong, their relationship is not jeopardized. Mutual trust enables them to ride the bumps. If John fails in a small way – misses an appointment or neglects to repay a small loan – Michel does not infer that John is disloyal or uncaring; he simply assumes that something has gone wrong. John forgot, was too busy, or was preoccupied with other things; Michel knows that John is his friend, and he can accept that John has other things on his mind too. All this suggests that Michel and John have a good relationship and that their trust is mutually beneficial and a good.

Relationships really do go better with trust; in fact, most go very badly without it. But praise for trust cannot be unqualified: there are moral caveats. When we think of a trusting relationship, the positive moral tone of the word "trust" suggests a benign context. In the story just told, John and Michel probably sound like nice people because of the way the trust between them is described. John will trust Michel to do things that he, John, thinks are good, and Michel will trust John on the basis of his own values. If the two men have a close, trusting relationship, whether it is a friendship or a business partnership, they probably share many values; this much can be inferred from the story so far. But all this says nothing about who John and Michel are or what they are doing. If the two men are bank robbers, terrorists, drug traders, or pedophiles, the trust in their relationship is not a social good. It serves their own relationship and projects and might be deemed good with reference to their values and goals, but it will only facilitate their harming other people. In such a case, it is misleading at best to think of the trust between the two as contributing to "social capital" – that general availability of social connections which facilitates knowledge and economic development. If John and Michel are drug dealers, then the fact that they have a smoothly working partnership, based on mutual trust and trustworthiness, is so much the worse for the rest of us.[9]

Disturbing cases of trust and trustworthiness are described by Primo Levi in his moving book *The Drowned and the Saved*. Levi writes of Auschwitz, noting that the history of the camps has been recorded almost exclusively by those who, like himself, never fathomed the bottom. He suggests that it was the "worst" people who were the fittest and who survived the camps; the "best" all died. To bear life after the camps, Levi suggests, victims have amended their memories so that the most painful things are screened out, fashioning for themselves a kind of consolatory truth. He discusses various forms and degrees of collaboration in the camps, taking care not to blame anyone for what they did under such utterly desperate circumstances. Many prisoners were craftsmen accustomed to take pride in doing good work. They were employed in the camps, where some did their jobs well, thus preserving for themselves a degree of identity and self-respect, while at the same time contributing to the appalling death system. Some prisoners, a "special squad," were *entrusted* with the running of the crematoria. These people were regarded by the German camp administrators as *trustworthy* in their jobs; they were *trusted* to continue in their "good work." Of such people, Levi comments that love for a job well done is a deeply ambiguous virtue.

The use of such words as "trust" and "entrust" in the context of Auschwitz is jarring because we are inclined to use "trust" according to our own values, and we do not value the efficient running of these camps. From the point of view of German camp officials, these prisoners could be "trusted" to do their job; they were "trustworthy," so far as the internal operations of the camps were concerned. Obviously, such trust and trustworthiness are not to be commended from an external moral point of view in which the efficient organizing and running of death camps are not regarded as goods.[10]

Trust, then, is not always and in every respect a "good thing." It is sometimes a good thing, sometimes not, depending on evidence, the risks, the relationship, and the broader ethical context of that relationship. From his writings, we may infer that Primo Levi valued trust but only in appropriate contexts. Acknowledging the ongoing political violence after the Second World War and reflecting on such horrors as the massive slaughter in Cambodia under the Khmer Rouge, he states that he can see no need for political violence, that any problem can be solved around a table provided that goodwill and reciprocal trust are present. When Levi writes in this way, we find trust in a more familiar context. When we think of it as an aspect of relationships that may facilitate agreements and prevent violence and atrocities, we find it in its natural moral context – facilitating something good – and we deem it good. But that is not to say that either trust or trustworthiness is always, in every context, good.

WHO TRUSTS? WHO IS TRUSTED?

This book is primarily about people trusting other people, as individuals. These cases seem to me to be central ones and likely to be those that we think about first when we hear about problems of trust, and issues of trust. Interpersonal trust is a central factor in friendships, in family life, and indeed in all good working relationships between people. It is also the foundation of social trust, when we trust people as anonymous individuals, in their roles in institutions and groups. Without trust between individuals, we would not have trust within and between groups and nations.

Interestingly, however, it is not only individual people whom we trust. We also speak of trusting and distrusting animals, objects, institutions, nation states, and God himself. Before turning to my main topic, which is personal and interpersonal trust, where the subjects and objects of trust are individual human beings, I will make some comments about these other cases, both because of their intrinsic interest and because they serve to illustrate the wide range of contexts in which we speak of trust and distrust.

Animals

We often think of ourselves as trusting animals. For instance, it seems clear that blind people trust their seeing-eye dogs. Watch a blind person walking with his dog towards a curb. The dog stops; the man stops. The dog moves ahead; the man follows. He trusts the dog to guide him, to see whether there are dangers or obstacles. If the dog goes ahead, the man does so as well, counting on the dog to have made a good "judgment" about the obstacles that lie beyond. Dogs may also be trusted to guard sheep or cattle, or even children and the family home. Horses and donkeys can also be objects of trust. Tourists riding donkeys on mountain paths have to learn that the animals naturally keep to the outside of the path; after some moments of panic, the rider is likely to learn to trust the donkey to know its way and not fall off the precarious path.

A somewhat different, and particularly dramatic, case of trusting animals is that of Charles Russell and Maureen Enns, two researchers from Canmore, Alberta, who spent four months living in a primitive cabin in northeastern Siberia. Although the territory was heavily populated by grizzly bears, Enns and Russell took no guns. Russell argues that when grizzly bears lash out at people in such areas as Banff National Park, they do so only because of the aggressive approach that humans in the area have characteristically adopted. In these places, humans tease bears with food, shoot rubber bullets at them, chase them with helicopters, and wear bear bells that make an annoying sound. Russell says, "I go on trust. These are intelligent animals. If people would put themselves in the bears' position, they might understand them better." He and Enns encountered grizzlies frequently and reported that they were able to keep themselves safe by acting unprovocatively and speaking softly to the animals.[11]

It would appear, then, that animals can be the objects of our trust. Furthermore, there is behavioural evidence suggesting that they can be subjects of trust, that they themselves can trust or distrust. A dog trusts its owner, but does not trust strangers, and so it barks loudly when they approach the house. A horse trusts the girl who usually rides it, but baulks when a new rider gets on. A dolphin trusts one trainer, not another. Still more fascinating is the fact that animals seem, in some contexts, to trust each other. In *Peacemaking among Primates* Francis de Waal describes how chimpanzees groom and stroke each other to maintain peace. He quite naturally sees the animals as seeking to reassure each other; they groom and stroke each other to overcome animosities and conflicts. One might say that they do this to restore trust.[12]

Objects

We speak as though even mundane everyday things can be the objects of our trust. The social philosopher Rom Harre offers the example of a mountaineer and his rope. Think of the man clinging to a rope while he dangles over a cliff. He is counting on that rope to support him. Similarly, a person might trust a life jacket to hold him up should he fall into the water. In Katherine Govier's novel *Angel Walk* a woman living on an island makes her two-year-old son wear a life jacket all summer. The boy cannot swim, and his mother is relying on the life jacket to keep him safe if there is an emergency. At the end of the summer, they leave the island for the mainland, and she throws the life jacket into the lake. It sinks. She had been wrong to trust that jacket: if her son had fallen into the water, the jacket would not have supported him.[13]

We may also think of trusting or distrusting computer hardware or software. A man buys an expensive new computer and the latest software to enable him to do a complex accounting chore. If a number of unexpected things go wrong, he may lose confidence in the system and come to be suspicious of it. The system does not seem to function as it should; it is unreliable. Perhaps there is something wrong with the hardware or the software, or both. In an indirect sense, people are still involved when we speak of trusting such objects as life jackets, ropes, and computers; it would be a mistake to think that we can place our confidence in such objects instead of trusting people. (We might trust a life jacket instead of a lifeguard, but then people manufactured, tested, and distributed the life jacket.) When we assume that an object will serve its function, we are, in effect, assuming that the various people who manufactured and marketed it did their jobs honestly and properly. If these objects do not perform, someone somewhere made a mistake. The complexity of computers is such that mistakes somewhere along the line are quite probable. Any computer user has learned that trust, or confidence, in computers should be qualified, and precautionary measures such as making back-up files should be taken.[14]

The Dead

Would it make sense to trust someone who is dead? The question seems at first a silly one, but it has been raised and taken seriously, and it raises some interesting issues.[15] Trusting means positive expectations about how another's actions will affect us. Expectations bear on the future; trust and distrust are attitudes that look forward. We might naturally think, then, that if the dead are truly and literally dead, they cannot act. And if this is the case, it would seem that they cannot do anything that would affect us and cannot properly be the objects of our trust or distrust. Of course, the matter changes if we assume that the dead are not so in the complete sense, but live on in heaven, hell, or some other realm and are capable of intervening in events on earth. In Charles Dickens's well-known story "A Christmas Carol" Ebenezer Scrooge's old partner, Marlowe, appears from a world beyond the grave to convince Scrooge that he must change his way of life. Marlowe comes back "from death" and talks. Scrooge, terrified and confronted with Marlowe's powers and presentations, does trust him, to the extent of believing him and reforming on the basis of his exposure to Christmases past, present, and future. In this story, being dead does not prevent Marlowe from acting. In fact, his post-mortal status and powers give him a unique authority.

If the dead live on and can affect us, then they can act benignly or malevolently towards us, and it makes sense to trust or distrust them. In this metaphysical framework, questions of whether to trust the dead really do arise. However, for many modern readers, such assumptions will not seem plausible. If we assume, on the contrary, that the dead literally are dead, then it will follow that they cannot act after death. From this viewpoint, it makes no sense to trust or distrust dead people in terms of expecting them to do various things that may affect us.

Nevertheless, people sometimes speak of trusting or not trusting those long dead. One might say, for instance, "I wouldn't trust Kant on sexual morality. After all, he was a bachelor all his life." That is to say that Kant is not to be believed, should not be regarded as a trustworthy source, on matters of sexual morality. The claim is that when Kant speaks to us about sexual morality, he is not to be believed because he lacked the necessary experience to write about this topic. Kant does speak to us, though not in the metaphysical manner in which Marlowe spoke to Scrooge. Though dead, Kant speaks to us through his writings, and because this is so, for those of us who read him, issues of trust may arise.

Consider another example. A grandmother dies and leaves a will in which nothing is provided directly to her grandchildren; she is relying on their parents to make arrangements for them. The question then arises as to whether this will was a sound and appropriate one, whether her arrangements were realistic. One of her children might express confidence in her mother, saying that she could nearly always be *trusted* to do the right thing. But the reference is to actions the grandmother took before her death. What lies in the future is the impact of the will and how her adult children will handle it. In this sort of case, trusting a woman after she is dead would mean believing that she showed good judgment in the way she drew up the will, that the arrangements she specified would work well.

Groups and Institutions

As for institutions and groups, we often speak of trusting or distrusting the city council, the Hudson's Bay Company, Revenue Canada, the Alberta government, France as a nation state, or the United Nations. We express our confidence or trust in the postal service when we mail a letter; our level of trust in another nation state when we vote for arms and disarmament politics; our distrust in a bank if, having

noticed many errors in its administration of our account, we cancel
that account and move our money elsewhere.

Trust in individuals and trust in institutions often interact and go
together. Consider, for instance, the case of a volunteer mediator
working under the auspices of the Better Business Bureau. Two disputing parties come to meet with her. The situation of mediation calls
for trust: given that they have come for mediation, these parties, who
are in a situation of some conflict and stress, have indicated that they
trust the mediator to be impartial, not to divulge confidences, to
understand them, and to have the skill and motivation to work with
their case. If they reach an agreement, they must trust the mediator to
state that agreement accurately and handle the necessary paperwork
appropriately. If their case has been submitted to a court and has been
resolved in mediation, it must be withdrawn at the right time and in
the right way. Disputing parties have enough trust in the Better Business Bureau as an *institution* to submit their case. When they meet the
mediator for the first time, they have to trust her at least enough to
begin; they do this because they trust the surrounding institutions.
Then, as the mediation proceeds, they will build on this trust or lose it
depending on how the mediator acts as an *individual*. Her actions in
turn will be based on mediation training, which has come from
practitioners schooled under the auspices of such *institutions* as the
Alberta Arbitration and Mediation Society or the Justice Institute of
British Columbia. If the mediator is not trustworthy as an individual,
the disputing parties are likely to lose confidence in the Better Business Bureau and related institutions. But if there were no confidence
in such institutions, they would not come for mediation in the first
place. The case illustrates the fact that interpersonal and institutional
trust may depend on each other.[16]

Trust is an attitude based on the past and extending into the future;
it reduces the complexity of the world for us, but leaves us with some
risk. It is in all these cases a matter of positive expectations and dispositions: we confidently assume, usually on the basis of partial, not
complete, evidence, that the trusted thing will perform in such a way
that we will not be harmed. When we trust, we assume that competence and appropriate motivations on the part of the agents in question underlie this expected performance. This can be said implicitly of
animals and of institutions (because people function within them),
but it cannot be said of ropes and life jackets or of the literally dead.
In these cases, there is neither competence nor motivation, except
indirectly, through the trustworthiness of people who are capable of
action. When we trust objects, we assume that those objects will function adequately, that they will do what they have been made to do

and what we are counting on them to do; we are, in effect, trusting that people have made them properly. And when we trust the dead, we imply that we can rely on, or count on, what they have left behind – products they created when they were alive.

God

For religious believers, trust in God is paramount. It is a unique and special case, one that is profoundly important and likely, through religiously derived conceptions of human nature, to affect attitudes of trust towards individual people and institutions. For some, belief in a Christian God is reason to trust human beings, whom they regard as creatures made in God's image. For others, such belief warrants acceptance of original sin, and it provides a basis for generalized suspicion and distrust. Religious beliefs have supported inclusive systems, a sense of brotherhood and sisterhood among all human beings. They have also supported exclusive systems, in which a contrast between True Believers and the Others is the basis for suspicion of outsiders. Whatever the effects of religious belief are on our attitudes to other people, there are bound to be some.

In the case of trusting God himself (or herself), trust is closely tied to faith. There are at least three dimensions to this trust. One, a presuppositional dimension, is faith in the existence of God. In order for the question of trusting God to arise, one must believe (and that on the basis of objectively insufficient evidence) that he exists. A second dimension is trust in God as an agent in human history, involving a sense that he is somehow implicated in its direction and meaning. The belief that God exists and has some role in history implies a disposition to interpret historical events in ways consistent with those beliefs, and it may greatly affect the meaning given to those events, as can be seen in Jewish and Christian fundamentalist beliefs about the significance of the establishment of the state of Israel. A third dimension of trust in God is a sense that he with whom one communicates in prayer is a divine force with a role in one's personal existence and the meaning of events in one's own life.

Clearly, such matters are profoundly important for religious believers and affect their attitudes towards human nature and the trustworthiness of other human beings. But such issues will not be explored in this book because they do not arise for agnostics, of whom I am one. Whether God exists or not, we have to conduct relationships with other people, whom we may trust or distrust, and we have to manage our own actions and emotions, which raises questions about our trust in ourselves.[17]

In this book I do not explore issues related to trust in animals, objects, dead people, or God. Questions of social, institutional, and political trust are discussed only insofar as they are inseparably connected to interpersonal trust.[18] My interest here is in trusting ourselves and trusting other people as individuals. Thus the book is about personal and interpersonal trust and distrust, about grounds for these attitudes, and about means for managing distrust and seeking to restore trust, when appropriate.

CHAPTER TWO

The Focus of Friendship

We human beings are naturally interdependent and unwilling to spend our lives alone. Part of being human is needing other humans. To enjoy life, we need to share and construct it with others. We cannot flourish as human beings unless we take an interest in other people for their own sakes, and this we do primarily through friendships. Friendship is not the only relationship where trust is important; attitudes of trust and distrust are highly significant in all human relationships. Nevertheless, it provides an important context for reflecting on the nature and significance of trust, because trust is absolutely central and necessary to it. Trust is certainly possible, and actual, outside friendship. But friendship is not possible without trust.

WHAT IS FRIENDSHIP?

Being a friend is not a fixed role in life. We expect friends to be available to do things, to hear us out, to be loyal, and to provide help or care when we really need them. And we expect ourselves to do the same for them. We count on, rely on, and trust our friends. We ourselves, in the role of friends, are expected and trusted to do various things and to accept various obligations towards our friends. Friendship is an informal, largely undefined relationship that people can negotiate and construct for themselves. Friends have differing relationships, and their expectations of each other also vary.

The fluidity and openness in friendship is one of the things that makes trust between friends so important. There is no determinate list of things a friend should do, no fixed role specifying just what it is to be a friend. We choose what to do with our friends. We trust them to be there for us, to go on liking us, to be loyal, to keep confidences, to share with us, to care for us; and we expect ourselves to do the same for them. But just how much is required is flexible. In thinking of someone as our friend, we trust that person to do the right thing for us and know what that is.

It is no accident that we speak of people *making friends*. Friends find each other, choose each other, and construct a relationship. In making friends, we respond with affection to a whole person. Most fundamentally, we value a friend as a whole person, not because she is witty, athletic, white, Chinese, a Christian, a musician or psychologist, but for the particular person that she is. Friendship is based on affinity and similarity, but also on difference: the chosen friend is different from other people we know and is treated differently. The aspect of friendship most discussed in contemporary moral philosophy is just this: friendship is partial and thus apparently at odds with the impartiality that a moral perspective seems to demand. We cannot love everyone equally or be friends equally with all. In modern industrial societies, most people have between three and seven friends, but between five hundred and twenty-five hundred acquaintances.[1] We may like and enjoy our acquaintances, but a relationship that is merely one of acquaintance is not characterized by mutual care or intimacy, and hence is not a friendship and not necessarily a relationship of trust.

When we develop friendships, we have contacts based on some degree of mutual attraction. We talk together, do things together, come to like each other, talk more intimately, acknowledge each other, and help and care for each other. As friends, we feel a bond, feel committed to each other. We appreciate the fine and special qualities of our friends: one's warmth and patience; another's keen mind, fairness, and sense of humour; still another's idealism and deep generosity. And we feel cherished and valued by our friends, whom we have chosen and who have chosen us. We are born into families and exercise only limited choice as to our co-workers and colleagues, but we choose our friends. When friendship lapses into a sense of tired duty, it is friendship no longer. In a meaningful friendship, there is mutual care and trust. Each friend cares for and supports the other, and receives care from the other in return. Helping the friend, we are at the same time actualizing or realizing ourselves.

Trust that the other person will grow and develop, and that we are able to care for her as she does so, gives us courage to go ahead with projects and activities. Having friends, we can better face and accept the risks in life and proceed confidently. To care for another person, we must be able to see inside that person's world as though we ourselves were inside it and have a sense of what life is like for him or her, what that person is striving to be, and what he or she requires for growth. As friends, we help one another to grow and develop, sometimes nurture and protect, advise or exhort. In deep friendships, we can encourage the striving and development of another person without losing ourselves. We can feel life's triumphs and tragedies in the heart of another and reach out to that heart without diminishing our own lives.[2]

Friends enjoy being together, like each other, and may even love each other. They share confidences and care for one another. Each appreciates and cherishes the other for what he or she is. Friends meet some of our deepest needs. This fulfilment would not be possible were it not that we like or love our friends for themselves, for what they are. If our involvement with our friends were purely self-centred, we would not regard them as independently worthy beings; they would not be our moral equals or individuals with whom we could grow and share our experiences. If we were purely self-centred in our friendships, our attitude would be implicitly exploitative. An exploitative "friendship" is not a friendship at all, but only a pretence at one. A friend is another self, an equal self, and we trust our friends to value us in this way. We trust that the social surface of friendship – that it is an affectionate, caring relationship – is also its reality: the friend genuinely likes and values us as persons and is not merely using us for some purpose of his own. True friendship requires valuing and cherishing another person as a separate being with his or her own emotions, needs, insights, and position in the world. If the other person is not seen in this way, he or she is not acknowledged and accepted as a person in his or her own right, but only as an instrument to fill another's needs and desires. The supposed friend who cultivates a relationship only to make better career connections or visit a summer cottage is not a true friend. Neither is he or she a person to be trusted.

Through friends, we extend our experience of the world. We hear our friends' stories and jokes, share their hopes and fears, participate in their successes and failures. Metaphorically as well as literally, where our friend has travelled, we can go. If she is raising a handicapped child, we may gain a sense of the struggles, pains, and joys from years of hearing her experiences. We acquire understanding and appreciation for aspects of life that we have not directly experienced. C.S. Lewis put it this way: "We want to be more than ourselves ... we want to see with other eyes, to imagine with other imaginations, to feel with other hearts, as well as our own."[3] Because we have friends, we experience more of the world. They tell us their stories and their problems. From them we learn a style of response that may be different from our own. In this way, friendship provides an opportunity for moral growth. Through our friends, who share their experiences with us, we gain new insights and a chance to expand and amend our own ideas. A friend can tell us what harms her, what offends her, what gives her courage and hope, what sorts of initiatives she would take. Not only do friends give us company, support, and joy, but they open new windows on the world by providing us with vicarious experience. To a degree, we can become these other selves. Friends enlarge our world, and it is trusting intimacy that makes this enlargement possible.

Our joys and successes are heightened, our sorrows lessened, when they are shared with friends. Human beings naturally seek out others. Aristotle said long ago that without friends life would not be worth living, and this claim holds true for most people today. When things are going well, we seek conversation, fun, and good times with our friends. We seek pleasure in their company, and company for our mutual pleasure. If things go badly, friends are a source of help and consolation, lightening our burden of worry and despair. Solitude is sometimes to be cherished, but its pleasures and consolations exist by contrast. Were we never to have the company of good friends, life would be a misery. Human beings are not by nature solitary. In most prison systems, being put "in solitary" is one of the worst forms of punishment. Our nature is to go outside ourselves, to seek other people to enjoy and love, empathize and identify with, care for and cherish. We need and want these relationships, naturally seek them, and are lonely and miserable if we cannot find and retain them.

In *I and Thou* Martin Buber said: "It is not as if a child first saw an object and then entered into some relationship with that. Rather, the longing for relation is primary ... *In the beginning is the relation* as a category of being, as readiness, as a form that reaches out to be filled, as a model of the soul ... the innate you."[4] Buber emphasized intimate interpersonal relationships, which he understood to be the foundation for truly human development. A child comes into the world with an instinct and need to relate to other human beings. It is the nature of human beings to seek out another: I seek You. The connection is fundamental: without You, there is no I. The Self alone is incomplete, reaching out for relation like a cupped, outstretched hand waiting to be filled. The other person is not an object to use and manipulate, but a living being who can be present to us in a reciprocal relationship. In human encounter that is genuine and complete, we accept and acknowledge the Other. This does not always mean harmony of purpose or belief. We may disagree; we may confront. Intimacy is not the same thing as harmony, and it need not be grounded in sameness. Where we differ in response, in feeling, or in belief, we should acknowledge and communicate those differences. Failing to do so will cut us off from each other.

A special feature of friendship is intimate talk, which clearly presumes trust. Trusting our friends to take an interest, to sympathize, to understand, and not to betray confidences, we tell them what has happened to us, how we feel, what worries us, what excites us. Much of the joy of friendship is due to the fact that with friends we can divulge our feelings; we need not try to keep up a front or make an impression. Confident that our friends appreciate and respond to us for what we are, we feel relaxed. We need not pretend; we can be ourselves. Friends tell each other things that they would not tell just anyone, trusting each other to keep them confidential.

Such exchanges are central and important in friendships, especially those between women. Psychologists refer to such revelations as "self-disclosure": we disclose ourselves when we reveal our experiences, emotions, and needs to our friends. This sort of intimacy is a key to the joy and healing force of friendship. Being intimate is not only an emotional relief; it contributes to our knowledge of our own selves and our own feelings. By talking things over, we come better to know ourselves, gaining an enhanced awareness of who, what, and how we are. From a moral point of view, we can grow and develop. To a friend we may confide anxiety about a child or a concern about personal unattractiveness. In such contexts, we may receive advice or reassurance. But if not, there is still relief in simply telling someone. Joys too are better for being shared. Excited about a new relationship, promotion, hobby, or pregnancy, most people feel the urge to tell someone. Who? Families and lovers, of course, but also – and most significantly – friends.

In his famous essay on friendship, Aristotle claimed that it was the very basis of human flourishing. Plato had regarded friendships as phenomena of the fluctuating, unstable, and devalued world of sensory experience, and as requiring justification with regard to something higher than this mundane life. According to Plato, friendships could be so justified because our love for our friends (based, Plato thought, on their physical attractiveness or beauty) could lead us to the appreciation of beauty in other people and ultimately the eternal form, Beauty Itself. Unlike Plato, Aristotle valued friendship for itself, as it exists in the experienced world. That we seek and value friends testifies to our social nature: human beings do not want to live alone. Aristotle regarded friendship as an expression of human nature and a necessary condition of human society. He distinguished true friendships from those based purely on pleasure or utility. People (for him this meant free men; he assumed that women and slaves were incapable of friendship) could have friends of pleasure, with whom they enjoyed activities, or friends of utility, who were useful to them for some purpose or other. But Aristotle believed that the deepest and best friendships were founded on mutual appreciation of good moral character.[5] In perfect friendships, people support each other in their virtue. Their mutual knowledge of their virtuous characters is the basis for their trust in each other; each can be confident that the other would not wrong or betray him.

The moral seriousness of friendship has also been a theme in some contemporary philosophy. In his book *Living Morally*, Laurence Thomas explains the friendship as a relationship in which friends develop their moral characters and help each other to become the best people they can. Friends are not afraid to "tell it like it is" when they see each other going astray, Thomas says. They work out together how to behave in life, what sort of life to lead, and what sort of person to be.[6] These comments fit many friendships of early adult life, when young people are chosing educational programs, careers, and mates. Struggling to shape their adult lives, many young people exhaustively explore possibilities with others. Often, parents or other adults do not play the key role of listening patiently and engaging in endless discussions; rather, the friends of late adolescence who together work out what is worth doing, how one can do it, and how best to live.

But virtue and the development of moral character and a way of life are certainly not all there is to friendship. It is more than cooperative moral criticism and mutual cultivation of virtue. Shared pleasure and plain fun are also important. Typically, friends enjoy each other's company, being together, and doing things together. They may dine together, swim together, see movies together, sing or dance together, or share other favoured pursuits. Friendship brings joy and pleasure. For all his emphasis on virtue, Aristotle also granted that pleasure was a feature of friendships. In fact, he judged friendships based on pleasure to be more authentic than those based purely on the usefulness of the friend. Where there is pleasure, there is some valuing of the relationship for its own sake and not merely as a means to some further purpose. A friend of utility is one with whom we have friendly relations because she is useful to us – a woman we play tennis with because we both need exercise or another whose well-behaved children make convenient playmates for our own. There is nothing wrong with these useful relationships as such, provided that they are understood to be what they are and not confused with deeper friendships.

Kinships are unalterable and unchosen, making them different from friendship, which is a voluntary relationship. A sibling, aunt, or cousin may become a friend as well, but it is still one thing to be a relative and another to be a friend. Friendship is essentially a relationship of equality, hard to sustain where there are significant disparities of age or status between people. At its best the relationship between parents and their adult children can be wonderful and fulfilling on both sides. But even when it is, it lacks equality. The parent has known the child from birth, has known his or her vulnerabilities and dependencies over a lifetime, and has played a large and essential role in making that child into the adult that he or she has become. The adult child remembers this; so does the parent. In such circumstances, parent and adult child are not, and can never become, psychological equals.[7] To become so, they would have to do the impossible: blot out the past. Between the parent and an adult child there lies always the history of the childhood itself: the memory of long phases of adult authority and care and nearly complete dependence on the part of the child. These factors continue to count against equality, even if an aged parent has become completely dependent for her own care on the child she nurtured decades ago. Our parents can never be our equals, and for this reason even the best relationships between parents and children are not in the fullest sense friendships.

Nor is the relation of neighbour the same as that of friend. We do not choose our neighbours; we move somewhere and find them. If we are lucky, we trust them and enjoy their company, but neighbours as such are not friends. A good neighbour is available for casual chats, occasional help, and recourse during emergencies. We may ask him to fetch the mail and papers or watch the house when we travel; we may do similar small chores for him. Like friends, good neighbours trust each other. But trust between neighbours is restricted to particular functions and is not as full and deep as the trust between good friends. Typically, with neighbours there is little intimacy or deliberate cultivation of shared activities. If we are fortunate, our neighbours are amiable, helpful, and undisturbing. Some of them may become our friends. But to be a neighbour, even a good neighbour, is not yet to be a friend.

The same can be said of the relationship of co-worker. With our co-workers we have important activities and training in common and ample opportunity for contact. We see co-workers daily and may talk and chat with them frequently. Still, the relation of co-worker as such differs from that of friend. It does not typically involve intimacy, shared activities outside work, or choice of relationship. The career ethos of some social groups and the scarcity of prized jobs in professions leads many people to move to find suitable work. Often, we rely on work situations to provide a basis for our social life, which can lead us to seek friends primarily among colleagues. In congenial working situations, we have cordial relations with co-workers. We are certainly familiar with them, and if we are lucky, we trust them in their roles on the job and depend on them to be pleasant and supportive. But relationships with colleagues are largely defined by working roles. For this reason, they are not friendships. To confuse such relationships with friendships is likely to put stress on them and inhibit people from seeking genuine friendships off the job.

This tendency was illustrated in several popular television situation comedies of the seventies. On *Mary Tyler Moore* the central character, Mary, worked in a newsroom. Whenever she gave a party, all her co-workers were invited. One episode even had her say, "You guys are my family." Another popular show of the same period, *WKRP in Cincinnati*, featured a group of people working at a marginally successful rock radio station. It also portrayed camaraderie and closeness among colleagues. When disc jockey Johnny Fever thinks God is talking to him, he turns to co-workers Andy and Venus and eventually to his boss, Mr Carlson, to try to find out what it means and whether he is going crazy. The popular television series *M.A.S.H.*, which dealt with an American medical unit based in Korea during the fifties, was similar. Isolated from family and other friends by war, the central characters were depicted as extremely close friends supporting each other through bizarre wartime tribulations.

But there is a crucial respect in which such depictions are misleading. We rarely choose our colleagues, and when we do, it should not be primarily on the basis of personal liking or affection. We function with them in institutional or professional roles. To develop a relationship of collegiality into one of friendship requires extending it outside the workplace and developing a broader range of shared activity, intimacy, loyalty, and more personal bonds. Whatever the old television sitcoms may suggest, there is a difference between co-workers and friends.

A variation on the colleague is the comrade, or co-worker in the context of a voluntary organization working for a common goal. Such cooperative work provides the context for many activities and important conversations. Comrades share disappointments and accomplishments. In the nature of the case, they are likely to have important beliefs and ideals in common. If they like each other, become intimate, and develop bonds of personal loyalty, the relationship of comrade becomes one of friend. But unless and until this happens, comrades are not friends. They are loyal, not to each other and a special relationship, but to something outside themselves: the common goal.

Letty Cottin Pogrebin, a recent chronicler of North American friendships, cites two other relationships to be distinguished from friendship: pals and confederates. Pals enjoy doing things together, often pairing up for one particular activity. They get together and have fun, but they are not exactly friends. Their relationship is based on common enjoyment of some activity, not on affection and loyalty to each other. Pogrebin gives an example of two men who jogged together for many months, enjoying each other's company and having interesting intellectual conversations. When one moved a few kilometres away, the jogging ceased and so did their relationship. These men were pals, not friends. Confederates are more like friends of utility. They have the sort of relationship where they use each other to a common purpose: the joker and the straight man, for instance, or the popular girl and the shy girl. The popular girl feels more secure flirting when she is with someone else who is no competition in sexual terms. The shy girl acquires status and vicarious excitement because she has a popular "friend." So they go about together, each meeting the needs of the other. Confederates have a friendship of utility.

Horst Hutter, the author of a recent monograph on friendship, maintains that deep friendships are comparatively rare in contemporary industrialized societies because people tend to interact within patterns required by institutionalized roles.[8] The teacher chats with the principal; the professor meets with her student; the dentist asks his patient about his holiday; the boss has lunch with the secretary. When they run smoothly, these relationships may be enjoyable and friendly. But they are largely structured by social roles, and for that reason they do not amount to friendships. When they work well, there is reliability and trust, but not the intimate trust of friendship. Little intimacy is possible in such contacts, and the equality that is characteristic of friendship is often missing from them.

What Hutter suggests is illustrated by the case of Judy and Karen, who did not become friends because social roles kept them apart. Judy first met Karen when her daughter Anna was nine and had to change schools. Anna had been placed in a school for the gifted. Then, though bright and precocious, she was unable to handle its demands and moved back to the neighbourhood school. Judy and her husband had not quite agreed on how to respond to the problem, and Judy was terribly upset. Karen was the principal of that neighborhood school. Judy arrived in her office, nearly in tears, to tell Anna's story and plead for a place for her in this "ordinary" school. Right away she liked Karen, who struck her as warm, sympathetic, and understanding and seemed at the same time highly competent.

She felt that she could have poured out her heart to Karen and would have loved to have her as a friend. But the roles of "principal" and "parent" were the basis of the connection between Karen and Judy, and they worked to kept them apart. Karen had so much authority and responsibility. Though well educated and articulate, Judy could not be Karen's equal in the school, which was the only context where they ever met. She always liked and admired Karen, but was never able to break through the barrier of those roles, parent and principal. How could she ask "the principal" to go to a movie or out for coffee? Over the next several years, Judy saw Karen many times and talked with her occasionally at meetings and on the phone. Their liking was mutual, but they never became friends because social roles interfered.

Modern social life contains many obstacles to friendship: lack of time, social and geographic mobility, feelings of competitiveness and resentment, urban isolation, fears of violence. Hutter finds in industrialized societies widespread attitudes of competitiveness, resentment, and suspicion, which, he says, create a formidable barrier against against civil social relations and still more against meaningful friendships. He fears a developing "commodification" of social relations, wherein colleagues, acquaintances, and even sexual partners come to be treated as *things* that we need to possess. Modern society, he claims, is structured so as to make us need friends and intimacy, but at the same time it reduces our opportunities for friendship and intimacy. We tend to be isolated and occupy ourselves largely with private concerns; these factors work against friendship. But at the same time they make us need trusting friendships more than ever. Hutter suggests that the result is that lonely people set out on a frantic search for sexual intimacy.

But this bleak analysis seems to be based on armchair social criticism rather than on specific empirical data about friends and friendships. Studies indicate that even busy North Americans have several close friends, deeply value their friendships, and would like to spend more time with friends.[9] Despite mobility, stress, consumerism, competitiveness, and resentment, we *do* have friends, and we trust and rely on them. We value our friends and try – sometimes a little desperately – to make time for them. To be sure, there are in modern life many obstacles to the development of friendships. But judging from common experience and the evidence cited in other accounts of friendship, most people succeed in making and maintaining friends and find their friendships extremely rewarding.

Friendship is a close reciprocal relationship between two equal people who care deeply for each other, enjoy shared activities, exchange confidences, know each other well, are loyal to each other, and want to spend time together. It is a chosen relationship: friends together construct their shared activities, their expectations of each other, and their mutual obligations. We find and make friends and friendships, structuring relationships according to mutual desire, need, and possibilities. The relation of friend is different from that of lover, parent or relative, colleague, comrade, neighbour, confederate, or pal. Our friendships nourish and replenish us and are a source of fun and joy. They provide a context for building a meaningful life, our character – indeed, our very selves.

Time is a limited resource that we give to our good friends, and its scarcity is one of the things that makes friendship special. We trust our friends, who are special to us, and part of this trust is our confidence that we are special for them too: they care about us enough to take time for us. As in other relationships characterized by trust, we allow ourselves to be vulnerable in friendship. We open ourselves to another's pains and problems, not only to his or her triumphs. If friendship ends, we are likely to be sorry, often hurt. If it ends in betrayal, we are bound to be hurt. Are friendships worth the risk? The question does not really arise: human beings by nature want, seek, and enjoy friendship.[10]

TRUST AND FRIENDSHIP

Deep friendships illustrate all the central aspects of intimate trust between human beings. This trust is based on shared experience and intimate knowledge of the other person. With such a background, we make the unquestioning assumption that the friend is loyal and dependable. We take it for granted that she will not betray us and that we can count on her to care for us, to help out in emergencies, and to be reliable about minor matters. We have experienced this support already; we feel that we know her, and we expect her loyalty and dependability to continue into the future. This trust involves positive expectations grounded in experience. But those expectations transcend the experience; we assume our friendships will move forward into the future, even when circumstances change. We take for granted that our friends will continue to like us and act well towards us.

Friendships are based on choice, affection, and attachment. With a friend, we have a sense of being liked and valued for ourselves: that is how friends act towards one another. We trust that the friend is not just pretending, that he or she genuinely does like and value us. Trusting, feeling accepted by another whom we regard as a worthy and dependable person, we are assured in our self-esteem. We feel safe and secure with our friends. We have a confident expectation that good, not harm, will come to us from this relationship; friends are people we trust. These positive expectations are based on our sense of the friend's integrity and genuine affection.

We have a positive attitude towards our friends and interpret their actions in a positive way. If a friend makes a slightly ambiguous and possibly insulting remark ("You sure look tired" or "That's a rather dramatic purple vest you're wearing"), we do not take offence. We trust her, feel confident that she likes us, and interpret the comment as non-insulting. Trusting our friends means that we can feel relaxed with them. We are at ease. We are willing to let ourselves be vulnerable.[11] In the context of friendship, trust means that we expect affection, loyalty, and dependability; we feel confident and relaxed; we interpret what the friend says and does in a positive way; we can accept our own vulnerability.

Trust in this sense is absolutely necessary for friendship. If we distrust another person, we are anxious and doubtful about her responses to us; we worry about how she will act; we feel uncertain about what she means and suspicious when minor things go wrong. In the company of a person whom we distrust, we feel uneasy. We cannot relax; we cannot be open and intimate because we are fearful that the amiability of the other person may be on the surface only. Perhaps she seeks to use us, exploit us; perhaps she is only pretending to like us; perhaps she will betray us, let us down. We feel insecure, nervous, perhaps even fearful. Obviously such a relationship cannot be one of friendship. A friend is someone we find affectionate, supportive, and loyal, someone whom we believe will stand by us, someone we trust. We can have many different relationships with people whom we do not trust, but friendship is not one of them.

When we trust friends, there are things we assume that they will not do. They will not deceive and manipulate us, try to exploit us, or use us merely to gain access to other people or material advantages. They will not spy on us – not have detectives follow us, go through our correspondence, or report us to authorities. They will not make fun of us behind our backs, divulge our confidences, steal our money, or sexually abuse our children. Our friends have it in their power to do terrible things to us, and we to them. A relationship of friendship is based on an implicit assumption that such things will not happen. Malicious harm, betrayal, and abuse are unthinkable. Positively, we expect friends to be good for us, to do us good. But even more significant is the negative side: the vast range of possibly harmful things that we feel confident our friends would *not* do.

In trusting our friends, we depend on them. We assume without question that they will care for us by helping when we need support. We count on them to stand by us in moments of emergency or personal crisis, and we expect ourselves to do the same for them. A characteristic example is that of Robert, who was deserted by his wife and left in charge of three distraught children at a time when he was terribly disturbed himself. After months of juggling work, disturbed children, and household chores, he desperately needed a few days to himself. Robert called his old friend Laura and asked her to take care of his children for a weekend. For Laura and her husband, who had two lively boys themselves, the timing was not convenient. But seeing Robert's need, they came through.

Friends exchange confidences, have intimate communications, tell each other things they would not tell just anyone. This confiding requires trust that the other will listen and understand, will continue to accept us, keep secrets, and not use confidential information against us. Talking with friends means being able to tell them what we would not tell just anyone and have our feelings and stories acknowledged. A friend will empathize with us, react, comment, question, perhaps contradict us, work out what things mean, share joys, commiserate, seek solutions for problems. To share intimate confidences with another person means trusting that person to accept and care, to be and remain loyal. The fact that intimacy is essential to friendship means that trust is essential too.

Intimate confidentiality is mutual: we not only tell things to our friends, but we listen to what they have to say. And this too requires trust: openness to the other, acceptance of her as a person in her own right, as one who feels and experiences from her own viewpoint and is honestly sharing her feelings and experiences. As friends, we listen and hear gladly, sharing when we can share, responding with feeling and honesty, differing gently and constructively when we differ. We accept that a friend has her own perspective on the world, and we take that perspective seriously even when it differs from our own. What has happened to her? How did she feel? What did she think about it, and how is she going to respond? We are interested because she is a friend, and listening, we come to know. This openness also requires trust. Our friends are other people whose feelings, beliefs, and situation may differ significantly from our own. Because we accept and care for them, we trust them to tell us the truth as they see it, and we are open to learning from them.

Trust in a friend is based on shared experience and accumulated knowledge over time. With a friend, we have played or worked together, shared joys and pains, lived through triumphs and crises. Trust in a friend is based on accumulated evidence – sometimes a great deal of evidence. Yet for all this evidence, for all the many years we may have known our best friends, we can never say that we completely know them. Changing circumstances may result in changes in people, as in the case of the friend who has been relaxed, affectionate, and flexible but later becomes tough and hard to keep in touch with when she accepts more economic responsibility within her family. People change, and so do circumstances. In trusting a friend, we assume that that she will not cease to like us, that she will never betray us, that whatever she does, whatever she becomes, she will seek to continue our caring relationship. Of course, these are assumptions, and they cannot be guaranteed, but in good friendships we make them without question. In friendships, we reveal ourselves, give of ourselves, let ourselves feel and care. For these reasons we can be hurt or harmed; we are vulnerable. In being friends, we accept this risk. In fact, so completely do we accept our vulnerability that we are unlikely to recognize it at all.[12]

Friendships can tolerate a certain degree of distrust, provided that it is restricted to certain areas. We may know that a friend is careless about small loans, and when we lend him twenty dollars, we may doubt that we will ever get the money back. He is generally a trustworthy person, but careless about money. Or we may cherish a friend and trust that he cares for us, while recognizing that he sometimes overestimates his own ability to get things done and can be unreliable about the details of plans as a result. We like him and appreciate him as a person, but would not trust him to proof-read a lengthy technical manuscript or arrive on time with party treats for sixty people. In good friendships, trust is central and strong. But that does not mean that it must extend to every single aspect of a friend's behaviour. Friendships, after all, are between people who are imperfect and know each other to be so.

According to a *Psychology Today* survey, adult Americans regarded loyalty as the most important quality of a friend.[13] This result points to the centrality of trust in friendship: a loyal friend is one in whom our trust is not misplaced. He or she is the friend we can count on, one who cares for us as the person we are and not for our wealth, reputation, beauty, popularity, or connections. The loyal friend is one who will not betray us or let us down, who keeps our secrets, keeps his or her promises, and comes through for us in emergencies. Trustworthiness in a friend is truly a necessary element for friendship. However entertaining and fascinating he might be, the acquaintance who tells tales behind our back or is pleasant because he wants an invitation to the summer cottage is not a friend. If we know that he does not keep confidences, he will not fulfil our needs the way a friend does. More than anything else, a friend is an equal intimate whom we trust and in whom that trust is not misplaced.

Trust is essential in virtually every aspect of friendship. It is built into our understanding of who and what the friend is. We regard her as affectionate and loving, as one who accepts and cherishes us for what we are. We assume that we are special for her and she for us. We allow her to know us, and she allows us to know her. She does not hide herself from us; when she seems to be open with us, she is really herself, not just someone trying to make an impression. She is what she seems to be; she means what she seems to mean; we need not probe through an appearance to access what might be underneath.[14] If we sense that another person is pretending to be something that she is not, or putting up a kind of screen between herself and us, we cannot experience the very special pleasures of friendship. The open and genuine communication of friendship requires intimacy and openness between people who are freely committed to a frank and honest relationship, a relationship that is special and acknowledged to be so by both parties.

TRUST AND CHILDREN'S FRIENDSHIPS

Children's friendships are based to a large extent on play and shared activities. Until adolescence, they play together more than they talk together. Their friendships depend largely on proximity at home or at school and, where such proximity is lacking, on cooperative support by parents who make arrangements. There is evidence that children as young as six are sensitive to violations of trust and regard trustworthiness as a key attribute of a friend. Peter Kahn and Elliot Turiel interviewed children ranging in age from six to eleven to discover their attitudes about trust and friendship. They asked questions based on stories in which a friend failed to meet expectations.[15] Kahn and Turiel distinguished three categories of trust: moral trust, psychological trust, and social-conventional trust. As they used these terms, moral trust is the expectation that a friend would respect basic moral principles – keeping promises, not lying, not stealing, and so on. Psychological trust is the expectation that a friend will be understanding, kind, and helpful when a person is in trouble and needs support. Social-conventional trust is the expectation that a friend will more or less conform to accepted social conventions – dressing neatly when going out to a restaurant, for instance. These researchers found that the children they interviewed saw moral and psychological trust as essential to friendship. Violations in moral trust – acts such as stealing and lying – had the most serious effect on friendships. Social-conventional trust seemed to be relatively unimportant.

Younger children, ages six and seven, were barely able to say why violations of moral and psychological trust made them unhappy with their friends, but they were unhappy nevertheless. They were inclined to state their reactions in terms of what they liked and disliked. They did not like it if friends lied to them or took toys. They clearly perceived violations of moral and psychological trust as incompatible with friendship. A real friend would play with you if you were sad (psychological trust) and would not lie to you (moral trust). Children ages eight and nine tended to focus on the magnitude of the violation – how many times the friend failed to return a toy, did not show up to play, told a minor lie – and how serious were the consequences. By ages ten and eleven, children were able to discuss how and why the violation of an important expectation affected their relationship with a friend. In all cases, moral and psychological trust were central to their idea of friendship.

My own discussions with some sixty Calgary schoolchildren ages nine to eleven also suggested that trust and trustworthiness are central in children's friendships.[16] Asked what a friend is, many children said a friend was someone to "hang out with," to have fun with, and to talk to. A friend should "have a good sense of humour and be fun." In other words, a friend should be a pal. But there was a more serious undertone too. These children added that friends will cheer you up and help out when you are in trouble. Talk was important. You feel comfortable with your friends: you can talk to them about your problems, and they talk to you about theirs. You like your friends and they like you. You trust them – to keep secrets, to take care of things you might leave with them, to be there when you needed them. A favourite example was that of a pet. If you went on a trip and left your cat with a friend, you could trust him to take good care of it. Asked what was the most important thing in friendship, nearly two-thirds of these children referred to trust.[17] Two other favourite themes – "a friend likes you for yourself" and "a friend will help you out if you are in trouble" – also allude to trust.

Asked what they would do if they could not trust a friend, the children were baffled. The question hardly made sense. If there was someone you could not trust, she was not your friend. If a person was your friend, well, you could trust her – to keep secrets, take care of your things for you, and help in times of trouble. Trust was explained by these children in terms of expectations that were not to be violated. A trusted friend would not steal toys or money and would return borrowed property, care for property or pets if asked, keep promises and

secrets, refrain from gossiping, and tell the truth. She would be someone you could rely on and count on. She would never blackmail you
or threaten you; she would be there when you needed her. She would
like you for yourself, not just for your possessions or connections, or
for what you could do for her.

If a friend acted in an untrustworthy way, you would feel unsafe
and insecure, embarrassed, insulted, and sorry for yourself. You
might even be frightened if you had told this friend things that you
did not want other people to know. Some children said they would
feel "ripped off" and cheated. They would be mad and angry and not
want to be friends any more. One boy said he would feel "cheap,"
thinking that he had too freely given of himself. If he had trusted
someone who was not a good person, well, he had made a mistake;
this would make him feel stupid. He would blame himself, but from
the experience he would learn not to make such a mistake again.
Finding that a friend was disloyal would make a person feel foolish
and inadequate, and perhaps less likely to try to make new friends.
You might feel that there were signs you should have recognized; you
should have known this person was not a real friend, so the fault was
in you. Or you might feel that the reason this false friend did not care
about you was that you were not a worthy person, not worth caring
about. In other words, discovering that you had a false friend would
weaken your trust in yourself.

In their study of adolescent friendships, William Rawlins and
Melissa Holl found that the preservation of established trust was the
"overarching concern." Rawlins and Holl interviewed thirty-two
high school juniors, half boys and half girls, in a small city in the
northeastern United States.[18] They draw an interesting distinction
between teenage *popularity* and *friendship*. Among teenagers, popularity is a matter of public reputation and acceptance. A popular person is one regarded as likeable and desirable as a companion or date.
Friendship, on the other hand, is private and intimate. It is a close relationship between two people who trust each other, have chosen
each other as companions, and acknowledge and accept each other.
Somewhat paradoxically, teenagers who are "popular" may have
few or no close friends. Their public reputation and status may be
intimidating and function to prevent others from becoming close. For
adolescents, friends should above all be trustworthy, accepting, and
positive (not critical) towards their friends. The worst thing that a
friend could do would be to undermine her friend's public image by
telling negative stories in public or revealing secrets.

The girls interviewed by Rawlins and Holl tended to have a best
girlfriend whom they continued to see and remained close to when

they were dating a boy. Boys had male friends, but tended to lessen their commitment to them when they had a girlfriend, who usually became their best friend. These teenagers made distinctions between various types of friendship. When they did so, the depth of trust and the kind of talk in the friendship turned out to be the crucial features. When trust in the friend was less, talk was not as significant to the friendship, and shared activities were relatively more important. In a best friend, a person could have "absolute confidence." The relationship would be intimate and exclusive.

One cannot simply *be* a certain kind of person unless other people accept one as that sort of person. Friendships are crucial for the development of identity during adolescence. Forming one's own identity and self-concept and experiencing intimate relationships with others are closely related. What a person is and how others see him or her are always bound together. In the case of adolescence, with its extreme self-awareness and real embarrassments, the linkage is especially tight. Somewhat paradoxically, the adolescent preoccupation with self leads to extreme deference to the opinions of others. Characteristically preoccupied with themselves, adolescents tend to assume that others share their preoccupation. A girl who has a pimple on her chin feels it and sees it in the mirror. She finds it terribly important, thinks it wrecks her appearance, and assumes that everyone will be looking at her and noticing just this feature of her appearance. Having one pimple, she will be an ugly person with blotchy skin; that is how others will see her. Adolescents tend to put on a show for an audience which they imagine to be large and critical. Uncertain of themselves, moving away from their parents as guides in life, they need positive support from friends. Keeping confidences and refraining from gossip and back-stabbing are especially important in friendships at this stage of life. A friend, a trusted other, supports the self and the self-image.

MEN'S FRIENDSHIPS AND WOMEN'S FRIENDSHIPS

At the psychological level, survival depends on having at least one true and trustworthy friend. In interesting ways the nature of that survival and the nature of friendship itself differ between men and women. Friendship is deeply affected by gender. Most women's friendships are with women, most men's friendships with men. Our society may be heterosexual, but it is homosocial. And men's and women's friendships differ considerably.

Although men and women mingle at school, at work, and in community groups, successful and lasting friendships between them are relatively rare. We seek people who are similar to us when we set about to make friends, and gender still marks vast differences in life experience. For all the lifestyle changes that have resulted from feminism, girls and boys still grow up differently. We find different circumstances even in the same family, class, or school, and respond to people and circumstances in different ways. Gender differences persist in adult life. Being a girl friend is a very different role from being a boy friend. And despite all efforts by men to do more to care for children, being a mother is a quite different thing from being a father. There are exceptions, but in general, women have more in common with other women than they do with men, and men have more in common with other men than they do with women. The pattern of friendships varies accordingly. Sexual attraction between men and women who become close friends tends to press relations of friendship towards romance and sexual intimacy, dramatically altering feelings and expectations. Friendship can survive as a component of sexual partnership, and when it does, the partners have an especially wonderful relationship. All too often, though, romance displaces a male-female friendship, and when the romance fades, the friendship ends.

Men and women tend to have different expectations and values about life and different styles of interacting and talking with each other. In general, women emphasize and value personal relationships more than men do. They want to feel connected, they feel uneasy when they are in a role marked as superior, and they cherish intimate conversation. A woman who is especially successful in her work or with her children is likely to downplay this success when talking with another woman, emphasizing instead various problems and difficulties she is encountering. She is anxious to relate as an equal, not to boast or even appear to be boasting.[19] Women friends like to be together and talk, and when they talk, common subjects are children, feelings, other people, and relationships.

Men, on the other hand, seem to value independence and status more than relationships as such. Many friendships between men are based on shared activities and have a strong "pal" component. Men generally like to joke, exchange anecdotes, have fun, and enjoy sports and other activities. When they talk, they are more likely to share information or discuss women, politics, or sports than to explore feelings, character, or relationships. There is a kind of intimacy that women cherish, which is at the very core of their friendships, and seems rare in friendships between men.

Obviously, such differences between men and women are general, not universal; there are exceptions to the pattern. Some men cherish closeness and have no interest in sports; some women are uncomfortable with much talk and little activity. Some girls and women seek male friends; some men seek female ones. But in general, women's

friends are women, men's friends are men, and the styles of relationships vary with gender. Women's friendships tend, on the whole, to
be more intimate than men's. Right from the girlhood tradition of
having a best friend, women place a high value on relationships with
each other, receiving considerable solace, joy, and support from each
other. They listen and are listened to, support and are supported,
identify, empathize, and care. They expect intimacy and care from
each other, and generally they receive it.

From Aristotle onward, the classic Western literature on friendship
exalts friendships between men. Legend had it that women could not
really be friends. For women, relationships with men would always
come first; women competed with each other to attract men. As
recently as the sixties, this was the prevailing myth about women
friends. Their friendships with each other were less important than
their quest for a man, and thus were vulnerable to relationships with
men. In the fifties and sixties, young women would not go out together for dinner, coffee, or a movie on a Saturday night. To do so was
shameful: we were supposed to have dates. To be seen together in
public on a Saturday evening would reveal the shocking truth that
women had to settle for each other because no man had chosen to pay
for our company.

Under the influence of the feminist movement, all this has
changed. Since the seventies, popular culture, always an expression
of changing lifestyles and ideologies, has shown considerable interest
in women's friendships. Contrary to the classic tradition in Western
philosophy and literature, contrary to early popular culture, contemporary popular culture tends to exalt women's friendships. The film
Beaches illustrates the trend, telling the story of two girls who meet by
chance and become extremely close. They are room-mates in college
and share early work experience. Eventually, when one is fatally ill,
the other cares for her. After her friend's death, she adopts and cares
for her child. A girlhood friendship becomes a deep, lifelong relationship between adult women. Through the daughter, the friendship
survives even death. Another film, *Thelma and Louise*, also shows intimate women friends. They go off on a holiday together, an "escape"
that is to be a major treat for both of them. Louise, the stronger
woman, is fiercely protective of the more innocent Thelma, who is
abused by her husband. When Thelma is assaulted by a man after a
dance-hall fling, Louise intervenes with force in an attempt to protect
her. They begin to fight back together against men who make sugges-
tive remarks and obscene gestures. Eventually they launch into a
criminal campaign. Together they head off on a madcap adventure of
crime, leading to murder and finally joint suicide. The adventurous

and implausible dynamics of their escapades are more characteristic of the violent adventure narratives of heroic men than of women's friendships. But the ideology of the film, which was a popular success, was to exalt the trust and intimacy between women who support and fight for each other – in this case, even to the death.

Ways of Talking, Styles of Intimacy

Men's and boys' friendships are often depicted in contexts of adventure, danger, heroism, and war. Physical tasks and quests are central to the story and men's relationships. These relationships are characteristically less intimate than those of women and girls, featuring little exchange of confidences about career success, family life, or sexuality and tending to pal relationships focused on common activity. Men may talk about computers, politics, sports, and guns and think they have had a satisfying, intimate conversation. Boys and men who want more intimate exchange often seek out girls and women. Particularly fascinating are recent investigations of female and male conversational styles. Men and women tend (with exceptions, of course) to talk in different styles and to different purposes. Girls and women converse in order to make connections with others and seem most comfortable with a relationship of same status, or equality. They seek to share problems and relevant experience and confirm each other's feelings. Most women tend to feel uncomfortable proclaiming their accomplishments and successes. Boys and men, on the other hand, approach conversation with an intense concern for who is up and who is down. They seek to confirm their status on a pecking order. Men are often unwilling to ask for help, take advice, or even to ask directions – much less confess feelings of failure and inadequacy – because that would imply accepting an underdog position.

These and other differences are described by Deborah Tannen in her entertaining popular book *You Just Don't Understand: Women and Men in Conversation.* Tannen, a sociolinguist, studies the way people talk. She argues that men tend to see themselves in a hierarchical social order. Women, on the other hand, picture themselves in a "network of connections" in which "conversations are negotiations for closeness." We want to feel connected and close to people we are talking to, especially when they are intimate partners or other women. When negotiating for closeness, we try to confirm and support each other. We tend to want to reach agreement or consensus, not victory in an argument. Women seek intimacy and connection with others, with whom they want to relate as equal and similar, not superior, beings.

Tannen stops short of saying that the characteristically female style is best. She thinks that both male and female styles serve important purposes. All human beings value and need both independence and intimacy. The male style tends to cultivate and protect independence, and the female style to cultivate and protect intimacy. What we should understand is that these styles differ, have different merits, and serve different functions. If we do not appreciate this fact, we are likely to be extremely frustrated.

Tannen offers enticing examples. "When men change the subject, women think they are showing a lack of sympathy – a failure of intimacy. But the failure to ask probing questions could just as well be a way of respecting the other's need for independence."[20] As far as Tannen is concerned, men and women approach conversation and social interaction so differently that communication between them is virtually cross-cultural. There is as much of a gap in style between men's and women's talk, culturally speaking, as there would be if an English lawyer were talking to an Iranian rug dealer or a Turkish housewife to a Jewish stockbroker. "Instead of different dialects, ... they speak different genderlects."[21]

Talk is an important element in friendship, crucially related to self-disclosure and intimacy. If Tannen is right about the differences between men's and women's conversational styles, then we would expect their friendships to be different too, and this difference would affect the nature of the trust between them. Indeed, this seems to be the case. Stuart Miller, a psychologist, interviewed one thousand Americans and Europeans, searching for "true friendship among adult men." He found so little intimacy, self-disclosure, or meaningful contact that he reluctantly concluded that men simply did not value or cultivate same-sex friendships in the way that women did. Most men had no real male friends, many tending to confuse acquaintanceship, pal relationships, or relations with colleagues with genuine friendship. Another social scientist, Michael McGill, studied five thousand men and women over a ten-year period ending in 1985. He concluded that few men had intimate friendships, and most did not seem to value friendship very much. McGill found that only one man in ten had a friend with whom he discussed work, money, and marriage, and only one in twenty experienced a friendship in which he disclosed feelings about sex or about himself. He regretfully concluded that most men's relations with each other were superficial to the point of being shallow.[22]

The characteristically male style of conversation seems not conducive to deep friendship or to the development of intimate trust. In fact, it would appear to inhibit expressing feelings and attitudes, revealing concerns, and sharing problems. Honesty about a whole range of topics is ruled out; one cannot express anxiety or sorrow or dismay, confess feelings of inadequacy, or accept help and advice. The traditional male sex role presumes a structuring of the world as a competitive place where a man must constantly struggle to prove his mettle and maintain his position. One author concluded that men's talk is really about proving manhood, commenting that conversation between men was "an ongoing pissing contest."[23] The contrast with women's friendships could scarcely be more dramatic.

Many men do not like to discuss problems or feelings, and for this reason friendships between them are less intimate than those between women. But this does not mean men are not close in another way; nor that they do not count on each other for help and support. Trust between men is tied more to action than to talk. When there is talk, it is of a different kind. And talk is not valued as it is between women. A man will expect himself to know somehow, without talk, that his friend is unhappy. When he responds, he will respond by doing something – loaning a car, taking the family out for dinner, or perhaps suggesting that they play golf or paint a fence together.

One older man went to considerable lengths to have a bottle of the very best whisky delivered in a distant city to his friend of sixty years, who was dying miserably of cancer. "I know he won't be able to drink it," the man said, giving careful directions to his granddaughter as to how she should deliver the gift. "It's the gesture that counts." Had he been at his friend's bedside, this man would probably not have been able to talk about death, the end of their friendship, or what his friend had meant to him over so many years since their high school days. And had he tried to do so, his friend, a frail man in his late seventies, would probably only have been embarrassed. Even if never to be consumed, the whisky was something they could manage emotionally. Men do care; they just express their concern in ways other than words.

Adventure films and stories model men's friendships in contexts of danger and adversariality. Men face challenges or enemies together, risk their lives together, and are loyal to the death. The excitement and hazard of adventure or war brings them close together in contexts where life is at stake, so that they can acknowledge their bonds to each other. They work together, are bonded to each other, love each other, try to protect each other, even die for each other. There is trust: these men depend on each other for their very lives. It is a profound trust, but one with an entirely different tone and basis from that of women's friendships, with their intimate talk, exchange of problems and feelings, and expectations of day-to-day small-scale

support. Many men cherish war experience and regard "war bud-
dies" as their best friends ever. These *are* deep, close, intimate, and
loyal friendships among men, very different from the friendships of
women.

The closest male friendships are often set in a context of battling
against a common *enemy*.[24] Competition between individual men is
displaced by competition between *us* and *them*. Perhaps for this
reason, close friendship and deep loyalty in a context of war or adventure may not survive the mundane realities of everyday life.
Men's friendships seem strangely polarized between pals having fun
together and warriors risking their lives for each other. The middle
zone is often missing.[25]

Perils in Female Intimacy

In significant ways, women's friendships can be imperfect. Women
are entirely capable of triviality, cattiness, deceit, disloyalty, and betrayal. They can be too captivated by relationships, or too dependent
on a single "perfect" friend to accept that that friend will have other
good friends or love relationships with men. Women may be so keen
to establish connection that they are unwilling to express honest and
constructive disagreement. Their quest for connection can inhibit
the very intimacy it is intended to facilitate. And the intimacy that
women establish makes them extremely vulnerable to betrayal.

Nancy Thayer's novel, ironically titled *My Dearest Friend*, tells of
one such betrayal. It describes an intimate friendship between two
young women, both wives of faculty members at a small college in
the northeastern United States. Laura and Dora spend a tremendous
amount of time together, enjoying glorious outings in the country,
shopping excursions, parties, activities with children, and luxuriously
long telephone conversations. They talk intimately about men, sex,
marriage, pregnancy, childbirth, children, their own pasts, and their
ambitions for the future. When Laura's husband leaves her for another woman, she is devastated. In one of many intimate exchanges,
she tells Dora that she has never had an orgasm, a revelation that
Dora reports to her own husband, Jake.[26] Dora works hard to care for
Laura; the two continue to spend long hours together, though less
exuberantly than before. Eventually Dora begins part-time teaching,
and Laura helps her out with babysitting and household chores. After
some months Dora is devastated to discover that Laura is having an
affair with Jake. Confronted, Jake insists that he wants a divorce to be
able to marry Laura. She really needs him, he says, whereas Dora,
who is working part-time, can manage her child and her work without his support.

Enraged and devastated, Dora feels absolutely betrayed both by her husband and by her "dearest friend." What hits deepest is Laura's appalling exploitation of intimacy: she lied about never having had an orgasm. She used Dora; she expected what she said to be told to Jake. She then used sex, and Jake's pride in giving her an orgasm, to manipulate their sexual affair into a relationship which he saw to be as unique and as demanding marriage. Laura calculatedly exploited the intimate talk of friendship, using it to manipulate both Dora and Jake. Hidden behind the warm person Dora thought she knew was a false friend, willing to manipulate and betray her to get another husband. The example is fictional, but the points it makes are real: intimacy can be exploited and friends can betray us.

Common pitfalls in women's friendships are explored by Susie Orbach and Luise Eichenbaum in their book *Bittersweet*. Therapists, colleagues, and friends since their college days, the two authors co-wrote the book to explore jealousy, alienation, and competition in women's friendships. Describing the quarrels, jealousy, animosity, rivalry, and pettiness that they and many of their clients had experienced, Orbach and Eichenbaum conclude that women's desire for intimacy can also work against good relationships. Women seek relationships and connectedness. They want to talk to their friends frequently, telling them all the significant things that are going on in their lives, share tears and laughter, and feel in constant touch. In fact, women want so much to be connected to others that they may have trouble accepting differences and acknowledging disagreements. They expect a strong connection, one that takes a lot of time and energy. The danger is that women may expect so much from their friends that they cannot get it, given the stresses of busy adult lives.

When women are disappointed, they begin to feel anger and distrust. They tend to avoid expressing these feelings to their friends because they do not want to rupture relationships; they do not want to disagree, to admit to being jealous and frustrated, or to express other awkward feelings. Ironically, women's longing for closeness can pull them apart; such failures of frankness mean that communication is flawed and notes of inauthenticity slip into the friendship. When women are unable to acknowledge difference and disagreement, they deprive themselves of opportunities to resolve their conflicts, put their friendship on a realistic adult basis, and re-establish intimacy and trust.

Orbach and Eichenbaum hypothesize that women unconsciously model female friendships on their own original closeness to their mother. For most women, Mother was the first intimate partner. She was the one with whom the daughter was extremely close in early years, and from whom she (apparently) did not have to separate in order to develop into a mature person. For boys it is different: for them too, Mother was the first intimate, but she was also the parent from whom the boy must distinguish himself in order to become a man. From the point of view of daughters, Orbach and Eichenbaum suggest, mothers were desired as total intimates. But they were always imperfect intimates because the practical circumstances of life meant that they were unable to offer total attention and unremitting devotion.

It is just such total intimate dedication, Orbach and Eichenbaum speculate, that women seek in friendships with other women. (They are not speaking of sexual intimacy in lesbian relationships, but of close friendships between women.) In seeking this complete intimacy with closest friends, women are almost certain to be disappointed. Most adult women have rather full and hectic lives outside their closest female friendships. They have husbands or romantic partners, children, work, parents, community commitments, and other friends and are thus in no position to devote themselves to a single friend. Given the intense demands that many women are inclined to make on friendships, trouble awaits. There are too many competing claims. Wanting more company and support than an adult friend can realistically give, women easily become jealous and resentful. They are set up, emotionally, to expect and want far more from their female friends than many of them are able to give. Their friendships often involve a sort of merged attachment attractive in its connectedness and intimacy, but hazardous to personal growth when taken to extremes. A woman wants to find herself. Craving connection, she may look to others to define what she is. Closeness and connection are valuable, but they have their limits. Orbach and Eichenbaum recommend acknowledgment of conflicting emotions and opinions and honest communication about difficulties as strategies for coping with envy, rivalry, and alienation in women's friendships. We must accept that liking and loving are compatible with differences of belief, lifestyle, and emotion. It takes trust and confidence to acknowledge these differences and try to deal with them honestly.

When Aristotle said that "no one would choose to live without a friend" and referred to friends as "other selves," he was thinking only of friendships between men. He assumed that women's friendships were not relationships between morally mature people and that they deserved no special attention. In this respect Aristotle represented his age and many to follow: he studied and exalted friendships between men. In contrast, some contemporary reflection on friendship seems to exalt relationships between women, implying that friendships between men are generally inferior to those between women. Women's friendships generally involve far more intimate talk and self-disclosure than those of men, and women seem to value their same-sex friendships more than men do.

But such claims need to be qualified. Women's friendships are by no means trouble-free. Male friends trust and support each other; intimate talk is not everything. They may establish a kind of quiet intimacy that does not depend on talk. There is such a thing as quiet companionship, which can be relaxing and fulfilling. If two people experience together a beautiful mountain hike or a spectacular sunset, they may be close and share the occasion without putting their feelings into words. This too is trusting friendship.

THE RISKS OF FRIENDSHIP

When we trust our friends, open ourselves to them, reveal our secrets, rely on them, and depend on them, we make ourselves vulnerable. If our friends have been dissembling, or if they change in ways we do not expect, we can suffer great harm as a result. There are friends who cease to be friends, friends who betray us, and false friends – people who appeared to be friends but never were. A friend may simply lose interest in our well being because she has acquired new interests and other friends; she may come to find us unattractive and boring, or limiting in various ways. She may let the friendship lapse or suddenly break it off, leaving us feeling hurt and vulnerable, lest she share her intimate knowledge with others who are not our friends. We may think that we have a friend in a co-worker or political colleague, only to discover that when the context of the relationship changes, the relationship ceases to exist. Anyone has a right to end a friendship. But some reasons for doing so are selfish or trivial, and some ways of ending friendships injurious and disloyal. When friendships end, we are often hurt. We have given our affection and trust, have allowed ourselves to be vulnerable, have assumed a reciprocity and lasting relationship, only to find that it is faltering or is over.

Even more disturbing are cases where the friendship was false from the beginning. The person who seemed to be a friend may have been using another person for some purpose of her own. There may be love and affection on the one side and only utility on the other. The other person in the relationship will feel betrayed and worthless. She has been manipulated; she is hurt, probably angry. She is likely to feel incompetent, even stupid. Why was she duped? Why could she not see through it? Someone betrayed by a false friend will feel more hesitant about forming new relationships and might be inclined to avoid friendships – to begin to distrust her current friends, to wonder what lurks beneath the warm and genial surface of her other relationships. She might quite naturally start to close off, to hold back from intimacy, to avoid even simple companionship. She may be fearful of relaxing, of letting herself go. To find that someone who was a cherished and apparently affectionate and loyal friend had been dissembling all along, had never cared, and was working actively against our interests is devastating. Two decades after Laura's betrayal, Dora still felt the hurt. The rupture between appearance and reality threatens confidence in the normal workings of the social world and could cast other established relationships in jeopardy. And yet, for all the naturalness of withdrawing, for all the difficulty of trusting again, isolation from intimate relationships is not the right response.

Although Aristotle was wrong to disregard women's friendships, he was right when he said no one would choose a life without friends. We do take risks when we make friends; we allow ourselves to be vulnerable to our friends. But if we did not take these risks, life would not be worth living. For most people, life without friends would not even be a meaningful option. They could not choose it and remain themselves.

Our vulnerability extends even after friendship ends. Our former friends may have possessions of ours, things given symbolic value within the relationship. They certainly know many things about us, some of which we would not want to become public knowledge. Because of their knowledge and their role in our lives, these people retain a power to hurt us, even after the friendship is over. This lasting power further illustrates two basic facts about trust and friendship: friendship is based on trust, and when we trust, we are vulnerable. We love and need our friends; life without them would be scarcely bearable. And yet our friends can hurt us, even after a friendship has ended quite painlessly. Should we avoid closeness to protect ourselves? The answer cannot be yes, for in avoiding the intimacies and joys of friendship, we would deprive ourselves of too much in life. Rather, the solution lies in picking the right friends in the first place.

We should not make friends with people who are malicious or cruel, who gossip or are willing to betray others. They are not worthy friends, and were we to cultivate them, we would place ourselves in jeopardy. Some day they might betray us. Picking the right friends becomes a matter of trusting ourselves. Annette Baier, who wrote about the need to trust former intimates, says: "We simply have to develop our taste in people, then trust it. If it fails us, then our friends may let us down. But if we do not trust it, we will have no friends. The ethics of trust in friends, then, throws us back on the ethics, or prudence, of trust in ourselves. Like all trust, it can be misplaced. Like trust in our friends, it is an indispensable condition of a bearable life."[27] Even though we might on occasion make a mistake and choose the wrong friends, it would not make sense to choose, for that reason, to have no friends at all. We cannot get along in life trusting no one, barricading ourselves against all who would invade that inner sanctum that is the self.

We need friends – for companionship and enjoyment of life, co-operation and sharing of activities, communication, maturation, and moral growth. To be sure, we are vulnerable to our friends and take risks when we are friends. The amiable colleague who wants to chat over lunch might really want nothing more than to steal our latest research ideas. The warm and sympathetic woman next door could be a spy for the national security organization. A person who has been betrayed by a friend may contemplate such possibilities, and we all could be suspicious in this way all the time. But we cannot conduct a rewarding and meaningful life in this manner, and if we try too hard to protect ourselves, we will only harm ourselves.

Friendship requires trust: friends cannot control each other. When we trust, we accept our vulnerability. Most friendships will not last a lifetime; some will end with pain. All leave us vulnerable, even when they are over. We may be unlucky enough to have friends who betray us or friends who were false from the start. Yet acting only on these possibilities will not give us a meaningful life. We need to be open to each other. We need friends who are close. And to cultivate and maintain close friendships, we need to trust each other.

CHAPTER THREE

Trust and the Family

Once upon a time a woman put up ten thousand dollars to bail her husband out of jail. He was there because he had been arrested for attempting to slit her throat. She forgave him. She let him move back in with her. She listened to him; she believed him; she thought he wanted to be reconciled with her. But life did not run smoothly; they did not live happily ever after. In the end, he killed her.[1]

This story tragically illustrates the psychic centrality of the family. For better, for worse, people do value their family connections. Women, especially, often try desperately to retain family connections, even in cases where they have been beaten or abused. One thing that makes many of us want to preserve our family connections and go to immense lengths to keep families intact is that we need intimate companions and may not know where else to find them. The good aspects of good-enough families are so essential to human development and thriving that even members of bad families may cling desperately to them.

What is a family? How should a family operate? Is it better for people to live in families than alone? Is it possible to live and work in families while maintaining our individuality, autonomy, and self-respect? Family relationships and duties pose many problems. Roles in the family are changing: caring for children, providing for the family, and domestic work are now shared by men and women – though seldom on an equitable basis. But heterosexual gender roles are far from being the most controversial aspect of contemporary families. The hottest political topics are gay and lesbian families and the "family values" cherished by the religious right. Gays and lesbians are challenging the old definition of the family with mom, dad, and the kids. At the same time, and in vocal opposition, conservatives are pushing a return to so-called family values as the source from which solutions to all our social problems will flow. According to "family values" advocates, if men and women would just refrain from getting divorced, if men would only remain employed to provide for the needs of the household, and if women would just stay home to bake cookies and wait for the children to come home from school, things would be right with the world. The need for welfare, unemployment, and old-age support would greatly diminish; children would behave well in schools; juvenile delinquency would virtually disappear; unemployment would be wonderfully reduced. Families would care for their own, and governments would save a lot of money, which they could use to reduce their deficits and pay off the debt.

Women and men should be suspicious of this agenda, not least for its assumption that a man who wants to be the sole provider for a family can readily do so in the contemporary economy. So-called family values are old-fashioned patriarchal values based on the conviction that the man is the head of the household. They assume a narrow conception of what the family has been, what it is, and what it can be. The father is the provider and authority figure; around him the family is to live, move, and have its being. Such families limit opportunities for women, undermining their autonomy and self-respect and encouraging them to find their identity through their husbands and live through their children. Worse yet, men in patriarchal families have perpetrated appalling abuse on wives and daughters. The dominant male claims authority over their very bodies. The good old days of the *Leave it to Beaver* family were not as good as many people thought. While the religious right calls out for family values, others reflecting on the family have become increasingly doubtful.[2]

After more than a decade of intensive press exposure of battering, incest, and abuse, many people – and many women especially – are becoming suspicious not only of so-called family values but of families themselves. Confidence in the nuclear family as an institution is diminishing. From a feminist point of view, a major underminer of confidence in the family is that families have worked to keep women down. For all the changes in women's and men's work, women still have more responsibility for children and household tasks than men do. Studies indicate that women work an average of fifteen hours more per week than men, because of extra work in the household.[3] It is a lot of work to be a wife and mother. And women's work, so easily and so naturally taken for granted, is taken for granted in the home most of all.

Married women with jobs outside the home are still handicapped by the notorious "double shift." Many sacrifice career and educational opportunities by moving with their husbands to enable them to pursue their careers. Gone are the days when a woman could lose her job just because she was married. Nearly gone are the days when a young woman would not be hired because she might become pregnant. But problems of family mobility and pressures of domestic work still function to limit women's opportunities. Young women are told they can "have it all," but in practice this is far from easy. Family responsibilities and loyalty to a husband and his career remain major obstacles for many women.

There are worse problems in families than restriction of opportunities for women – problems of violence and physical or emotional abuse. In families, people live intimately and are deeply vulnerable to each other. In those where there are women and men, women are vulnerable to men. Thousands – in fact, millions – of women have been battered and abused by their husbands and ex-husbands. For many women, home is more dangerous than the street. Patriarchal traditions, which gave men authority over their wives and daughters, have not entirely died. In male-headed families, women are vulnerable. Somehow, for whatever reasons, women, like men, still seem to want to live in families of some description. Why? To avoid loneliness; to have a home where we have companionship and company; to share life with others; to have a sexual partner, a sexual life; to bear and raise children; to link ourselves with the future and the broader society; to connect through our children with the rest of life. For most women these are good, or overwhelming, reasons.

For most people, the family means home. To feel safe and secure at home, we must trust others who live there. If home itself turns out to be somewhere from which we need shelter, the world is a fearful place indeed. Trust begins within families.[4] Children must be nurtured and cared for; when this happens well enough, they trust their parents and come naturally to trust other people and the world at large. From the trust developed within the family, they can move on to trust themselves, form friendships outside the family, and participate reliably and responsibly in society at large. Without a foundation of trust in the family, trust in other contexts has little chance to develop and survive.

The fundamental family relations that shape us as individuals are almost never a matter of choice. We enter our first family because we are born, the product of our parents' passion and desire for children, or because we are adopted, chosen by our parents. The relationship between a child and its adult parents is fundamental for individuals and for society itself. If women did not give birth to children and ensure that they were cared for, human society could not persist. Growing up in an intimate group and being strongly attached to particular adult human beings who supply love, care, and the material necessities of life is essential for human development. Membership in a family is a basic aspect of human life. We are social creatures who need affection, companionship, love, and intimacy to maintain our humanity.[5] We grow up in families we do not choose, but when we have grown up, most of us choose to live in families. We need support and sympathy, connection and commitment.

WHAT IS A FAMILY?

A man and woman, married to each other but with no children and no intention of having them, constitute a family. A man and woman living together unmarried in a committed intimate relationship also make a family, whether they have children or not. A lesbian or gay couple living with children, however acquired, constitute a family. A man and his children, living in a household without his former wife, constitute a family. Adult siblings living with their elderly mother, whom they care for, form a family. Heterosexuality is not essential for a family, nor is the presence of two sexes within a household. A marriage ceremony between the partners is not essential; nor are children; nor is the biological reproduction by adult partners of the children they are raising. Within a family there may be two generations, three or four, or only one.

It seems impossible to pin down the *essence* of a family without arbitrarily favouring some particular culture, historical period, or lifestyle.[6] Among the aristocracy of the eighteenth century, households included dozens or hundreds of servants and hangers-on, and bonds between parents and children were slight.[7] In modern Hong Kong the extended family remains more common than the nuclear one, and mothers-in-law continue to exercise considerable authority over young brides. Anthropologists report that, among the Zinacantenacos of southern Mexico, the basic social unit is identified as "a house." This "house" may include from one to twenty people. The Zinacantenacos speak of parents, children, wives, and husbands, but do not have a word to mark off a wife, husband, and their children as "a family," distinguished from other social units. Tribal peoples, apparently, speak readily of lineages and clans, but they rarely have a word for the nuclear family of mother, father, and children.[8]

Wittgenstein spoke of "family resemblances" between things that do not share a neatly definable essence. His favourite example was games. Wittgenstein claimed that games have no common essence;

there are many kinds of games from ring-around-a-rosy to chess, tennis, card games, the Olympic games, ball games, and many more.

... we see a complicated network of similarities overlapping and criss-
crossing: sometimes overall similarities, sometimes similarities of detail.

I can think of no better expression to characterize these similarities than
"family resemblances"; for the various resemblances between members of a
family: build, features, colour of eyes, gait, temperament, etc. etc. overlap and
criss-cross in the same way. And I shall say: "games" form a family.[9]

Charmingly, Wittgenstein's notion of *family resemblance* fits families
themselves. They resemble one another in various ways, sometimes
closely, sometimes less closely. There is no fixed essence, but rather a
variety of similar features. Married, common-law, or single-parent;
lesbian or gay; nuclear or extended; with or without children – families today have a family resemblance to each other. They are similar
in various respects, and they tend to serve similar functions – providing for intimacy, companionship, sexuality, nurturing, home, and
the care of children – without sharing a common logical essence. But
for any supposedly necessary feature of a family (man, woman,
marriage bond, children, common household), it seems easy to find
an exception. There are families without a man, families without a
woman, families without children, families without a home, families
with three living generations, families with only one living genera-
tion, families with two living generations. Most families are founded
on the intimate partnership of two adults and provide (or have provided or intend to provide) for children.

But not all: in 1986, national statistics taken in the United States
indicated that only 7 per cent of households fit the old fifties pattern
of breadwinning father, full-time mother, and at least one child under
eighteen. The most common household – near half of all households
in the survey – had an adult male wage earner and an adult female
wage earner, with or without children. A Canadian social survey in
1995 showed that 44 per cent of families had a man and a woman,
married to each other and with children; 30 per cent had a married
man and woman and no children; and 14 per cent had a single parent,
male or female, with children. Common-law relationships between a
man and a woman with children constituted another 5 per cent, and
common-law relationships between a man and woman without children 7 per cent.[10]

Yet these statistics seem to omit entirely the following small family.
Judy and Jill are a lesbian couple living in Vancouver with their twin
sons, Bob and Michael. Judy was over forty when she gave birth to

the twins. Her friend Alex, who lives with his partner, Joel, in Montreal, is their biological father. He and Joel knew Judy from their years as graduate students, and when Judy told Alex about her intense desire to have children, he agreed to donate sperm. Frozen, the sperm was flown from Montreal to Vancouver. Jill and Judy inserted it using a syringe. After a rather difficult pregnancy, Judy gave birth to healthy twin boys. She and Jill are both their mothers. Judy went back to work about nine months after the twins were born; a nanny helps to look after them. Alex and Joel keep in touch with the women and their boys. Judy, Jill, and the boys are a family. Alex, the father, and his partner, Joel, are close friends.[11]

Asked to envision a family, few of us would think first of all of such a grouping. Is it a family? Yes, though hardly a "standard" case. But it is not the only "non-standard" case. Few of us would think of the typical family as that of an older heterosexual couple with two children adopted from the same young, handicapped woman, who was unable to care for them herself. Or of the single-parent father who got his child by making contractual arrangements with a surrogate mother. Though widely publicized, such reproductive innovations are still statistically rare and have not penetrated our deep emotional expectations about parents and children. For all the changes in customs and morals, the word "family" still calls up images of mother, father, and children.

In the nuclear family of the fifties, a full-time male wage earner was supported in his efforts by a wife working in the home and available to respond to various exigencies, such as the illness of children and elderly parents. Now, when both adult partners work, there are frequent conflicts between responsibilities at work and those at home. Although women are no longer available for permanent domestic duty, many social institutions fail to take this fact into account – as every working woman who has had to cope with school professional days is painfully aware. The nuclear family continues to have a considerable influence on social institutions, on emotions and expectations, and thus on daily life. Although it is disappearing in reality, this "ideal" family persists in our institutions and imaginations.

HEARTH AND HOME

Characteristically, a family lives in a household, although not every family is contained within a household. Family members may leave for a time, as when a man takes a job in another country, sending part of his wages home and returning every few months to visit his wife and children, or a grown child leaves for a summer job or university elsewhere, still retaining emotional and financial ties to her family of origin. Nor does every household constitute a family. Non-family households are, in fact, rather common, as, for instance, in the shared-accommodation arrangements that frequently occur among students.

For most of us, though, family, household, and home coincide. Home is a special place of safety, warmth, security, and comfort. At home we can relax, put down our guard, and be ourselves. We have recourse to home to rejuvenate and replenish ourselves. From the public world, we come home to relax, eat, sleep, clean ourselves and our clothing, and be ourselves in our own secure place, which we have established as separated off from the broader world. Home should be secure and safe, cozy and warm. There we take shelter from the wider world and receive emotional support from companions. We can let go emotionally, lapse into rages, weep, fight, throw tantrums, or sulk. Not that this behaviour is especially welcome at home, but it will be more tolerated there than among friends and colleagues. We can express ourselves in the physical surroundings of home, in selecting furnishings and decorations, food, plants, pets, and sleeping arrangements. Most people can take a home for granted. They have a place which is theirs, which provides considerable privacy and respite from the wider world. Robert Frost described home as the place where, if you have to go there, people have to take you in. We have, or should have, a virtually unquestioned refuge at home.

Home can be the sanctum it is because of boundaries. There is a respect for people's living space; the outside world does not enter without permission. We trust others outside the household to respect our boundaries and treat our home as a private place. To a considerable degree, people are able to preserve control over who is in the home. Those who do not live there must ask permission to enter, typically by knocking or ringing the doorbell. If they are not given permission, they will go away. The idea that home is a reserved space for those who live there, set off from the public world, enterable by outsiders only when they are granted permission, is one that few of us would relinquish. To have the privacy of our homes, to feel safe and be able to refresh ourselves emotionally and physically, we have to assume that others will not enter at will; that means that we trust them to respect our rights over our private space. The special nature of home is founded on social norms that we trust other people to respect. When our home is violated by outsiders or becomes an unsafe place, we feel a special horror. Victims of domestic robbery often report being disturbed as much by the sense of invasion as by financial loss.[12] The idea that unknown persons have broken through the physical and psychological boundaries of home to rifle through desks, drawers, and cupboards, seeing all the paraphernalia of our domestic lives, is profoundly disturbing.

At home we should feel safe – safe from the outside world because we trust that people who do not live there will not enter unless invited, and safe with others who are in the home because we trust that they will respect our boundaries and possessions, and support us emotionally, physically, and economically. In Western cultures, it is important to have one's own private space within the home, whether this is a separate bedroom, our own workspace, a drawer no one pries into, or merely a single journal or bundle of letters. We trust that others who live with us will respect this privacy. The husband trusts his wife not to go through his papers and decide which should be discarded. A mother trusts her children not to root through her underwear drawers or rifle through her correspondence and papers. Children quickly gain a sense of their own possessions and their own space, which they expect their parents and siblings to respect. Home should be safe and secure, a place of respite for individuals and families. And it can be so only because we trust each other to respect boundaries.

Home is not only a psychological state but a physical place. If we keep possessions, run households, and take refuge in several different physical places, then to that extent we have several homes. The cottage is an obvious example. When we travel temporarily to work or study, we acquire a secondary temporary home. Even a hotel room may become a "home away from home," invested with minor domestic comforts. For whatever reason, Western societies tend to place great value on the privacy and cosiness of home. Those who have no home are to be pitied, even when they are relatively affluent individuals who have no home because they have chosen a nomadic style. Travel may bring on a longing for home, family, and domesticity, a longing so acute that even mundane objects such as vacuum cleaners and dish towels can make us feel lonely and wistful.

Far more pitiful than the traveller without his family are the literally homeless, forced to exist on the streets, sleeping in the open or under bridges or staircases, using public toilets and washing facilities, and begging for food, work, or money. With nowhere to go for rejuvenation, the homeless tend to look tired and dirty all the time. They live constantly under the public eye; they can assert no boundaries over a physical place that is their home. For them, the world is a cold and brutal place, without warmth, security, or companionship.

Most of us are fortunate enough to have homes, and most make our homes with other people. Typically, the family lives together at home, providing love, companionship, support, security, and nurture. Much of the significance of the family lies in the fact that it provides this physical centre of intimacy and privacy, where we have companions and can restore ourselves. From the safety of home, we move out to the public world and back again. Those who can take home for granted have a safe and comfortable place to be, a venue for self-expression and material maintenance, a place for physical and psychological restoration. To be unsafe at home is a special horror.

LOVE AND CARE IN THE FAMILY

Unique in its emotional significance, the family has been called a system of love objects. Three-quarters of the people surveyed in a Yale University study were prepared to define the family as "a group of people who love and care for each other." In the same survey, 71 per cent of the people interviewed declared themselves to be very satisfied with their family lives.[13]

Trust is central in every family relationship. If a family is functioning well enough, the children within it are fed, nurtured, cleaned, taught, loved and cherished, and given a sense of sexual and personal identity. What can we say about contemporary homes and families? As sons or daughters, we acquired from our family of origin our genetic, psychological, and social heritage, our location in the world, and our most basic cultural and intellectual knowledge. As adults, most of us live in families of some sort: as wives, husbands, partners, parents. For most of us, it is our families that provide our main locus of abiding affection and mutual support. In families we are not simply individuals; we are interconnected. We grow up in households, guided and cared for by others, sharing in communal tasks, and subject to customs and expectations that make us what we become. We identify with something greater than ourselves. We have obligations of support and cooperation, and we acknowledge those obligations because we grow within them and grow into them. Ideally, in a family household all are committed to all. Family members depend on each other considerably, in ways both practical and emotional.

There are, of course, many families in which things go wrong, and bad families can do devastating harm to their vulnerable members. But the fact that bad families exist does not prove that there are no good ones. There are vast numbers of good and good-enough families that provide company, nurture, intimate relationships, warmth, and security for their members. Most of the time, most of us need and appreciate our families. Intimacy is necessary for flourishing in a human life. We live with a small number of people, typically others in our family, sometimes friends, to whom we are deeply attached and whom we love and cherish as the particular people they are. At an abstract level, we may acknowledge that the moral value and human dignity of a faraway stranger is equal to that of cherished loved ones. But to say this is not to say that we value our loved family members *in the same way* as we value distant strangers. With strangers, we have no history of relationship and connection, no love, no debt, no intimacy, no detailed sense of a shared fate in past or future. And it is just these things that are essential in family relationships. Members may fight and irritate each other, but they usually love each other deeply and to a considerable degree accept responsibility for each other's well-being. We have special relations and special obligations to our families, households, and family members because we are part of them and they of us. If we did not favour them in significant ways, we would not have these intimate relations. Without them, we could not develop and flourish as human beings.[14]

HOW SHOULD FAMILIES FUNCTION?

In what is referred to as the "traditional" nuclear family, women were accountable for virtually all childcare and for the emotional well-being of all family members, especially husbands. Men were primarily responsible for meeting the family's economic needs. When something went wrong, the response was almost automatic: it was mom who dealt with relationships and emotional problems – blame mom. Understanding that placing such demanding responsibility on women was unreasonable, the psychiatrist D.W. Winnicott argued that mothers can be "good enough" without being perfect. The good-enough mother provides sufficient physical and emotional care for an infant to thrive and develop, but does not sacrifice her whole life and being in order to do so.

More recently the family itself has tended to be deemed responsible when things do not go well. The family therapy movement developed throughout the sixties and seventies. In this movement, therapists regard the family as a *system*, a small system of closely interrelated and interdependent people operating by unexpressed rules. People trust each other to act according to these rules, though they seldom understand what they are. Suppose that something goes wrong: a teenage daughter is anorexic. She is the "presenting patient," the one who presents symptoms, but family systems therapists do not assume that she is the only one with a problem. There is something deeply wrong with the interactions of family members. The tacit rules, implicitly

trusted by all members, are not working as they should. Family therapists of the Milan school used brief, sometimes paradoxical, interventions (daughter should take dad to a picture show; mom and dad
should leave all the housework to the oldest son; and so on), seeking
by behavioural change to alter the interactions, and the tacit rules, of
the family system.[15] The technique often worked. Not only was it
fairer than simply blaming mother, but it was more efficient.

But despite its theoretically innovative character, much of the
theory and practice of family systems therapy was conservative to the
point of being sexist. The theory was based on the assumption that
"normal" families with well-defined boundaries between the generations and the sexes and honest open communication were basically
all right. Family systems therapists generally presumed that families
were units in which married mothers and fathers lived with their biological children and roles were clearly divided along the lines of age
and gender. In the ideal family of family systems theories, communication lines were open and relatively non-authoritarian. But in other
respects such families were straightforwardly patriarchal in the manner of "ideal" North American families of the fifties. Fathers were the
breadwinners and had more power in determining family affairs than
mothers. Mothers worked in the home and took most of the responsibility for caring for the children. Sons and daughters were brought up
in clearly differentiated gender roles. These families were generally
assumed by therapists and academics to be functional and healthy
and to require no therapeutic intervention. Any notion that there
might be significant similarities between "sick" and "healthy" families was usually rejected.[16]

But far from being essential for mental health, these "normal"
nuclear families put everyone at risk. Women were isolated, economically dependent on their husbands, handicapped in personal and career development, overburdened by childcare and household duties,
and given too much responsibility and power with regard to the family's intimate and emotional life. Men were economically exploited,
exposed to heartlessly competitive industrial relations, alienated from
life in the home, encouraged to repress their emotions, and discouraged from developing meaningful relationships with their children.
Children were vulnerable to a variety of harms ranging from too
intense mothering to physical battering and sexual assault. With the
identity and self-esteem of men dependent on their status as wage
earners in an unstable external economy, such families were especially
vulnerable to economic downturns. What is wrong with the call for a
return to family values is that it ignores the many respects in which
these supposedly traditional families simply did not work very well.

Dysfunctional Families?

Far from presuming the normal functionality of fifties nuclear families, many counsellors and therapists of the eighties and have nineties followed the ideas of *codependency theory,* according to which precisely the opposite is the case. In these circles the tendency is to believe that most families, even the most apparently "normal" ones, are *dysfunctional*. If we find ourselves in trouble, we should not trust our families: they are likely to be the very ones who mixed us up in the first place. A plethora of books advise injured adults who have been by-products of "toxic parents" how to recover from childhood abuse. Prominent theorists such as John Bradshaw have proclaimed that over 95 per cent of North American families are "dysfunctional."[17]

Dysfunctional families fail to provide an environment in which children can thrive and develop without suffering emotional damage. Children have to trust their parents, and yet (apparently) they should not. According to this theory, we are nearly all survivors of some childhood *abuse* from which we must recover. If we dispute the interpretation, thinking that our families were functional and normal and did not abuse us, we are deemed by codependency theorists to be "in denial." If we suspect that we were abused, we almost certainly were. If we do not suspect it, we almost certainly were; we are "denying it." In this event, we should not trust our own impressions and memories. Families are unhealthy places for children to grow up in. There is almost always something deeply wrong. Codependency theorists advise us not to trust our families. If we are inclined to do so, that means we should not trust ourselves.

On this theory, those of us who do not remember abuse, who deny being abused as children, are "in denial" because we are unwilling to acknowledge unpleasant facts about our pasts. A logical problem here (one that, regrettably, has made the theory seem more plausible in some circles) is that this theory is impossible to refute. If a person thinks he was abused, he was abused. If he does not think he was abused, he is in denial: he really was abused and is simply unable to face his past.[18] So either way, he was abused. Given the logic, it is surprising that only 95 per cent of families are dysfunctional – why not 100 per cent?

Obviously, to make Bradshaw's theory even superficially plausible, one has to define the term "abuse" very broadly. It includes not only sexual assault, physical beating, or gross negligence but being encouraged to assume adult responsibilities, not being informed of family secrets, having to compete with a more favoured sibling, or being encouraged to become an "overachiever." Bradshaw's notions of abuse and dysfunctionality appear to be seriously inflated and have been convincingly criticized as such.[19] The idea that adults are "adult children" with a wounded "child within" encourages people to think of themselves as victims, perpetuating self-indulgence, immaturity, and a simplistic understanding of human development. Codependency theory is contradictory in its assumption that our parents can be held responsible for their mistakes whereas, being "adult children," we are (blameless) victims of their abuse – victims needing tender care in order to recover.

Adults who think of themselves fundamentally as sons or daughters may find the analysis tempting. We all have feelings of anger and resentment and problems in living, and they must have had some cause. Tracing these problems to childhood abuse gives a ready account of our inadequacies, and twelve-step programs provide a direction to emotional stability and self-improvement. But if we think of ourselves as mothers and fathers, rather than daughters and sons, our viewpoint should change; parents are highly vulnerable to therapeutic rewritings of the past that isolate them from their children. A case in point is that of Barbara. She lost contact with her talented young daughter, who became convinced that her parents had warped her childhood by encouraging her to pursue science and mathematics. When they denied her extra money at one point during her university studies in literature, she wrote her parents off completely, accusing them of abuse. Even when Barbara's handicapped son died as a result of a tragic accident, her daughter refused to be reconciled with this "abusive" family.

Ten or twenty years from now, do we who are parents want to be rejected by our own children, ostracized and accused of abuse because we encouraged a daughter to study physics or a son to take up jazz dance? Because we moved several times when a daughter was in elementary school? Because we placed a son in a French-immersion elementary school? Or because we did not? Because a daughter did some babysitting, a son had a flyer route, or children had to share a bedroom when money was scarce? Because we did not have the moral energy to insist that our children cut down on sugar and eat vegetables? Because we missed a music recital for a business trip? No one should place confidence in any therapeutic approach that allows "victims" or "adult children" to work out a version of the past with a therapist and cling to it dogmatically, placing blame for current problems on something that parents did wrong decades ago.

Codependency theories assume that a newborn human being has a flawless pre-family self that would have developed into something quite perfect and wonderful had its parents only done a good job in rearing the child.[20] One can make this claim true by definition: a person did not do a "good job" unless his or her child turned out to be perfectly "healthy" by the standards of health set in codependency theory. But the notion of a flawless pre-family self has nothing to recommend it. In fact, it is just plain naive. The newborn infant has no natural self, good or bad. It has a genetic heritage affecting skills, talents, and personality. A human being, a person, a self, grows into being in a family and a broader culture.

The Myth of the Perfect Mother

In reflecting on trust and families, we need to strike a balance between the fifties assumption that "normal" nuclear families are quite all right and the contemporary tendency to regard virtually all families as dysfunctional. When we think about families, it is especially important to develop a realistic conception of motherhood. Perhaps as a result of infantile recollections, the belief in the all-powerful mother persists in our culture and practice and in theoretical writings on motherhood and the family.

It is easy – terrifyingly easy, I think – to blame mother for everything that goes wrong. Mother is responsible for all, does all. Unwittingly, even some feminist writers seem to echo the sentiment. They may claim that mothers in contemporary societies are handicapped by their relative powerlessness because those societies are inadequate in so many ways. But if societies were to reform in feminist directions, mothers would do everything "perfectly," and the world would be full of self-directed and happy people living in justice, harmony, and peace.[21] Many writings suggest an unfortunate lack of realism as to just how much mothers can do to shelter and nurture their children and protect them from the hardships of the world. Anyone who has been a mother knows from experience that there are hurts in childhood and adolescence that mother cannot fix. For instance, Johnny, who had developed muscular thighs by the age of seven, was teased at school for having fat legs. He came to dislike sports and gym because he did not want to change with other boys who might "bug him." Andrea, who as a teenager was rather attractive and exceedingly intelligent, went right through high school without ever having a boyfriend or a date. She did have a male friend, an extremely nice young man with whom she chatted at school and on the subway. But he was a Muslim, and his parents would not allow him to date non-Muslim girls. Both situations deeply hurt these children, and their mother was powerless to change them.[22]

Mothers are not perfect and they are not omnipotent. Even if they were perfect, their children would suffer hurts and bruises in the tumult of childhood life which their mothers could not prevent.

Besides, mothers have their own lives to live and deserve some independence as autonomous, self-respecting beings. Even in ideal societies these realities would remain. No one should fall into the trap of trusting mothers to do everything and blaming them if they do not – not in our present society and not in an ideal one. To trust women too much as mothers is worse than unrealistic and naive; ultimately, it is cruel.

A mother can be "good enough" without being "perfect" – whatever perfect would mean in this context. A mother can be good enough without abdicating her autonomy and relinquishing every shred of independence to fulfil every infantile want of her children. The same, obviously, may be said of fathers. And a family too can be good enough without being perfect.

TRUST AND THE GOOD-ENOUGH FAMILY

In the good-enough family, if there is an adult couple – heterosexual or homosexual, married or not – that couple has a working, intimate relationship. Partners supply each other with care and companionship and cooperate in earning a livelihood and running a household for themselves and any dependents. These adults provide tolerably well for the physical and emotional needs of any children in the household. If there is only one parent, there is no adult intimacy, and that parent has the sole and challenging responsibility of providing for the needs of the children. Difficult as this situation is, many women and men have met the challenge. Some single-parent families are good-enough families.

In the good-enough family, there is no sexual abuse or domestic violence, and material resources are adequate for health and day-to-day maintenance. Good-enough families may lack many desirable characteristics, and life within them may be far from perfect. There may be less-than-perfect justice and equity between members.[23] But despite their flaws, good-enough families provide a home, security, nurture, intimacy, and many other essentials to the adults and children who are their members.

Reflecting on these essentials, we can see that *trust* is a fundamental aspect of the good-enough family. Adult partners must trust each other as dependable, reliable, and caring companions who are committed to each other, the household, and an ongoing relationship. Children must trust adults to care for them and provide security. And adults must trust children enough to give them space to grow and develop. Of necessity, a good-enough family is one in which there is substantial trust between members. In these families, women and men can preserve their autonomy and self-respect. And in these families, all members will be safe.

In a good-enough family, adult partners have an intimate relationship that gives them company and support. They are able to communicate feelings, ideas, and concerns, and to rely and depend on each other. We cannot comfortably depend and rely on someone whom we do not trust. Nor, in most cases, can we relax and be sexually or emotionally intimate with another person whom we do not trust.[24] To be intimate with another person, we must trust him or her to accept us as we are; we must trust that we love each other, that the other person is fundamentally honest, caring, and committed to the relationship. Intimacy, whether physical or emotional, requires trust in many ways.

TRUST, SEX, AND INTIMATE PARTNERS

It may be undesirable, but it is true: people are perfectly capable of maintaining sexual relationships with others whom they do not trust. Such involvements, though highly risky, are apparently rather common. There is considerable room for untrustworthy behaviour in sexual relationships. Partners may lie about emotions and intentions, previous involvement, HIV exposure, venereal disease, birth control, orgasms, and much else. They may hold back verbally or emotionally, hesitating to express what they want and need. However, sexual *intimacy*, as contrasted with sexual *activity*, does require some level of trust. If we distrust a partner, fearing that he or she has not been honest about crucial matters, we are unlikely to relax, fully express our feelings, or respond freely to him or her. In these respects, distrust and lack of ease with a partner inhibit intimacy and sexual pleasure.

In sexual relationships, we are vulnerable. We expose our body to another, open ourselves, and disclose our selves and our feelings. And we are at risk, emotionally and physically. Sexual contact evokes strong feelings, and rejection after sexual contact will be emotionally hurtful. Physical vulnerability is obvious. Even with birth control and access to abortion, vulnerability to pregnancy is still a factor for women in heterosexual relationships. Men are vulnerable to manipulation and deception. Women may trick them into parenthood before they are ready or deceive them about whether offspring are really theirs. The risk of AIDS looms even larger than that of pregnancy. Sexual relations are literally life-threatening; promiscuous people pose serious risks to their partners. So far as HIV exposure is concerned, we do not sleep only with our partner, but with everyone our partner has ever slept with. Trust should be paramount because life itself is at stake. From the point of view of common sense or plain self-interest, it

is abundantly obvious that we should not enter into sexual relationships with those whom we do not trust. Sexual relationships
should presume trust. But in reality, many do not. People frequently
become sexually involved, quite spontaneously, with others whom
they scarcely know, much less trust. And such people take enormous
risks, often causing tremendous harm to themselves and others.

Within the context of a good-enough family, where there is an
enduring relationship between partners, risky behaviour with an untrustworthy partner on the basis of a sudden flamboyant passion is
unlikely. But people are still vulnerable in sexual relationships. Ideally,
in such relationships there will be understanding about whether pregnancy is desired and, if not, how it is being prevented. There will be
honesty about feelings and needs. There will be confidence between
partners about sexual loyalty, both for emotional reasons, as a basis for
intimacy, and to remove fears about AIDS and venereal disease. Sexuality in committed relationships implies expressing our feelings, being
intimate, and experiencing pleasure and physical satisfaction with a
familiar partner. In this context, we would expect and find a degree of
trust, and also a degree of prudence, exceeding what we would find
for casual sex.

But even in long and deep relationships, there are many failures of
communication, triggers of unhappiness, and acts of disloyalty. If a
woman loves someone enough to live with him, sleep with him, and
plan a life with him, then surely (we would think) she is not going to
fake orgasms or trick him into becoming a father before he is ready
to take the step. But these things do happen. There are countless
ways, large and small, in which loving partners can be untrustworthy
with regard to sexuality. The emotional and physical risks of sexual
activity and the harmfulness of sexual betrayal argue against casual
sex and for honest and committed long-term relationships, where
intimate and deep trust is developed and maintained.

In a good-enough family, adult partners trust each other enough to
be close and to have a satisfactory sexual relationship and a healthy
intimate life. But sensitive to high divorce rates and broken relationships, many men and women hold back from sexual and emotional
intimacy and commitment. They fear that they will lose their autonomy and independence if they succumb to marriage or living together. One twenty-seven-year-old woman wrote to a national paper
to say that she and her partner in a relationship that had lasted over
five years felt unable to commit themselves to getting married. Their
parents had not stayed married, and they could not imagine doing so
themselves; between them they had witnessed eight marriages, four

divorces, two common-law marriages, and one separation, and they had so many half-siblings, step-parents, and step-grandparents that they could hardly keep track of them. This woman said that her parents had had such a transient style in their relationships that she herself was incapable of making commitments to a partner. The details were poignant and impressive, but there is a flaw in the account. The young writer told her story as though she had no good model for responsible partnership and parenting, and hence no choices about commitment in her own adult life. She wrote as though her distrust of commitment were an inevitable result of her past experience, apparently oblivious to the real possibility of living a life of loyalty and responsibility, of choosing a path different from that of her parents. Her own choice was to enrol in Harvard Business School instead of getting married.

Many men and women want intimacy, commitment, and a family-based household, but fear that it may result in confinement and restraint, in a lack of freedom to pursue careers and economic self-sufficiency.[25] In a close relationship, people are dependent on each other and likely to fare better if they can acknowledge that fact. Obviously, if we depend on others, we are better off when those others are trustworthy. When they are not, we are at risk. If a woman trusts her husband to repair the roof and he fails to do it but tells her that he has, the family is at financial and physical risk. If a man trusts his wife with confidential talk about his workplace and she gossips irresponsibly, he, his colleagues, and his job will be at risk. Trust and trustworthiness in intimate relationships are extremely important.

Adult partners in a good-enough family will have an intimate relationship that is, for the most part, satisfactory. They will depend on each other in mundane matters and cooperate reliably in earning a livelihood, running a household, caring for its children, and arranging leisure activities. They will be good companions, friends, and sexual partners and will generally meet each other's dependency needs in an intimate relationship. On the whole, they will be honest with each other and not keep deep secrets from each other. They will keep promises to each other, and neither will seek to exploit or manipulate the other. They will like each other, appreciate each other, and express their affection honestly. They will be emotionally intimate and have a satisfying sexual relationship. Their love and companionship will not be based on roles mandated by social convention or on affectation and pretence. They will be loyal to each other, not using intimate knowledge to mock or attack each other with family and friends outside the relationship. They will be able to handle conflict moderately well, having styles of discussion and argument where each can express what he or she wants and feels and resolutions can be worked out without one party always getting her or his way.

All this is not to say that there will be no problems. But adult partners are able to cooperate in earning a livelihood and running a household, and their relationship meets many of their sexual and companionship needs. They are friends, companions, sexual partners, and collaborators in living a life and establishing a home.

CHILDREN AND TRUST IN
THE GOOD-ENOUGH FAMILY

For a child, to trust is natural. Children are born into the world predisposed to trust their parents and others who care for them. In fact, they will go to nearly any length to maintain their trust in their parents.[26] Children are vulnerable, dependent, and needy. To a child, the thought that her parents might fail to provide care and might even seek to harm her is nearly unbearable. She will do almost anything to resist such conclusions. Things have to be really grim before children renounce trust in their adult caretakers.

The trust of infancy and early childhood is implicit and unquestioning. The infant is predisposed to trust, and her trust develops because she is cared for. Her physical needs are met. If she is wet, she is changed; if cold, wrapped in blankets; if hungry, fed; if uncomfortable, held and rocked. Initially, infants are scarcely aware of the distinction between themselves and the rest of the world. With dependable physical care and emotional comforting, they learn that others are stable, reliable sources of ease and thus learn to trust in their caretakers, typically parents and for much early care predominantly mothers. Erik Erikson referred to this early trust as "basic trust." Basic trust is born of reliable care. Writing in the heyday of the *Leave It to Beaver* family, Erikson assumed that this care would be provided by mothers:

the amount of trust derived from earliest infantile experience does not seem to depend on absolute quantities of food or demonstrations of love, but rather on the quality of the maternal relationship. Mothers create a sense of trust in their children by that kind of administration which in its quality combines sensitive care of the baby's individual needs and a firm sense of personal trustworthiness within the trusted framework of their culture's lifestyle. This forms the basis in the child for a sense of identity which will later combine a sense of being "all right," of being oneself, and of becoming what other people trust one will become.[27]

This early trust is absolutely fundamental in personal development. It is the first trust, essential for developing a positive attitude to other people and the world at large and fundamental for developing further trust. People who, in infancy, do not receive this fundamental reliable care and do not learn that they can count on adults and the world at large are likely to experience enormous difficulty learning to trust in other contexts. In fact, Erikson maintains that resolving the dilemma of "basic trust versus basic mistrust" is the fundamental task of the first year of human life. As infants, we either find the world benign, comforting, and reliable or we discover it to be fearful and unreliable.

In growing from infancy to adolescence, a person moves from complete dependence to considerable independence. In good-enough families, adults care for children and provide the basis for this development. Parents in such families strongly identify with young babies and their needs. Infants are virtually helpless and tremendously vulnerable and appealing in their innocence and dependency. In the first year of life an infant is a being with appetites and needs who develops affectionate contacts with his parents and becomes integrated with them. A baby knows how to express his needs and stake a claim on his parents.

By providing reliable care and loving support, parents launch the infant on a process of personal development. Because they care for her and she can trust them, she is able to develop into a person. Discussing the process, D.W. Winnicott observes that well-cared-for babies relatively quickly establish themselves as persons. With less-reliable care, many babies tend to become restless, "suspicious," or apathetic. The idea of oneself is developed against a background of contrast: the not-self. For infants, this means the main adult caretaker. When the not-self (mother, father, or other adult caretaker) is unpredictable, an infant will develop a less-firm sense of self. The idea of self and the reference point of not-self are necessarily connected and develop together. Basic to the development of self in the first year of life, Winnicott says, are handling, holding, and "object-presenting."

The social environment in which an infant finds herself is crucial for her early development. She moves from absolute dependence to relative dependence towards independence. If a baby does not get support from parents or caretakers at this stage, she cannot turn into an authentic person.[28] It is through the sensible and consistent care she receives as an infant that a child is able to develop unity of personality, becoming "a dweller in the body." In adapting to her mother and father, she gains a sense of external reality, establishing for herself the distinction between self and the external world of stable objects and reliable other people. To gain a clear sense of herself, she needs to experience regularity in the world, a regularity that will at the same time provide for basic trust.

A young child needs a sense that the world is durable, reliable, and good, and that he has a secure place within it. His surroundings provide this security if he has a stable home, however humble. Fancy toys, expensive household appliances, high-tech consumer goods, a large bedroom, a new crib, and colourful clothing are unnecessary. What the infant does need is a secure home where adults keep him warm, fed, and clean, where they hold him and love him, and where the surroundings are durable, reliable, and good. The security of home protects a baby from intrusions of a world that he cannot comprehend and at the same time from some of his own uncontrollable impulses.

In a good-enough family there is good-enough parenting. This means that care is kind and reliable and that the infant is physically and emotionally secure. He is not anxious; he can be confident that he will be fed, changed, and loved by familiar people in a familiar environment. He is sheltered from the outside world, protected, and made secure by those who care for him. With this basis, he has acquired basic trust and is able to develop into a more independent being.

As the child develops, her parents allow her more freedom to explore, and she moves from complete dependence to an increasing degree of freedom. At this stage, too, trust is a key. Freedom is possible only insofar as parents are able to let go. For this they must trust the child, whether it is a matter of letting her walk across the room without support when she is two, play unsupervised with another child at seven, use public transport on her own at twelve, select her own clothing and take responsibility for her schoolwork at fifteen, or drive the family car at eighteen. Growth to maturity requires both that the parents trust their child and that the child trusts her parents.

To develop and learn, even to have a sense of self, infants and children must trust implicitly in those who care for them. Without basic trust, human beings cannot progress from infancy to childhood. In early childhood we need to trust others in order to learn language, social customs, or fundamental social skills. Later, children continue to trust their parents or caretakers, but the trust need not be implicit and unquestioning or total. Children are exposed to other children and other adults in school, community, and church activities. They acquire ideas from these sources and from the popular media and many interests and beliefs from sources outside the family. Children will learn that adults who care for them are not all-knowing and perfect, and cannot manage every situation and provide every sort of knowledge. They may find that their parents have broad areas of ignorance and incompetence, painful inadequacies, temperamental peculiarities, and embarrassing idiosyncrasies. The immigrant child may have to translate for her parents. The daughter of a single-parent father may find him inept at judging friendships between girls or participating in parent-teacher interviews. A son may realize that his mother's cooking is sadly lacking.

But despite these detected gaps in their competence, the child must trust parents overall; she must be confident that they will continue to be fundamental sources of emotional and physical security. To mature comfortably, we should be able to take it for granted that our parents will be caring beings who will continue to do their best for us. To a striking degree, people do this, even as adults. When her ninety-five-year-old mother died, one woman in her late sixties commented, "Now I really have to grow up."

For nearly everyone, maturity develops in a family. We progress from almost complete dependence to lesser dependency and then eventually to something close to autonomy. The family provides a home, offering physical security, companionship, and emotional support. It establishes language, norms of personal contact, and the whole basis for later learning, setting early attitudes towards the outside world. In a good-enough family we receive reliable and loving infant care, establishing a sense of external reality, basic trust, and a primitive sense of self. Later the family continues to meet our needs, providing opportunities for developing independence. Children who have brothers and sisters have the benefit of a social life with siblings, giving them companionship and experience at handling rivalries and conflicts.

A good-enough family is not perfect, and the trust within it is not perfect either. Here as elsewhere, there are many degrees and contexts of trust. Family members will trust or fail to trust each other in different ways and to different degrees. A woman may trust her husband to be sexually faithful and take good care of the children, but feel uneasy lest he forget to pay household bills on time. A girl may trust her father to be loving and caring and give good advice about school, but have little confidence in his ability to find a good music teacher. Obviously there can be significant gaps in trust in the good-enough family. Still, we can see how fundamental trust is.

A good-enough family can persist only if its members believe that it is good enough and are committed to it. Such a family presupposes trust or confidence by members in its own being and merit and commitment to its own persistence, as well as interpersonal trust between and among its members. To function as a family, to persist as a family, people need confidence in their family unit and its survival. By maintaining homes in which children are cared for and nurtured, adult partners in a family provide the basis for further trust in friends, teachers, and members of the broader society. Rearing children, they will eventually produce mature people who have acquired language and customs and can function in society at large. In this sense the family serves as the bedrock of trust, the basis for all trust outside the family. Trusting and confident people exist in the broader society because they have matured within good-enough families. Thus families can be said to create trust.

Yet at the same time, families presume the existence of social trust and viable communities and economies outside themselves. They exist and operate within communities.[29] The good-enough family requires trust between adults, between children, and between adults and children. Those relationships exist in the context of a broader society and are unlikely to survive if social institutions are malfunctioning or brutal. One might say that the good-enough family reproduces trust. In a context of social trust, it may raise children who can enter the community as people capable of maintaining sound relationships. From relationships of intimacy and closeness involving confident and trusting adults, it provides care and nurture, producing children who have trusted enough to become functioning adults.

Although no families are perfect, many are good enough. As Winnicott remarks, "A surprising number of people can look back and say that whatever mistakes were made, their family never let them down."[30]

CHAPTER FOUR

Problems of Trust in Families

The film *Ordinary People* shows a family committed to upholding a public image of success. Beth and Calvin are the middle-aged parents of Conrad, a miserably unhappy sixteen-year-old who attempted suicide shortly after the accidental death of his older brother. Calvin is a successful defence attorney, and Beth a stay-at-home wife who has established her role in life as that of wife and mother in a happy, successful family. The family lives in an elegant older home. Beth does not want to acknowledge Conrad's problems and brightly insists that everything is "great." She is furious when Calvin admits to friends that their son is seeing a psychiatrist. When Calvin suggests that they might visit the psychiatrist, Beth is deeply affronted. That would mean admitting that they were not functioning perfectly well on their own, something she is absolutely unwilling to do. As the story proceeds, it becomes apparent that Beth has never loved Conrad as she loved his brother. She cannot give him her complete attention or show him physical affection. Although she pretends, somewhat ineffectively, to be a normal mother to Conrad, he is not fooled. He can feel his mother's lack of warmth; he can remember her attitude to his dead brother; and he can recognize the discrepancy. Eventually he tells his father what he perceives. Genuinely concerned for his son, Calvin begins to reflect on Beth's concern for appearances.

With the help of his psychiatrist, Conrad learns to express his feelings and stop blaming himself for the fact that he survived while his brother died. He begins to recover. Watching as Beth stares coldly into space while Conrad hugs her, Calvin realizes that she has been living a lie. She wants desperately to preserve the picture of a perfect family living in the perfect household, to maintain a comfortable and entertaining life for herself, with a wealthy and devoted husband. But beneath this quest for perfection is little real love for her second son.

Calvin confronts Beth with her preoccupation with appearances and her responsibility for Conrad's suffering. The film ends with Beth leaving home, the implication being that Calvin and Conrad, who genuinely care for each other, will maintain a more honest and intimate home together. To keep up Beth's notion that everything was "great," the family had been living a lie.

Notoriously, there are deep problems of trust in many families. These include pretence and hypocrisy, seriously flawed communication, falseness, lies and deception, family secrets, infidelity, breakdowns in intimacy, sexual abuse, and family violence. Often these aspects are related. Infidelity is likely to lead to lying, deception, family secrets, and a breakdown in intimacy between adult partners. Secrets may necessitate lies and deception, which, when discovered, undermine trust. Sexual abuse and violence destroy trust and any sense of security, bringing great suffering and harm.

COMMUNICATION: LIES AND DECEPTION

Complete openness within a family is not desirable or even possible. We want privacy and need to keep some aspects of life to ourselves. A major problem for women has been maintaining some sense of separate identity and projects within the family. Still, the warmth and love that people need is provided in family life only if there is considerable openness in communications. If we are generally able to express our feelings and verbally communicate our conflicts, our wants and needs can be acknowledged by other family members, who can either try to meet them or explain why they should not. In families, children learn to recognize and express their feelings and needs, and gain a sense of themselves and of others by sharing them with parents and siblings. By interacting, acknowledging responses, and learning to recognize and resolve conflicts and acknowledge the needs of other family members, children can gain a positive image of themselves and others. All of this works only if a family has what is basically a clear and straightforward style of communication. With seriously flawed communication, a family may begin to disintegrate. In the family, as elsewhere, too many hidden meanings, sarcastic remarks, innuendoes, or outright lies will lead to suspicion and mistrust.

Failures in communication are common in closed families that demand strong conformity and preservation of the official family image. Beth, Calvin, and Conrad lived in such a family. Conrad's visits to a psychiatrist were appalling for Beth because they undermined her belief that the family was successful and able to function on its own.

A source of stress in many families is the difference between male and female styles of communication.[1] Most women and girls feel comfortable talking about their feelings and find relief in sharing their problems with other people. This communication style allows them to get support and help. It means that most girls let their parents know what is going on in their lives. Problems with friends, school, and activities tend to be known and understood by their parents, who can then attempt to help out. Boys are less ready to admit having problems. They sulk, grouch, or act out.

Pedro, who was twelve, was depressed and crabby for more than an hour until finally, after repeated aggressive questioning from his parents, he admitted that he was worried about spending time with them watching televised election results. His problem was nothing to be ashamed of – only that he had a lot of homework to do that night – but somehow he felt that it was shameful to admit it. Pedro's inclination was to clam up and worry about the homework himself, rather than tell his parents and ask for advice. In the case of more substantial problems, this characteristically male style can have tragic consequences. In closed families a member who does not agree with the beliefs or practices of the others is usually branded as sick or deviant and will often become that way in response. There is intense pressure for all members to have the same opinions, feelings, and desires. A family that is functioning as a closed system will go to great lengths to maintain a picture of perfect conformity. To present that perfect picture, central features of family history and family life are kept hidden and are not open to discussion. Relationships are seeded with landmines because there are so many threats to emotional survival.

Family members need to trust each other, and to do this they must communicate openly and honestly with each other. If one finds that the other has been dishonest about a serious matter, that trust will be undermined. The husband or lover who lies about his activities or friends, the woman who pretends to have an orgasm, the child who has lied about doing his homework or friends who smoke – all undermine the ability of others to trust them. Robert's trust in himself was shattered when it finally came out that his wife, Barbara, was having an affair. For many months he had sensed that their old intimacy was gone, and he had asked her repeatedly whether her feelings for him had changed. Barbara denied any change. Then she suddenly left him and the children, saying she was in love with her boss. It turned out that she had been deceiving Robert for two years, and there were some appalling details. She had asked for expensive lingerie for Christmas, and then after he had given it to her, she had worn it only to work. Robert was shattered. After being deceived so persistently and betrayed so thoroughly, he had trouble trusting again in an intimate relationship. He experienced considerable difficulty trusting other women, and for a time he lost his confidence in his own judgment, thinking how "stupid" he had been not to have detected Barbara's deception.[2]

In such cases, children may be greatly shaken. If they lose trust in their parents as a result of repeated parental lies or dishonesty, they may find it difficult or impossible to believe what other adults tell them. To learn from adults, children need to believe them; so the problem is serious. If we cannot trust family members in this way, then we "cannot trust the universe, including our internal universe of thoughts, feelings, and perceptions."[3] It is in the family that we first and most intimately define ourselves, our relationships, and the broader world. When family communication is seriously flawed, when myths are rigidly upheld against counter-evidence, when discussion is closed, lies common, or interactions based on pretence, the whole system is faulty.

Honesty means different things in different contexts. One family may practise it as strict factual accuracy, another as meticulous respect for personal property, yet another as emotional openness and spontaneity. When honesty means saying what we think or expressing what we feel, it should be tempered by a sensitivity to context. The mother who thinks her teenaged daughter looks lumpy and unattractive will be ill-advised to say so just as the girl is setting out on her first date or rushing off to an important job interview. In being honest with our children and our partners, we need to exercise some restraint, tact, and proper timing. Sensitive honesty presumes common sense and prudence. We cannot simply blurt out painful truths at any old moment. Telling the truth in a confrontational way can be an attempt to impose change on another person or, worse yet, a way of fighting. But tactful and balanced honesty helps to build a realistic picture of the family and enhance trust between members. Dishonesty and pretence, obviously, have opposite effects.

Lying is the most verbally explicit form of deception, the form giving the clearest linguistic indication that a speaker is trying to manipulate others into false beliefs. A lie is an explicit statement, uttered so as to lure the audience into assuming that the speaker believes what he says (when he does not). "I was at the school doing extra work on my report," says Jill, who was in fact at the home of a drug-using friend her parents have forbidden her to see. She says it straight, implying that that is where she was, that is where she believes she was. It is an outright, straightforward lie. Jill intends to deceive her mother, manipulating her into believing a falsehood, so she can get away with breaking the rules.

But lying is not the only means of deception and certainly not the only one that undermines trust. We may deceive by omission and evasion, by not telling. A girl who was shoplifting may deliberately avoid responding to questions about where her new clothes came from. She does not lie: she deceives by misleading, by giving partial information which, though true, conveys a false impression. Beth did not lie to Conrad in words. She lived in falsehood – lived to uphold a mythical representation of her family life that was not true to her own emotions.

Writing of life in communist Czechoslovakia, Vaclav Havel said that his people had lived a lie and had done this for so long that they became morally ill.[4] They had to pretend to believe in an ideology and a regime that they knew were not working, and they mouthed so many empty slogans that they hardly understood what they meant any more. With less excuse than the inhabitants of a totalitarian society, many of us lapse into living a lie. We have a notion of how things should be, and we talk and act as though they were that way, keeping up a falsely cheerful façade and refusing to attend to unpleasant realities. Pretence is innocent enough in limited circumstances, as when children pretend to be circus performers, princes, or dinosaurs. But when it becomes the basis for a way of life, it is a profoundly serious matter. Pretence can amount to living a lie, and when the truth is known, a whole way of life will be revealed as deeply flawed because it was founded on hypocrisy.[5]

We often pretend in order to keep up appearances, something that is important in many families. By convention, adult partners tend to present a public image of harmony and smooth functioning. It is standard practice to show a solid "front" to the public world and even to fairly close friends. While loyalty to a partner is desirable and necessary, and we should not expose every minor quarrel and domestic misery to the world at large, such pretence can be emotionally stressful and psychologically unhealthy – as it was for Beth, Calvin, and Conrad. It can also be harmful by preventing the family from getting help and exposing vulnerable members to damage.

FAMILY SECRETS

Nearly as much as lying, family secrets work to undermine trust. A family secret is not merely information kept from others; it is significant information, nearly always with negative emotional implications.

Family secrets usually involve intimate or threatening matters: addiction, imprisonment, suicide, illness and death, migration status, abortion, adoption, infertility, sexual orientation, affairs, incest, or violence. Virtually every family has its secrets: the mother who gave up her first child for adoption, the institutionalized aunt, the alcoholic uncle, the cousin who had an abortion.[6] Clearly, family secrets are a violation of therapeutic recommendations that people communicate honestly, express their feelings and concerns openly, and articulate and attempt to resolve their conflicts through cooperative discussion. Family members try to hide unpleasant truths in a attempt to protect others from shame and anxiety. But even when people have good intentions in trying to keep things hidden, secrets tend to undermine trust within the family.

The main problem with family secrets is that they are seldom fully concealed. Usually, some people know the secret and others suspect it. In families, secrets tend to separate people from one another; a line is drawn between those who know and those who do not. The daughter who had an abortion tells her sisters, but not her parents. The father having an affair reveals it to his brother and son, but not to his wife and daughter. Thus secrets tend to create barriers within families. Another problem with secrets is that deception is often necessary in order to maintain them. Such deception is, of course, likely to undermine trust, especially if it is clearly detected, but even when it is not. People are likely to sense that something is not quite right. Facts may be hidden, but feelings are not. Vulnerable family members, especially children, may suspect that central information is being withheld, become anxious, and lose their sense of trust. They may invent explanations that are as fearful and threatening as the truth and may blame themselves for the inexplicable fact that something seems wrong with the family. For family relations, openness is nearly always better than secretiveness.

SEXUAL INFIDELITY

In most intimate partnerships, people want and expect sexual loyalty. In his recent book about sexual infidelity, Frank Pittman, a family therapist, estimates that 85 per cent of men and women believe that monogamous relationships are ideal. Nevertheless, some 50 per cent of husbands and 30 to 40 per cent of wives report having had affairs.[7] One would assume that loyalty between non-married partners would be no better. Pittman takes affairs seriously, and he argues that his colleagues tend to underestimate the threat that they pose. His fellow family therapists, Pittman thinks, are trying too hard to be modern and liberated. In doing so, they miss something that should be absolutely obvious: the destructive effect of sexual betrayal on what were committed relationships.

Pittman's views confirm the centrality of trust in intimate relationships. His main argument against affairs is that they lead to secrets and deception, thus undermining trust between partners. It is not uncommon for people to be sexually unfaithful to their spouses or partners, but it is relatively uncommon for them to admit it openly. Affairs are kept secret from the partner and other members of the family. When an affair is ongoing, it requires many practical arrangements that necessitate deception and outright lies. Keeping all the details straight, to make sure one is giving a plausible and consistent narrative, will be stressful. Living under such pressures, the person having an affair is unlikely to be open or intimate with his or her partner. If the relationship was not flawed before the affair began, it will soon become so. While their intimacy is disappearing, there is another person with whom the disloyal partner can be intimate and open: the lover, called by Pittman the "affairee."

Affairs nearly always require secrets; they lead to deception, lying, and breakdowns in intimacy. Undermining trust, they undermine intimacy. When the affair is discovered, the many attendant lies are often as harmful to the marriage or partnership as is the affair itself. Unless restorative action is taken, affairs are likely to destroy what was a workable partnership. They break the bond of marriage or partnership and cause a person to fall out of love with his or her partner. It is an illusion, a self-deception, to think that the partner is safe because the affair is a secret and she knows nothing of it. The very fact of the secret makes the defecting partner an ally of the affairee and establishes a rupture in the marriage or relationship. A man who is having an affair need not keep secrets from his lover, but he does have to keep secrets from his wife. That very fact will make him feel closer to his lover and more distanced from his wife, will increase intimacy within the affair and diminish it within the marriage.

The deceived partner is likely to feel utterly betrayed when she finds out about the affair and the deception that attended it. The very act of love, her most intimate act, was founded on falsehoods; she may think to herself that her home and identity, the very core of her domestic life, have become untrue. On the basis of years of practice as a family therapist, Pittman has come to regard nearly all affairs as self-indulgent, unrealistic, and harmful. Lying, secrecy, and deception are at least as harmful as sexual disloyalty itself. "It's not whom you lie with. It's whom you lie to," he says.[7] Pittman has harsh words for adults who have committed themselves to marriage and children and who nevertheless feel entitled to indulge their every sexual wish. Contrary to popular wisdom in therapeutic circles, he insists than an affair begun on a whim in an unusual circumstance or unlikely moment can destroy what was a fairly satisfactory marriage and home.

People have implausible excuses for their sexual disloyalty, and these are too easily accepted by others who do not want to be "judgmental" and underestimate the harm that sexual disloyalty to a spouse or committed partner can bring. "One young man had an affair in order to impress his heroically adulterous father-in-law. One woman insisted she had affairs during episodes of split personality. A man claimed he was kidnapped by visitors from outer space and offered sexual opportunities with them. He had felt it his patriotic and scientific duty to investigate the situation fully."[8] People deceive themselves about the reasons for their affairs and the effect that they are having on their marriage. A man who is having an affair and keeping it secret will feel guilty and distanced from his wife. The fact that he can relax and be open with the affairee, yet has to hide things from his wife, with whom he will feel uncomfortable, means that his affair will become more fulfilling and relaxing than his marriage. Thus the affair is likely to be the favoured relationship if he has to choose between them.

It is misleading to insist upon a distinction between deception and secrecy in such cases. Whether the disloyal partner is lying, deceiving, pretending, or keeping a secret does not especially matter: the fact is that he or she is deeply involved in ways which affect him or her physically and emotionally and which his or her spouse does not know about. Marital intimacy and eventually marriage itself will be undermined. In most marriages and other intimate partnerships, sexual disloyalty and deception about it will amount to betrayal. One partner has broken a tacit or explicit promise to preserve his or her sexuality and sexual intimacy for the other. When this happens, women and children tend to be the most vulnerable.

A common effect of affairs is for people to end up distrusting marriage itself. Like the young woman who complained of her parents' multiple marriages and separations and her numerous step-parents, step-grandparents, and half-siblings, disloyal partners and people who observe them come to believe that there is something wrong with being married. Marriages do not seem to last, so marriage must be a faulty institution. Observing that others can apparently be happily married and yet their (apparent) security and comfort can be destroyed by sexual whim and indulgence, many people come to believe that the institution is not to be trusted. Pittman claims that this is the wrong conclusion to draw on the basis of the evidence. Seeing multiple affairs, divorces, separations, custody battles, and the like, people should not lose their faith in marriage. Rather, they should distrust the sexual indulgence that can wreak such havoc by bringing what were apparently good marriages to sudden and irrational ends. What causes divorce, Pittman argues, is not the fact that marriage is a flawed institution, but the sexual indulgence and disloyalty that we have come to tolerate or even expect. He contends that when people are in a committed relationship, and especially when they are married with children, they should not feel free to indulge every sexual wish and whim.

The belief that marriages are unlikely to endure can be a self-fulfilling prophecy. For the young woman who complained about her uncommitted parents, the belief that she cannot achieve a lasting marriage in which she is a responsible parent may become true because she believes it. People who distrust marriage and committed relationships will have a hard time remaining in them. They are thus likely to have unsuccessful marriages and to acquire further personal experience to back up their lack of confidence in marriage. As in so many other contexts, distrust tends to perpetuate and confirm itself. Once marriage is viewed as unreliable and unstable, we are less likely to try to make it work.

To ride with the daily ups and downs of a household, especially one with growing children, we need a certain amount of trust or faith that we will persist with what is, in essence, a basically good-enough relationship and home. We need to think of ourselves and our partner as surviving daily challenges. Commitment requires belief in itself. To remain in a relationship, partners have to trust that it is viable and can endure. The idea that marriage is unreliable because such relationships can so easily be destroyed by affairs may be unreasonable. Perhaps it is sexual impulses that should not be trusted. Following their impulses into casual affairs leads people to break up good-enough families and satisfactory homes, thereby incurring tremendous damage to their spouses and children and exposing themselves to emotional turmoil, financial cost, and considerable practical inconvenience.

Secrecy and the later exposure of secrets are especially destructive of trust for children, who tend to be the most vulnerable family members when a marriage ends. Children try to preserve a favourable picture of their parents and have a deep need to view them as loving and dependable people. If they discover that one parent has only been pretending to love the other, that one parent has been lying about what he is doing, they feel devastated because their very life seems to have been centred around a pretence. In cases where parents have seemed to their children to have a good relationship, the impact can be all the more devastating. The child's whole picture of the world is put in question. Home is the foundation of everything else, and it is no longer the secure place it seemed to be. Trust in parents, especially the parent whose affair necessitates the break-up, is seriously affected, as is trust in the institution of marriage, commited relationships, and the adult world in general.

Pittman's account of marriage and affairs gives trust an absolutely central role as the basis for intimate partnerships. He argues convincingly that it is not sexual yearnings for other partners or even outside sexual relationships as such that constitute the real betrayal of the partner. Rather, falsehood and pretence, secrecy and lying, destroy the trust that genuine intimacy requires. For women and men, trust in the partner is the essential foundation of a secure home.

VIOLENCE AND SEXUAL ASSAULT

When home is a place of violence or sexual assault, any notion that it is a place of security or comfort is destroyed. Common-sense thinking about home and family depicts the home as a secure and comfortable base for public life. As late as 1960, experts were estimating that incest would occur to only one in a million people. Freud had many female patients with stories of sexual abuse by fathers and uncles. But he could not believe that society was so rotten at its core, and to resist that conclusion, he came to regard those stories as indicative of infantile sexual longings. Recent evidence suggests that sexual abuse and violence within families are far more common than they were formerly thought to be.[9]

A recent newspaper account in Canada estimated that one in every three adult women and one in eight men had at some time been sexually abused. In a recent book on families in the United States, Stephanie Coontz quotes a poll, based on self-report, which suggested that one in seven persons had been sexually abused. As for violence, a common estimate for Canadian households is that one in ten is characterized by domestic violence. A poll undertaken by Carleton University in Ottawa indicated that slightly over half of Canadian women had, at some time in their lives, been abused by a male partner – a husband, partner, or boyfriend. Among native Canadian communities in the far north, estimates are far higher: one is that some 80 to 90 per cent of households experience violence against women.

Obviously, these figures are not precise, and reporting techniques in this sensitive area are not altogether reliable. Victims of abuse or violence may be more likely than others to respond to surveys and interviews, so that studies inadvertently generate an unrepresentative sample. Some statistics do not distinguish between abuse in the home and abuse elsewhere, or between verbal and physical abuse. The Carleton study, for instance, used an extremely broad definition of "abuse."[10] But even allowing for imprecision and overestimation, such evidence shows that the home is far from the safe haven that we have mythically assumed it to be, especially for the women and children who are most commonly the victims of violence. In one memorable statement, the U.S. surgeon general said that the home was a more dangerous place for American women than the streets.[11]

Ninety-nine per cent of the kidnappers of young children are their own parents, and most sexual and physical abuse of children occurs in their own homes. There are many patterns of abuse, but most abuse is of women and girls and is perpetrated by men. Ninety-two per cent of the victims of child sexual abuse are girls, and 97 per cent of the offenders are male. Though men are more often victims of violence than women, this is not true for domestic violence, where the large preponderance of victims are female.

So far as trust is concerned, the issue is too obvious to merit much comment. Violence, sexual assault, and physical abuse impose gross harm on victims, undermining any trust that the perpetrator is a loving, caring person and the home a safe place to be. For children, sexual assault by a father or mother constitutes a fundamental rupture in the world, a profound violation of their sense of how the world should be. The idea that a parent is someone loving and caring, someone meriting authority, who can nurture and give direction and advice, is absolutely shaken when that parent turns out to be a sexual abuser. What he does hurts; it will feel confusing, painful, and wrong. Sexual abuse by a parent or relative is virtually always accompanied by an attempt to impose secrecy; the child is made to feel responsible, bribed, threatened, or otherwise intimated into silence. Typically, abuse is accompanied by a sense of feeling dirty, worthless, and shamed, feelings that are only worsened if – as is so often the case – the attempt to impose secrecy on the victim is successful.

Needless to say, the effects on the victim's self-esteem and self-trust are likely to be devastating. She may repress all memory of the abuse, only to recover it later under the influence of some particular trigger. Though the concept of abuse has been stretched, and the dysfunctionality of families in general exaggerated, by theorists of the codependency movement, sexual abuse in families is a real fact of life. Families in which there is sexual abuse or violence really *are* "dysfunctional" – or worse. Whatever its nature, sexual abuse in the family is bound to be painful and to leave persistent and terrible effects. For the battered woman, home and family offer no comfort, only fear. A wall with spots, a supper that does not suit the dominant lord, a crying child or messy living room, can spark a serious beating.

The victim's sense of the abuser (especially if he is a parent), other family members, the family as a whole, the broader world, and her own self will be seriously affected. If the abuse is not revealed and ended, the victim lives in a world of shame, deception, and secrecy, a false world in which he or she plays a part in a pretence that cloaks a terrible reality. Victims lose their innocence and are robbed of their childhood. In this sort of context, appeals to traditional family values are quite beside the point. If anything, patriarchal practices and the privacy of the nuclear family tend to facilitate sexual abuse of women and children. The family characterized by sexual abuse or violence is typically one in which women and children are submissive and powerless, economically dependent on the earnings of male breadwinners, and accepting of an ideology of male domination. A man who sees himself as the head of the household, who should and does prevail over his wife and children, can more easily see himself as entitled to sexual privileges. On this view, his needs are all-important, and he has the right to fulfil himself however he can. Family violence seems to be facilitated by patriarchal and traditional assumptions about family and gender roles. It is probably not a result of male backlash against increasing female power: domestic violence is even more prevalent in highly patriarchal societies than in our own.[12]

It seems unlikely that violence and abuse in families are more common in the nineties than they were in the forties and fifties or earlier periods of history. Probably they were always present, and what is distinctive today is not the frequency of such abuse and violence but public knowledge and discussion about them. Now victims need not hide their shameful secrets as they once did. Hundreds of thousands of women believed they were the "one in a million" case of incest and said nothing. Journalists and researchers who came across evidence of incest or other sexual abuse within families tended to dismiss it. If they tried to publicize it, they were told that it was incredible or "too depressing."[13] A positive front had to be maintained: whatever the truth might be, the patriarchal nuclear family had to be upheld as the "foundation" of society. Patriarchal power relationships and relative isolation in traditional families did not prevent abuse; if anything, they helped to make it possible. Appealing to traditional family values to solve this social problem is clearly beside the point: the patriarchal nuclear family was more cause than cure.

Strangely, trust between men and women in battering relationships does not entirely disappear. Women often forgive their battering partners and become reconciled with them, temporarily at least. Repeated reconciliation and forgiveness are notorious features of battering relationships.[14] They can bring elements of sweet romance and make the relationship seem attractive again – until the next attack.

REFLECTIONS

A good-enough family needs trust at all levels – trust between parents or adult partners, trust between children and parents, and trust among the children themselves. In a single-parent family, the bonds between parent and children are especially important. For relationships to be genuine and supportive, for relaxation to be possible and problems to be solved, trust is essential. Without trust, there can be no real intimacy and security within the family. When the family lives in a home together, relationships between members tend to be intense. Contact is frequent and many things can go wrong. There are so many factors that can undermine the trust between members: hypocrisy and falseness, poor communication, lack of openness, manipulativeness, lying, deception, secrecy, and pretence. Understanding how they threaten intimacy and trust serves again to indicate just how important trust is.

But we should not in every case hold ourselves responsible for keeping the family together or for maintaining trust in relations between family members. In this context as in every other, there are cases when distrust and suspicious are warranted and necessary. We should, in many cases, try to trust, try to give our children or partners the benefit of the doubt. But trust should not be based on self-deception. We have no obligation to trust, or try to trust, when there is good reason not to. We should not try to bend our minds to believe things that we know are not true; we should not opt for implausible interpretations of what is going on, just to preserve a positive picture of the others. Trust is one thing, self-deception another, blind loyalty another, and gullibility yet another. As in other situations, trust only goes so far. Trying to force ourselves to trust by ignoring evidence is no good. If we do this, we will base our trust on self-deception and pretence. Such "trust" will not be genuine, and the family relationships that are founded upon it will be false and unreliable.

All trust is risky, and trust within the family may be the most risky of all. The old risk for women in marriage was to trust too much: to trust that the husband would be the breadwinner, would provide economically, and would be sexually loyal and loving throughout a lifetime. On such assumptions, many millions of women devoted their lives to unpaid work in the home, allowed themselves to be

economically dependent on their husbands, and left themselves
deeply vulnerable. Many gave up their own opportunities to work at
lowly jobs supporting husbands through a professional education;
others left interesting work to care for young children. Notoriously,
for many of these women, the foundation fell out. Their partners
were not loyal. They departed, leaving women and their children in a
precarious situation. Knowledge of the relative frequency of divorce
and break-ups, acceptance of the feminist view that women have
talents and should have opportunities to use them in broader public
work, and the economic advantage of having two wage earners make
this old vulnerability uncommon today. The new risk may not be
overcommitment, but rather a lack of commitment – losses because
we are unable to believe in lasting relationships.

Most people live in families in a home and work to make those
families viable. To do so we have to trust our partners and our children, and we have to be committed to our own relationships. Despite
all our problems, this trust is still possible for many people. And
when we understand its importance, we can use it to communicate
honestly and openly, to transcend our lies, to share our secrets, and to
build a better life together. Trust in the family should not be categorical or absolute; nor will it be, given the real circumstances of daily
life. Like most forms of trust in this world, it will be partial, qualified,
and compromised. But nevertheless it will be real. Without a modi-
cum of trust, the family is doomed.

For all its flaws, for all its risks, our family is our first human circle.
Most of us have created another family that provides us as adults
with our companions and home. Good-enough families are founded,
not on heterosexuality and stereotypical gender roles, not on male
providers, not on biological reproduction, but on trust between
people who live together in a home, trust each other, and are committed to building and living a life together. Adult partners who trust
each other bring up children who trust them. Those children can then
move into the greater world with basic security and confidence. In a
good-enough family a child trusts her parents and begins to trust
herself.

CHAPTER FIVE

Self-Trust

In a poignant essay the American therapist Carl Rogers described the tragic case of a young German woman known as Ellen West. A sensitive and expressive woman who married unhappily and starved herself into slimness, Ellen West was treated by numerous psychiatrists and doctors, and spent several years in a sanatorium. Released despite doctors' knowledge that she was suicidal, she took a lethal dose of poison and died at the age of thirty-three. Rogers saw Ellen West as a person taught not to trust herself. She was distanced from herself to such an extent that she did not know or fully experience her own emotions. Instead, she seemed to feel as others told her she was supposed to feel. Her emotions, and her sense of her own emotions, were inauthentic, and as a result she had difficulty relating to other people. Coerced into conforming her love life to the dictates of her parents, Ellen ignored her own feelings and wishes. The result was a "respectable" self through which she tried to live. Lacking all confidence in her own responses, thought, and good judgment, she failed to trust herself.

At twenty, Ellen West was a lively young woman who had enjoyed a happy childhood. Then she fell in love with a young man to whom her father took violent objection. Her parents convinced her that she was not in love and persuaded her to give up the man. Unhappy, she began to overeat. Then, teased about being fat, she started to diet. If other people did not like what she was becoming, she would change herself to conform to their expectations. Rogers commented: "It is perhaps indicative of the beginnings of her lack of trust in herself that she begins to diet only when teased by her companions. She feels an increasing need to live her life in terms of the expectations of others, since her own impulses are unreliable."[1]

At twenty-four, Ellen fell in love with a fellow student to whom she became engaged. But her parents insisted that this love was not the real thing; she did not know her true feelings. This love was not right; she could not be feeling what she thought she felt. As a result of parental pressure, Ellen came to see herself as an "untrustworthy organism." Finally, disregarding and distrusting her own experience and feelings, she gave up the relationship. She could not decide what to do with her life. It seemed to be teaching her that her own feelings were not a reliable guide to action; only the experience of others could be trusted. Ellen turned to a doctor for help. She became extremely depressed and began to deny not only her feelings but her desire for food and the natural shape of her own body. She dieted ferociously.

When she was twenty-eight, Ellen West married a cousin approved by her family. By thirty-two she was starving herself, taking sixty laxative pills a day, and seeing analysts and doctors. Isolated from her own feelings and needs, she became progressively more detached from other people. Doctors saw her as an object, a strange, abnormal mechanism that had gone out of control. They argued about what sort of object she was. What was she a manic-depressive, a melancholic, an obsessive-compulsive, a schizophrenic? Suicidal? Ellen wrote, "I confront myself as a strange person. I am afraid of myself." Diagnosed as suicidal, she soon fulfilled the prophecy. Rogers could find no evidence that anyone treating Ellen had tried to relate to her as a person capable of autonomy and worthy of respect, one whose "inner experience is a precious resource to be drawn upon and trusted." The story of Ellen West offers a tragic illustration of the importance of self-trust.

WHAT IS SELF-TRUST?

The concept of self-trust was pivotal in a doctoral study by Doris Brothers. In 1982 she examined trust disturbances among young women who had been victims of rape or incest. Her sample was quite small: she studied twenty young women aged nineteen or twenty. Brothers distinguished three types of trust: trust in others (e.g., Mary trusts Celeste to look after her home); trust in the self when this concerns behaviour affecting others (e.g., Mary trusts herself to drive the school bus carefully); and trust in the self when this concerns a person's own attitudes and actions (e.g., Mary trusts her own judgment and instincts when she is making decisions). The third sort of trust is what Ellen West lacked. Brothers called it "self-trust."[2]

To determine self-trust in the young women she was interviewing, Doris Brothers questioned them about their attitudes and likely responses to various circumstances. How did they think they would respond to disappointments? How much confidence did they have in their own self-control? What were their expectations about success in jobs and careers? In personal relationships? How would they respond to other people's opinions about them? To efforts by others to control them? What confidence did they have in their ability to make decisions?

In posing these questions, Brothers assumed that a person with self-trust would believe that she could cope with problems she might face and deal with her own responses to things that might happen to her. To trust oneself is to see oneself as a person who can cope and function in the world, a person who does not need to be monitored, guided, advised, or controlled by others. Brothers believed that self-trust requires self-acceptance: when we trust ourselves, we have a sense of our own competence; we believe that we can control ourselves and make reasonable judgments about what to do. From this sense of competence and adequacy, we can be hopeful about our prospects for the future.

The results of Brothers's study were disturbing. The young women interviewed, all victims of rape and incest, experienced severe disruptions in trust, most of all in the area of self-trust. Although they had been violated by men, they tended to blame *themselves* for what had happened.[3] They devalued *themselves* and had a diminished sense of their own competence and good judgment. This tragic response may have been an attempt to render traumatic events intelligible and preserve a sense of the world as a tolerably safe place. (Why would this happen? What could make such a thing happen? I must have done something wrong. There must have been something I could have done to prevent it, and I didn't do it. It was my fault. So there is something wrong with me.) Paradoxically, blaming themselves was a way of making sense of the world and reasserting a degree of control. Sexual assaults by known persons would indicate that even relatives and friends do not love this person, will not take care of her. Even at home, intimacy is a dangerous thing. Attacks by total strangers (so-called blitz rapes or random acts of violence) would suggest that anyone might attack at any time. Either way, the implications of sexual assault are frightening. But by blaming herself, a young women could blot out some of the fear; if she was to blame, then by changing aspects of her own behaviour and style, she could prevent similar things from happening again. Blaming oneself in these cases seemed to be a way of preserving a sense of a safe world. It is as though a young woman is saying, "Somehow, I brought it on myself. Fundamentally, home and the world are still all right. There must be something wrong with me."

These results are especially tragic because lack of self-trust is a devastating handicap in life. Without it a person cannot achieve personal autonomy. She cannot make her own judgments and decisions; she cannot form her own opinions and beliefs. She drifts, responding to pressures and opinions, an easy victim for others with controlling personalities. By contrast, an autonomous person is capable of making her own decisions and choices and controlling her own life.

One helpful way to think about autonomy is to reflect on the thoughts we have and the procedures we implement when we are making choices and deciding what to do. In modern Western cultures, at least, individual autonomy is an important value. We have only one life to lead in this world, and most of us feel that we should make the best of it in our own way. That requires autonomy – independent judgment about what to believe and do. And autonomy absolutely requires self-trust. Ellen West, who had no self-trust and no autonomy either, let her parents and friends dictate to her. In her case, the results were disastrous. To exercise autonomy in planning and leading our lives, we need to discover our own talents, feelings, beliefs, and values. We need to define who we are, understand ourselves, think for ourselves, and set our own goals. We seek, within limits, to direct our own lives.[4] If we do not trust ourselves, we are incapable of judging, deciding, and choosing for ourselves. To make autonomous decisions, we have to ask ourselves questions about what we really want, need, and care about, and we have to seek answers to these questions from within ourselves. Of course, we may take advice and suggestions from others, and we should think carefully about what they have to say. But in the final analysis, it is for us to make up our minds about what to think and do. Although the opinions and suggestions of others must be taken into account, they should not outweigh our own beliefs, instincts, and feelings. To exercise autonomy, to live our lives as responsible and active individuals, we must value our own wants and needs. We have confidence in our own emotional, intellectual, and moral competence. And this is simply to say that, in order to make autonomous decisions, we have to trust ourselves. When self-trust is undermined, we do not rely on our own judgment and do not make our own decisions.

As the case of Ellen West so vividly illustrates, self-trust and autonomy are absolutely essential for a person's mental health and very survival. To make an autonomous decision, a person must be capable of introspection – looking into himself to reflect on what he feels, wants, and believes. He must be capable too of thinking back, remembering past events and feelings, and working out what they meant and mean, what their significance is for his identity, goals, and prospects. He must be capable of critical reflection and deliberation. All this requires self-trust, the abililty to rely on one's own critical reflection and judgment.[5]

THE ANALOGY BETWEEN TRUSTING ONESELF AND TRUSTING OTHERS

When we trust another person, we have positive expectations about that person's motivation, competence, and actions. We believe in his or her basic integrity; we are willing to rely on him or her. And when we do so, we make ourselves vulnerable to that person. Trusting, we accept our vulnerability. Trust affects the way we understand another person and interpret what he says and does. If someone we trust tells an off-colour joke or excludes us from a conversation, we do not take it as an insult. If he fails to call when he said he would, we do not conclude that he is no longer a friend. Trust between people is not an all-or-nothing matter. It can exist in various degrees: we may trust someone only a little, considerably, or absolutely. Our trust is often relative to situation and circumstance. We might, for instance, trust a person to do the gardening, but not to care for our children or manage our financial affairs. Usually, trusting involves expectations based to some extent on past behaviour. Still, trust goes beyond what evidence shows. Because circumstances and people change, predictions of the future behaviour of free agents cannot be guaranteed. Trust involves risk and vulnerability. When we trust other people, we are at risk; we are vulnerable to them, but we let ourselves be vulnerable because we feel confident that they will not let us down.

All these aspects of trust between persons hold true for self-trust. The expression "self-trust" is not metaphorical; we can literally trust ourselves. When we do so, we have positive beliefs about our own motivations and competence. We see ourselves as persons of integrity. We are willing to rely or depend on ourselves, accepting risks attendant on our own decisions and our vulnerability to their consequences. And we have a general disposition to understand ourselves in a positive light, an implicit sense of our own basic worth and integrity. A person who sees himself or herself as basically well intentioned and competent and as able to make reasonable judgments and decisions and carry out reasonable plans of action is one with self-trust.[6]

Like interpersonal trust, self-trust exists in degrees and may be relativized to various contexts. No one trusts herself absolutely and in every respect, and no one should.[7] We might, for instance, trust ourselves to give a public lecture or do the family laundry, but not to offer advice to a suicidal adolescent or find our way around in a Turkish city. To function as an autonomous human being, to be able to feel and value our own feelings, interpret our own experiences, and direct our own lives, what we need is basic, or *core*, self-trust. This means having a sense of confidence in ourselves as feeling, remembering, knowing, judging, and acting agents. To have this self-trust we do not need to be confident of our competence and motivation in every context.

Unlike self-esteem, which is closely related to it, self-trust is not a trendy concept. We do not hear much about it.[8] Many people, even those who are quite reflective, would not bother to ask whether or in what respects they trust themselves. Often, as happens so frequently in issues of trust, we become conscious of self-trust just when it is missing. In some respect, we do not trust ourselves, and because we do not do so just at that moment, we may become aware that "normally," we do trust ourselves.[9] Set out for a walk, cook dinner, read a book, or purchase an airline ticket – do we trust ourselves when we do such things? We would never think of saying so; we take it for granted that we know how to do things and can cope with what will come up in such mundane activities. In such matters, as adults who are sane and functioning in their own society, *we believe implicitly* that we are able to do these things. We can speak the language, are understood, know our names and addresses, can find our way around, and are competent and sane.[10] If this were not so, we could not function in day-to-day life. Does all this mean that we trust ourselves? Yes, to a degree – although we are scarcely ever aware of it.

Issues of self-trust come closer to the surface when we are challenged in some way and have to respond. Then we need our self-trust, and then it helps to have considered what self-trust is and why it is important. We have to make judgments about what is going on; we have to make decisions about what to do; we then have to carry out these decisions. In the interests of autonomy, we should do these things ourselves. If we are making decisions with a partner, he should not drown out or control our contribution. If we are insecure in our sense of our own values, motives, and capacities, we may lose ourselves too easily. We may follow a bandwagon or cave in, for no good reason, to the pressures of a dominating boss, colleague, or partner.[11] Or, for that matter, even to a demanding child. "Just say no," the saying goes, and often that is right. "No means no," to be sure. But we can want to say no, have a strong sense that we ought to do so, and yet not quite manage to do it. We can bend too easily to the suggestions and criticisms of other people, yield too readily to social pressures, or lack initiative in overcoming obstacles. Without self-trust, it is not possible to make effective decisions.

When a person experiences something, interprets what has happened, and later remembers and recounts what she has experienced, she may not think of herself as *trusting* or *not trusting* herself. However, should she or others begin to question her idea of what happened, the issue of self-trust will become obvious. Is it for others to tell her what she is feeling, what her experiences meant, or what she remembers? Self-trust may become an issue when a person has to decide whether she can depend on herself to implement a decision and act on her own values in a difficult situation, as is illustrated by the following example.

Joseph is a recovering alcoholic. With the assistance of an AA group and his supportive family, he has been dry for three months. Joseph has been invited to a wedding reception where alcohol will be served. He fears the event will be stressful, not only because of the alcohol but because some years previously he had a passionate affair with the woman who is about to be married. Officially they are now just friends, but it was she who ended the affair, and Joseph was very unhappy about it at the time. In deciding whether to attend the reception, he reflects on whether he can trust himself to cope with his emotions, have the will-power to stay off alcohol when under stress, and – if he does have a lapse with drinking – return later to his AA program. If he decides to go, he is in effect trusting himself to conform to his values in these trying circumstances.

In deciding whether to attend the reception, Joseph has to ask himself whether he will be able to stick to his decision not to drink. If, after reflection, he goes to the reception, he is trusting himself to cope with the situation and its aftermath. If he choses to stay away, he has decided his control is not good enough. Though he does not feel strong enough to attend, he can feel good about having the wisdom to avoid a setback in his struggle against alcoholism.

Another case illustrating the effect of self-trust is that of Linda, a single parent with three sons. She lives in an upper-middle-class district, but because of her recent divorce, she has a lower income than many others in the area. Her youngest son, Robert, has been in the first grade for five months but does not yet read. Linda speaks with Robert's teacher, Eleanor, at a parent-teacher interview. Eleanor says that Robert is rather slow at reading, slower certainly than many others in the class. She then suggests that he would be quite normal and would fit into a class better if he were in a poorer part of town where people are "slower." Describing the encounter, Linda said of Eleanor, "She destroyed my trust."

Linda heard Eleanor's comment as expressing stereotyping, prejudice, and hasty judgment. She discounted Eleanor's response, finding it so disturbing that she could no longer regard her as a competent teacher. In this instance, she trusted herself and she ceased to trust Eleanor – as a teacher, in any event. Linda reacted in this way because she relied on her own beliefs and values. She made a negative judgment about the teacher and preserved her sense that as a mother she was providing a reasonable environment for her family. If Linda did not trust herself, if she felt doubts about her own competence as a mother and had little confidence in her capacity to provide for her children emotionally and economically, she would have responded to the encounter in quite a different way. Perhaps she would have worried about her ability to bring up her children; perhaps she would have nagged Robert to speed up and prove that their family was as good as the others; perhaps she would have moved to another, less "threatening" district.

There are many dimensions of self-trust. We may be called upon to trust our perceptions and observations; interpretations of events and actions; feelings and responses; values; memory, judgment, instinct, common sense, and will; capacity to act, flexibility, competence, talent, and ability to cope with the unexpected. When we trust ourselves, we have a conviction that on the whole we are competent and sensible people who can do what the situation demands. Whether an issue of self-trust arises, whether and how much a person trusts herself will vary from one context to another. To lack self-trust in some restricted capacity or specific situation is not necessarily a serious handicap. Few people would be restricted or burdened by the sense that they could not rely on themselves to purchase a second-hand car, explore Istanbul unguided, or do suicide counselling. This contextual self-distrust may very well be helpful, inhibiting us from mistakes and rash behaviour and from accepting responsibilities that we cannot carry out. But core distrust of oneself – self-doubt in fundamental areas – is something else again. To lack general confidence in our own general ability to observe and interpret events, to remember and recount, to deliberate and act, is a handicap so serious as to threaten our status as an individual moral agent and our basic self-respect.[12]

If a person were to distrust her memory of her own childhood, her ability to understand the gestures and comments of other people, her instinctive feelings towards acquaintances and possible friends, her sense of her own interests and abilities as regards occupation and leisure activities, and her ability to define and implement future goals, she would lack self-trust in core areas. In such a case, she could scarcely function as a person. Absence of this core self-trust would make effective choice and personal autonomy impossible. To reflect on our beliefs and values, to work out a resolution in cases where those beliefs and values conflict, it is necessary to view ourselves as having worthy values, competently founded beliefs, and the cognitive and moral capacity to make good judgments and implement decisions. All this is simply to say that we need, in fundamental respects, to trust ourselves – to believe that we can do these things reliably and dependably and need not turn over our judgmental and decision-making powers to others.[13]

When we trust another person, we have experience with that person and evidence about her. We know her, to some extent, through what she does and says. We have a sense of what sort of person she is from being with her, doing things with her, and seeing and listening to her. With self-trust, our evidence is about ourselves. We have more evidence because we have been with ourselves our whole life. But despite all this experience, we do not have perfect self-knowledge. We can forget, misinterpret, overvalue or undervalue, or deceive ourselves.

When we trust another person, we are vulnerable to him or her. If that person acts badly, we are in a situation not of our own making, from which we must retrieve ourselves. If we trust someone to mail an important document and he forgets, we have to cope with the consequences. With self-trust, the predictability of success or failure may be greater: we should know better what is going on because it is, after all, our own self that we are trusting. This is not to say, obviously, that our self-knowledge is perfect. Risk remains: we are vulnerable to our own failings. As with every case of trust, self-trust is risky to some degree. We may be hurt or harmed if we fail to do what we trusted ourselves to do. So far as vulnerability is concerned, trusting another person and trusting ourselves are quite comparable.

CAN WE TRUST OURSELVES TOO MUCH?

The simple answer is yes. We can trust other people too much, and similarly we can, in various ways, trust ourselves too much.[14] Our trust can be too great, considering the evidence on which it is based. Or, although well grounded on evidence, our self-trust can be so complete as to have adverse consequences: we may rely too much on ourselves and too little on others, or become dogmatic in our belief in our own good character and good sense.

Our trust or distrust of ourselves is generally based on our knowledge and beliefs about what we are able to do and our sense of ourself, resulting from our experiences in life.[15] An example of a woman who came not to trust herself in a particular context because of something she did is that of Pat, who irrationally stood up in a canoe in chilly ocean waters. As a result of her sudden motion, she and her friend Susan capsized and barely survived the experience. Reflecting on her impulsive action, which had nearly cost them their lives, Pat said that she would never trust herself in a canoe again – an overstatement probably, but she took this instance of silly and dangerous behaviour to be evidence of something about herself. Pat has unforgettable evidence that she can get carried away when she is having a good time and that she is capable, on occasion, of acting so impulsively and carelessly as to endanger her own life and that of her friend. She knows this about herself because of something she once did; reflecting on it, she trusts herself less in this respect and in this context. A certain amount of caution and healthy self-doubt will result from this frightening experience. If Pat were to write off the episode and not reflect on it at all, one would say she was rash and overconfident with respect to canoeing. If, on the other hand, she had many times safely paddled her canoe through the harbour, she would feel a confidence, based on evidence, that she could do that again.

The young women interviewed by Doris Brothers trusted themselves too little in the area of sexual control. Coerced by others, they nevertheless blamed themselves for giving in, discounting the fact that they had been forced by their attackers. A person trusts herself too much if she trusts herself beyond what the evidence warrants, and too little if she trusts herself less than the evidence warrants, as the following contrasting examples illustrate.[16] When André successfully passed a driver's examination on the first try, he felt confident that he could drive alone to a distant city. He overestimated his ability, inferring too much from a single success. He underestimated the significance of inexperience and possible fatigue or hasty decisions; he had too much confidence in his driving abilities, and in this regard he trusted himself too much. Consider, in contrast, Betty, an older woman who has driven for forty years without accident and yet says that she would not trust herself to drive on the highway. She has ample evidence that she is a good and careful driver, and yet she somehow thinks of highways as more fearful than roads in town and would not have the confidence to drive on them. Based on the evidence of past performance and competence, André trusted himself too much and Betty too little.

In many ways we distort or misinterpret our own past actions. We may see ourselves as being more virtuous and competent than the evidence implies and become too self-confident. Or we may criticize and diminish ourselves, failing to take seriously even our substantial achievements.[17] Selective self-history is a well-known activity, often criticized in autobiographers. In our own story of life and the world, we may be the hero or the victim. Either way, we may exaggerate our own significance. A common phenomenon is the "partisan bias" in which people are, in effect, prejudiced in their own favour. An individual with partisan bias uses a double standard for judging her own success and that of others.[18] If a person has had three unsuccessful marriages, he may "know" that it was not his fault that these relationships failed. Yet he may believe that someone else with three unsuccessful marriages has been "proven" impossible to live with. A double standard: the self is judged far more leniently than the other. A converse syndrome can also be observed. Some people with little self-trust tend to employ a double standard in the other direction, discounting their own successes while inflating those of others and thereby handicapping themselves by underestimating their own power and competence. Both syndromes cause problems. Those biased in their own favour and trusting themselves too much are likely to be rash and overconfident; they may easily alienate other people. Those who trust themselves too little and undervalue their activities will not undertake new ventures and will suffer from diminished self-esteem.

Even when self-trust is backed up by evidence, it can be counterproductive if it is carried too far. Strong self-trust can prevent us from cooperating with others – refusing, for instance, to delegate work when we are in charge. One woman is superbly organized and competent; she can trust herself to get things done because she knows from experience that she can do the job herself and do it well. Her colleagues, children, and friends rely on her constantly and she always comes through. So it has been for much of her life. Even as a child, she took over domestic tasks from her parents. What this woman does is called "over-functioning." The classic joke about over-functioning is the one about the mother so accustomed to cutting her children's meat that she unwittingly assumes everyone needs such assistance and cuts her neighbour's meat at an adult dinner party. People who over-function take on too many tasks and prevent others from developing their competence.

Perversely, such people tend to encounter problems because they are so reliable and dependable. A dependable and capable person may trust herself more than she trusts others and for good reason: she has found from experience that she herself can and will complete various tasks, whereas other people are often undependable. As a result, she becomes unwilling to rely on others and assumes too many responsibilities herself. Such people have strong self-trust, which is supported by evidence and in that sense not irrational. Their self-trust can support their own autonomy and self-direction and can in those ways be an important asset. Because they are largely self-directed, such people are generally immune to social pressure and secure in their self-valuing. But such strong self-trust, though in one sense rational, can go so far as to be counter-productive when it leads to over-functioning. People who over-function characteristically take on too many responsibilities, overloading themselves with work and discouraging the development of competence in others.

In other contexts, strong self-trust can lead to dogmatism and inflexibility. Trusting our own perceptions and judgments, we may be sure that we are right and therefore unwilling to change our minds. Sometimes our confidence can go too far. We need basic self-trust; we need to value ourselves and have confidence in our own feelings and judgments. But our self-trust or self-confidence should not be absolute. Clearly, we can make mistakes about our own abilities and feelings, no less than about other people and external events. To close our minds to the comments and arguments of others, to assume that our own judgments and abilities are certainly and categorically right, is to be dogmatic and inflexible. Absolute self-trust will have negative consequences.

Obviously, absolute self-trust is never warranted. Everyone is fallible. Our own conception of ourselves should not count for everything, should not stand firm in the face of every bit of counter-evidence or counter-interpretation. Reasonable self-trust requires an honest and balanced appraisal of our motives, abilities, and actions, one that takes into account the responses of friends, family, and colleagues. Self-trust should not shield us from all suggestions, advice, or criticism. Nor should it inhibit us from collaborating with and depending on others. What is absolutely crucial is that core of self-trust and self-valuing. We must take our own feelings, beliefs, and responses seriously, make our own choices, for our own reasons, and be capable of acting confidently as we judge we should.

CHAPTER SIX

Self-Trust, Self-Respect, and Self-Esteem

When we have self-respect, we value ourselves for those things that make us persons: our consciousness, choices, capacities, and abilities. A person with self-respect has a sense that he or she is a human being whose interests and ends are valuable and who, as a human being, has dignity and worth. Having self-respect, a person can stand up when demeaned and insulted, with the conviction that these attitudes are not deserved. Allowing ourselves to be exploited, manipulated, or used over a long period of time is seriously undermining to our self-respect; if we become tools enabling others to achieve their ends, our sense that our own ends, goals, and interests are worthy is unlikely to survive.

To have self-respect, we must value ourselves as people. We must regard our own interests, values, beliefs, and goals as important and see ourselves as people with dignity and moral worth – people whose needs and goals are every bit as important as those of others. Self-respect and self-trust are necessary for achievement and success, whatever the undertaking. In any endeavour there are obstacles; if we do not regard our pursuits as worthy and achievable, we will soon give up. If we do not value ourselves and our plans, we will be plagued with self-doubt and unable to move towards our goals.[1] Self-trust requires having a positive sense of our own motivation, competence, and integrity. To persist, we must think that what we are trying to do is worthy and that the way we are trying to do it is fundamentally good. Without this faith in ourselves, we cannot continue effectively in life. If we doubt or distrust ourselves, we see ourselves as ill-motivated, incompetent, and unable to act independently. Doubting, losing faith, we are likely to downplay our qualities and potentialities; we see ourselves as unworthy, lacking integrity, unable to implement worthy goals, and inadequately equipped to deal with the world.

We often face challenges to our actions and beliefs. Obstacles present themselves; things go wrong; relationships turn out badly; others confront and criticize us. To preserve our own sense of our motivation and character, we need resources within ourselves to consider and respond to these sorts of challenges. This is where self-trust enters the picture. We must be able to assess what others say, reflect on our actions, values, and beliefs, determine the accuracy or importance of the challenge, and respond appropriately. This reflection requires relying on our own capacities of memory, deliberation, and judgment, and we will not be able to do so unless we trust ourselves. To discriminate between apt and ill-founded challenges from others, we need to trust our own memory, judgment, and conscience. With no resources to preserve our ideas, values, and goals against criticism and attack from others, we will be too malleable to preserve a sense of being a person in our own right and will therefore be unable to maintain self-respect.

Gross illustrations of this dynamic can be seen in the battered woman syndrome. Battered women can be so demeaned and (literally) beaten down by abusive partners that they come to believe they are worthless beings who deserve what they are getting. They come to accept abuse as a fact of life, something which is found to happen to them and which they are powerless to prevent. Tragically, abuse works to undermine self-respect and self-trust, the very inner resources that are needed to escape it.

Self-trust is necessary to maintain our self-respect. It is also basic in connection with self-esteem. Three basic distinctions help to clarify self-esteem:

a *Core Self-esteem and Situational Self-esteem*   Core self-esteem is our sense that fundamentally we are acceptable persons; situational self-esteem is our sense that we are competent and can act adequately in some specific context or situation. Clearly, one can have core self-esteem without having some types of situational self-esteem. A person may, for instance, be quite secure about her overall worth while nevertheless lacking self-esteem as regards her ability in basketball or her capacity to find her way around a strange city when she does not know the local language.

b *Comparative and Non-comparative Self-esteem*   Self-esteem may be interpreted as comparative: we esteem ourselves, or value ourselves, in comparison to other people. Examples are of a familiar type. A man takes pride in his muscular body; he feels even better about himself when he is in the locker room and compares his trim, strong body with those of other men his age. A girl prides herself on her singing; she entered a competition and won first prize. In each case, the individual's self-esteem is buttressed by the fact that he or she has evidence of superiority over many others. *Comparative* self-esteem is implicitly competitive: we cannot all be "the best," and most of us cannot be better than most others.[2] There is another, deeper kind of self-esteem which is *non-comparative* and not implicitly competitive. We may esteem ourselves simply as the human beings we are, without grading ourselves on any implicit comparative scale. We are individual human beings; we have feelings, desires, hopes, and fears; we love and are loved; we have talents and projects and a place in the world. As human beings, we have a dignity and a claim to respect, and it is these aspects of ourselves that can provide a basis for non-comparative self-esteem. The distinction between comparative and non-comparative self-esteem has immediate practical significance insofar as self-esteem is widely accepted as important for mental health and as a major goal in education. If we accept that it is desirable for everyone to have a good sense of self-esteem, then, to be coherent, we must assume a non-comparative conception of self-esteem. Comparative self-esteem sets one person against others; non-comparative self-esteem does not. If we understand self-esteem comparatively, life begins to seem like a competitive activity. It is obviously impossible for everyone to have well-founded self-esteem in the comparative sense: we cannot all be better than most others. It is desirable for everyone to have a basic and adequate sense of self-esteem; but to say this makes sense only if we understand self-esteem non-comparatively and non-competitively.

c *Inner-based and Outer-based Self-esteem*   There is a difference between our inner sense of self-esteem and a self-esteem based on the expressed attitudes of other people. In the absence of inner resources, a person denigrated by those around her is likely to feel incompetent and worthless. She will be unable to maintain a sense of self-worth and will lack core self-trust. If she has some inner sense of worth and competence, self-trust can enable her to preserve this. Self-trust makes possible independent judgments, an understanding that ill-treatment received is wrong, and a preservation of a positive sense of herself and her future prospects. Solid inner self-esteem is the stuff of terrific narrative, myth, and fairy tale. Cinderella always knew that she was better than a kitchen maid, even though she was consistently abused by her stepmother and stepsisters. How did she maintain that inner conviction that she was a worthy person deserving respect? Why and how did she learn to trust herself? The fairy tale never gave us the answers. Was the Fairy Godmother responsible? Some people can preserve a sense of identity and worth in the face of overwhelmingly difficult circumstances, and that is an inspiring fact. But the prominence of such heroic determination in myth and legend is no guarantee that such inner strength is common in the real social world. Many of us wish that we could stand up against denigration and lack of social recognition, but fear that we cannot. The sad truth is that many abused and downtrodden people are not like Cinderella in this respect.

What is fundamental for self-worth and self-trust is a person's *inner, non-comparative* sense of *core* self-esteem – that is to say, our fundamental sense of self-worth, our basic internal conception as to whether, fundamentally, we are worthy and adequate persons, regardless of how we compare or fare under competition with other people. This inner self-trust and self-esteem does not depend on specific performance in particular contexts such as sports, study, or cooking. It does not require comparison and competition with other people; it is not a matter of mentally checking our status or performance to see how well we are doing in comparison with others. Nor does it depend on luxury goods, a title, status in society, or overt praise from other people. This *basic core self-esteem* is really a matter of self-acceptance, an accepting of ourselves for what we are and a conviction that we are worthy persons whose needs and interests, beliefs and feelings, are absolutely as worthy of attention as those of other people. If we do not accept our motives and goals as worthy, if we do not believe that we have sound judgment and competence in key areas of decision and action, then we cannot trust ourselves, and we lack basic self-esteem.

If, on the other hand, we do trust ourselves, we can more easily protect our self-esteem in contexts where external recognition and acknowledgement are lacking. Like Cinderella, we can, when appropriate, tell ourselves that others are treating us wrongly, demeaning us unjustly, that we are not less worthy than they. If other people should demean or insult us, basic self-trust, supporting self-respect, will be a major personal resource for resistance.

SOURCES OF SELF-TRUST

Obviously, a secure family background tends to make for self-trust. If a person is loved and cared for during infancy and childhood and feels physically and emotionally secure, he or she can form an identity as an accepted, loved, and valuable person. Treated as lovable and valuable by those closest to him or her, such a person will naturally gain a sense of himself or herself as a worthy person meriting respect. If, in addition, a person's upbringing has cultivated the ability to think through issues, deliberate, and make decisions, she or he is more likely to be independent and capable of the autonomous thought and action that are essential to maintain self-trust in later life.

Important, too, are experiences of competence and success. Like other kinds of trust, self-trust is founded in part upon experience. We come to trust ourselves as capable and worthy persons because we have evidence that we can accomplish our goals, make reasonable decisions, and successfully conduct important relationships. Of course, success in action and decision-making is not sufficient for self-trust. Most people require some appreciation and positive response from others. The family is a crucial starting point, but rarely sufficient. Because family support is quasi-obligatory, where it exists, it may seem so normal as to be insignificant. The insecure teenager, told by her mother that she looks lovely, can all too easily dismiss the remark, saying, "You only think that because you're my mother." In the sensitive phase of adolescence, friends are crucial, and acceptance and praise from family members can be too predictable to be relevant. Self-confidence and self-esteem require acceptance and success outside the circle of family and intimate friends.

Unless there is strong support and acceptance outside the family, and in the absence of a heroically independent sense of self, those who lack love, security, and acceptance during childhood are unlikely to have self-esteem and self-trust as adults. Even within a secure home, an authoritarian upbringing can work against self-trust. People are told what to do and not encouraged to develop their own capacity to think things through, their own values, and their ability to make and implement their own decisions. For the same reasons, a rigid and dogmatic education is likely to work against the development of self-esteem and self-trust. If a person is trained to defer to authority and not to think for himself, he is less likely to be capable of doing so in later life. When one authority is displaced, he may seek out another, as is the case with many adherents of cults.

A person who does not trust herself and has low self-esteem will not think of herself as well motivated and competent. If, perchance, she should happen to accomplish something for which she receives praise and credit from others, her self-esteem may improve. But if her self-doubt is extreme, she may find herself unable to accept the recognition that others offer. She will tend to discount her success and attribute it to luck or the interventions of others, rather than to her own effort and ability. Only if she can experience and acknowledge her own role in achieving success will she have evidence to support trust in herself.

There is evidence that empathethic responses from other people can strengthen self-trust. Doris Brothers makes this claim in her recent exploration of trust and self-trust in the context of therapy.[3] She claims that all her patients have experienced "trust disturbances." A major purpose of therapy is to work to rectify those disturbances and enable the patient to use more mature criteria in his or her estimations of trustworthiness. Trust disturbances manifest themselves in various ways: some patients trust themselves scarcely at all; some trust others against all evidence, making themselves trustworthy people for others, but setting themselves up for exploitation and betrayal; some are generally suspicious of others, including her as a therapist. Brothers maintains that it is the consistent, reliable, predictable, and dependable behaviour of parents or caretakers that makes mature self-trust possible, and it is the reliable, predicatable behaviour of the therapist with regard to the regularity of appointments, consistency of session duration, fairness of fee arrangements, and so on that helps promote mature trust attitudes as a result of a therapeutic relationship.

These elements are important, but the most crucial of all is empathy. By her empathetic responses, the therapist shows that she acknowledges the feelings and situation of the patient; she does not discredit or downplay what he is feeling. The patient is thereby encouraged in his sense that what he is saying and feeling he really *is* feeling, that what happened to him and felt bad really *did* happen and really *did* feel bad. Because the empathetic response validates the patient's feelings and beliefs, and because that response comes from a person who is showing herself trustworthy, empathy helps provide a basis for self-trust.

TRUSTING OURSELVES AND RELATING TO OTHERS

A person who has a secure sense of self-worth and is confident of his or her ability to cope with the world need not put up a false front with others. Such a person will feel no need to cover up, pretend to be what he or she is not, or try to make a good impression: he or she can relax and act naturally. People strike others as trustworthy when they seem reliable, consistent, sincere, and genuine, and untrustworthy when they are unpredictable and undependable or when they seem to be putting on an act, hiding something, or trying to deceive or manipulate. Thus other people are likely to find the self-trusting person trustworthy. In the case of apparently inauthentic behaviour or impression management, people feel unable to sense the "real person" underneath and thus gain no understanding of the other's character.

In some situations, we trust ourselves and rely on our own judgment in order to *resist* undermining criticisms and interpretations put forward by other people. The example of Linda in the parent-teacher interview, discussed in the last chapter, illustrates this pattern. Linda trusts herself and as a result does not trust the teacher, Eleanor, whom she takes to have put forward a criticism based on facile stereotyping. This example may suggest that self-trust and trust in others are opposed or alternative attitudes; it may suggest that we trust ourselves more only if we trust others less. But such an opposition between self-trust and trust in others does not hold true in general. Because she trusted herself, Linda was able to maintain her trust in her son Robert and keep her confidence that he would learn to read well some day. Self-trust is needed to think through and make our own judgments about what is going on, what we have done, and what we can do. We need it to think things through for ourselves and to act on our own beliefs and values. Self-trust is as necessary for continuing to trust someone who is, in our best judgment, trustworthy, as it is for deciding, on the basis of evidence, that we now have grounds to be suspicious of someone we used to trust. Trusting ourselves may support us in trusting others or distrusting them, depending on the circumstances and on what we think is sensible and best.

Self-trust requires and is required by positive relations with other people. We develop as people because we encounter others, and we grow because of our friends and family, with whom we talk and share experience. In his philosophy of dialogue and encounter, Martin Buber argued that the growth of a self comes because another self is present to it. We need confirmation from other people.[4] For another's presence and response to confirm me, I must acknowledge that that other is genuinely another person, a self in his own right, making judgments on the basis of his own beliefs and values, and feeling and responding because he is the individual person that he is. A person whom I have dismissed as "just a party hack" or "your typical white, male scientist" cannot confirm me in my feelings or offer meaningful advice to me, and that not because of any intrinsic flaw in him, but because I have categorized and rejected him so as to make it impossible for him to do so. To receive empathy and confirmation from another person, I have to regard him as a worthy individual in himself, in his own right. I have to approach him with the attitude that he is a worthy human being. To do so, in certain fundamental ways, I have to respect and trust him. And for a genuine encounter, I also have to trust myself enough to expose myself to another.

In a meaningful encounter between two persons, each is conscious that the other is another and may differ from himself. Buber says, "The sphere of the interhuman is one in which a person is confronted by the other. We call its unfolding the dialogical." When people are really trying to make contact and to listen to each other as individual authentic persons, when they are not trying to impress, manipulate, or exploit each other, when the encounter is serious and not merely trivial, then there is a genuineness that Buber calls a kind of truth. This genuineness requires a sense of the other as a *person*. "The chief presupposition for the rise of genuine dialogue is that each should regard his partner as the very one that he is." In a situation of genuine dialogue and encounter, I acknowledge that the other person is unique and different from me, and I direct what I say to him as the person that he is. I sense him as a whole, as a unity, and in my listening and responses, I confirm him as what he is. In all of this, I trust the other person, and I assume that he is ready to treat me as his partner in dialogue.

This interaction, in that space between two persons that Buber calls "the between," requires self-trust. To encounter another and accept that she really is another distinct self, an independent person in her own right and not a tool to prop up my self-image or an instrument to be used in my plans and projects, I need a secure sense of myself. Confirming and responding to another person in this way does not require agreeing with her. I may disagree; I may confront her with that disagreement. But in a genuine interhuman dialogue, I must maintain the recognition that the other person is one who is unique and distinct from me, one with her own feelings, beliefs, and values, which need to be heard and merit respect. I can help that person to trust and realize herself without seeking in any way to impose on her. But I must trust myself to do so. Lack of self-trust or self-confidence can lead to failure to relax or to pretence, which make a person appear to others to be unnatural, potentially manipulative, and untrustworthy. Positive self-trust, on the other hand, not only results in more natural and flexible behaviour, but also facilitates the capacity for genuine dialogue with others.

In describing the characteristics of helping relationships, Carl Rogers cites features of a helping person that are crucial to a successful relationship. Within the term "helping person" Rogers includes anyone in a role that calls for nurturing or assisting another. Parents, teachers, counsellors, social workers, and therapists are helping persons in this sense. Aspects of the helping person that Rogers deems essential to the establishment of a successful relationship are trustworthiness, empathy, warmth, acceptance of the other for what that person is, understanding or trying to understand the other, and congruency.[5] By "congruency" Rogers means the fit between what the helping person feels or believes and the way he acts. If a person who feels angry tries to behave in a sympathetic, helpful way towards another, the opposition between his emotions and behaviour is likely to be sensed. It will make him seem insincere, not genuine – and therefore untrustworthy. A person who trusts himself has a secure sense of self-worth, an acceptance of his feelings, and a solid sense of his good judgment. All this provides him with the confidence not to hide, to "be himself." This ability to express one's self is essential for intimacy in close relationships.

A person who is insecure and constantly trying to make a good impression on another is unlikely to establish good relationships. Haim Gordon is an Israeli philosopher and theorist of education who used Buber's philosophy and existentialist literature (Dostoevsky, Kafka, Camus, Sartre) as the basis for an educational peace project involving Arabs and Jews in Israel. Gordon's idea was to have people discuss literary examples of life problems, of authenticity and inauthenticity, and on the basis of those discussions, move towards a situation where they could genuinely encounter each other in serious conversations. Progress was made, but there were many problems along the way. Describing the project, Gordon said that trying to put up a good "front," trying to impress the other person, worked against these goals: "the person who is concerned with making an impression is not giving all of himself to his partner in dialogue. He is giving only one side of his being, which he hopes or suspects his partner will appreciate ... if I always suspect that the person is trying to make an impression, it will be hard for me to trust him. And without trust, life is Hell."[6]

In the project, Gordon found that Arab men seemed to experience tremendous difficulty revealing themselves in dialogue. He speculated that one cause was their lack of emotional intimacy with their wives, who were culturally denigrated as inferior and unequal partners and with whom these men seemed to have little egalitarian exchange. Perhaps as a result, many of the Arab men whom Gordon worked with had apparently had little experience of divulging their feelings and concerns to others. They were constantly trying to make a good impression, which worked against straightforward and frank encounters.

The relation between self-trust and empathy works in two directions. Brothers found that empathy helps to develop self-trust. When a person has a sense that another reliable, caring person can identify with his feelings and is not discounting them, he is strengthened in his belief that he really does count as a person and that his feelings are real and significant. From another perspective, however, self-trust seems to be necessary for empathy and the willingness to understand

and identify with others. This connection becomes apparent when we think of the relationship from the other side, from the point of view of the one who empathizes with another.[7] She is able to adopt that other's outlook and point of view and better understand the other's perceptions and feelings. To enter into the emotions of another person, she needs courage and a secure sense of herself. She must have learned that it is safe to care, to relate to the other as a person. To empathize, to enter into the world of another and yet remain our own distinct self with our own distinct needs, beliefs, and emotions, we must know who we are and what we are doing, which is simply to say that we must be able to trust and rely on ourselves. For one lacking in self-trust, empathy from another can help to develop self-trust, and in this way, empathy supports self-trust. But from another point of view, self-trust supports empathy: it is only because she basically trusts herself that a person is able to empathize with another.

A person who trusts herself believes that she is a morally sound person worthy of respect, and that her practical, emotional, and intellectual competence is adequate for dealing with the world. These beliefs are social beliefs – beliefs about ourselves as members of a social world. And there is considerable evidence that social beliefs affect social reality: to a surprising extent, they *construct* social reality.[8] Beliefs affect reality. We tend to make ourselves into the sorts of people we believe ourselves to be. We have conceptions of ourselves, and to a considerable extent we seek out opportunities to act upon and maintain features of these self-conceptions. By acting as we do, we often inspire responsive behaviour that supports our own self-conception. For example, a person who is an extrovert and regards himself as such will seek out activities and occasions on which he can talk and relate to others. In these situations, he behaves in an animated and friendly way. He regards himself as a person who enjoys others' company, seeks out company, and is chatty and amiable. By and large, he gets the response he expects when he goes out into the social world. Analogously, a person who thinks that her own actions have little influence on events tends to seek out situations in which the outcome is determined by chance. Seeing herself as relatively powerless, she selects situations in which she cannot do much and need make little effort. Thus her view, too, will be confirmed. A person who sees himself as effective and competent, on the other hand, is more likely to seek out situations in which his actions will make a difference. If it turns out that he cannot act effectively, he will tend to explain his failure as being due to external circumstances, not the result of a personal failing or defect.[9]

In addition, we tend (often inadvertently) to inspire confirmations by others of our own picture of ourselves. Studies have indicated that people who are depressed behave in ways that tend to arouse depression, hostility, resentment, and rejection on the part of those around them.[10] Similarly, anxious people have a tendency to inspire anxiety in others, and cheerful people to inspire cheerfulness in others. If we do not trust ourselves, our lack of self-confidence and self-esteem is likely to convey itself to others in some way. If we are not confident that we can move ahead and get things done, others will not believe that either. Thus without self-trust we are likely to acquire the social handicap that other people will not be willing to trust us. If we have negative feelings about ourselves and our abilities and prospects, our actions tend to produce negative effects on other people. A natural corollary is that positive attitudes about ourselves and our abilities, including self-trust, will also communicate themselves to others. If we trust ourselves and have a confident, self-reliant attitude, that attitude will convey itself to others in our gestures, actions, and words. As a result, other people are more likely to trust us.[11]

Core self-trust and situational self-trust are key aspects of our self-conception. If a woman sees herself as strong, agile, and competent in emergencies, she might volunteer as a guide on lengthy backpacking trips. If her conception of herself is that she is an honest, dependable person, she would not seek employment in a questionable enterprise or find friends among drug dealers. How we see ourselves is an important factor in what we do with our lives, which opportunities we seek, and which we reject.

Psychological studies suggest that how other people respond to us seems to depend very much on how we see ourselves. In one set of experiments, people were paired and each given a different idea as to the partner's probable response to them. Those who regarded themselves as likeable treated the partner in a friendly manner, even in those cases where they were advised by the experiment that the partner did not like them. Those who saw themselves as unlikeable acted so as to elicit an unfavourable reaction, even when they were told that the partner liked them. Clearly, a sense of self-worth and competence is likely to be beneficial for relationships with other people. On the whole, self-trust has positive effects on a person's activities and relationships, whereas its lack has negative effects.[12]

A sense that we are unworthy and lacking in integrity and competence bodes ill for our personal happiness and leaves us open to exploitation and manipulation by others. To have goals and pursue them, to confidently experience and remember, to interpret reality

according to our own norms and style, to assert that our own interests and needs count – all this requires self-trust. With little or no
self-trust, we are constantly open to having our beliefs and values
put aside by others; we are thereby deprived of any internal source
of constancy that could provide for the appraisal of beliefs, values,
choices, and actions and the reconciliation of conflicting desires and
goals. Since pressure from outside the self is variable in nature, inte-
gration of the self must come from within.

To value self-trust is not to claim that our own sense of reality and
our own competence should count for everything. Rather, it is to
argue that they must count for *something*: they must count if we are
to understand, reflect, judge, choose, and act in key areas of life with
respect to our own experience, feelings, interests, needs, goals, and
life plans. To function as moral and cognitive agents, we cannot abdi-
cate to others decision-making in key areas such as memory, interpretation, judgment, intimacy, friendship, reproduction, occupation, and
use of leisure time. Our own sense of what happened, what experiences mean, what our motivations were, what we can do, must be
taken seriously and rejected only if we reach our own reflectively
grounded conviction that we have made a mistake.

A person does not take her own experiences seriously if she is willing to discredit and discount her sense of what happened merely
because someone else questions the account. ("You think he is prais-
ing your work because he's interested in it and thinks it's good?
That's not it at all. He's just trying to curry favour because he's up for
promotion and he's going to ask you for a reference.") Any event has
a number of possible interpretations. When we understand something one way, we should not close our minds to the possibility that
others, who understand it differently, have a more accurate interpretation than our own. Sometimes we should change our minds: we
should accept other people's ideas and reject our own. But when we
do this, it should only be after serious reflection. What were the reasons for our interpretation? Do they still hold up? What are the
reasons for the alternative one? How good are they? How plausible
are the accounts? What we should not do, and what we will not do if
we trust ourselves, is dismiss our own ideas merely because they are
called into question by someone else.

In autonomous thinking, we need to take account both of our own
view and of that of the other. When we trust our own judgment, we
rely on our autonomous consideration of evidence, information, reasons, and arguments. We do not succumb to correction based on an
assumption that someone else must have it right just because he is
someone else.

To preserve a sense of who we are, to preserve the conviction that we are worthy and competent, to hold to a sense that it is we who lead our lives, to function as a cognitive and moral agents, we need self-trust. We need to preserve and develop our belief in our own integrity and worth, our credibility as a witness to and participant in the world, and our capacity to remember and recount our experience. We must confidently depend on ourselves to think accurately, deliberate reasonably, make sound decisions, carry out sensible plans, and implement worthy goals. Only with self-trust can we conduct our own lives so as to lead an authentic personal existence not open to domination by other people, social convention, or passing fads.

LACK OF SELF-TRUST

Clearly, lack of basic self-trust is a tremendous handicap in life. Without it we will see ourselves as unable to confront challenges and contend with difficulties. We will tend to restrict our experience, avoiding new or potentially difficult situations and missing many opportunities. We will generally choose activities, even friends, who bear out our low self-image. We may be unwilling to love, thinking that no good person could love us in return. If we allow ourselves to be loved by an unworthy person, no good will come of it. "I couldn't deserve affection from anyone worth much," a person with little self-trust may think. She may not allow herself to love at all; she may unconsciously perpetuate her poor self-image by seeking unworthy partners. Low self-trust and self-esteem underlie the old Groucho Marx joke "I wouldn't join any club that would have me as a member." As is illustrated in the Ellen West case, lack of self-trust can be a handicap so extreme as to result in suicide.

In the German Democratic Republic (formerly East Germany), there was extensive spying by agents of the Stasi, the government secret police. After the reunification of Germany, with public access to the files, terrible revelations emerged. Many people found that they had been victims of spying by special agents, some of whom were colleagues, comrades in opposition political groups, friends, lovers, or even husbands and wives. Reactions by victims of these revelations varied, but common among them was a lack of self-trust. Belinda Cooper, an expatriate American who had worked with environmental opposition groups in East Germany, was a victim of spying and discovered that the Stasi had a file on her, as it did on all members of her group. One member had been a special agent.[13] Reflecting on matters later, she felt that they should have suspected something. The man had not seemed to share the political attitudes of the others; besides, he was unusually well off and had an expensive car. He had been admitted to a program on marketing to which it was difficult to gain access. In fact, the inner circle of the group had not entirely trusted this man; they felt that he was "mouthy" and should not be told about some of their more risky manoeuvres. However, they did not suspect him of being a Stasi informer, and later they came to think that they should have. Looking back, they blamed him for betraying them, but they also blamed themselves for not suspecting him.

Examining the role of gender in Stasi spying, Cooper found that the tendency for victims to blame themselves and begin to doubt their own judgment and competence was particularly common among women.[14] They felt they should have been more sensitive to nuances in relationships and should have known that something was wrong. The tendency for betrayal to result in self-doubt, discovered by Cooper in her interviews, was confirmed by several state officials charged with investigating allegations of Stasi involvement and requests, both from victims and from Stasi employees, for help in the new united Germany. On the basis of their extensive dealings with victims of spying, these men reported that victims had begun to question their whole system of communication and understanding because they had been so undermined by trusting the wrong people.[15] Betrayed by others, they came to lose trust in themselves and suffered grave handicaps in life as a result.

Lack of self-trust can lead to bewilderment and incompetence. Paradoxically, however, it can also result in delusions of grandeur and cruel attempts to dominate others, as has been argued by Andrew Bard Schmookler, Alice Miller, and others.[16] Schmookler claims that there is a tendency in human groups and societies for the most power-hungry and competitive people to gain control and exercise that control in domineering ways. Such people will struggle for the top, and if not successfully resisted, they will get there. If resisted, they are opposed by others who have to use aggressive, competitive, and brutal methods to struggle against them and who, if they succeed, will have thereby become usurpers trained in the cruel practice of power. In all likelihood, they will take over only to continue its exercise. Thus whoever rises to political power in a human society will tend to rule by domination. Human groups and societies almost inevitably feature relations between the dominators (usually powerful men) and the dominated (usually women and powerless men.)

Being dominated gives a person a sense of helplessness, vulnerability, and worthlessness. For those dominated, it is difficult to preserve self-esteem and self-trust. Though some fortunate people escape domination in adult life, nearly everyone is vulnerable to it during childhood. Parents, who are struggling themselves, who are often treated cruelly by the broader adult society, may have themselves been abused as children by their own brutalized parents. And all too often they take out their frustrations on their children. They may unconsciously re-enact scripts from their own childhood, choosing as victims the only people they can dominate and abuse. The sense of vulnerability and helplessness that children learn from such experiences is not forgotten when they become adults. It can have disastrous consequences in later life.

Children become adults, and as adults, they may try to compensate for their earlier vulnerability. Mistrusting other people and the world at large, they attempt to make up for their own lack of self-acceptance and confidence by self-aggrandizement and a quest for control over others. Some who have low self-esteem and little self-trust may try to buttress themselves with delusions of grandeur, constructing visions of themselves as superior or omnipotent. If such people gain political authority, they have an opportunity to exalt themselves by exercising tyrannical power over their underlings or even entire populations. Hitler and Stalin fit the model. Hitler had a desperately brutalized childhood. As an adult, he sought to be acknowledged as omnipotent and omniscient. He could not abide the thought of his own mistakes. There are many other persuasive examples, including those of Saddam Hussein, Nicolae Ceausescu, and Idi Amin.[17] The childhood abuse suffered by these men contributed to a sense of helplessness and a desperate lack of self-esteem, for which millions paid dearly.

In other people, lack of self-trust may result, not in delusions of grandeur, but in susceptibilty to the manipulations of others.[18] Such people become victims or tools of others whom they seem unable to resist. One example of extraordinary domination buttressed by lack of self-trust is that of the cult society, a totalitarian mini-society in which members are dominated to an extreme degree by leaders claiming a unique ability to interpret the word of God, spiritual truth, morality and standards for living – including, often, minute details of diet and hygiene – and fundamental matters of life direction, such as choice of spouse, numbers and timing of children, and occupation. Gurus can acquire astounding power over cult adherents.

Leaders are believed to have a special link to the divine or even, in some cases, to be divine. In such a framework of belief, it makes sense to trust the leader more than oneself. One should serve God or Krishna or the Guru or the Great Mother, whatever the cost to one's own needs or interests. Dominated cult members relinquish their sense of competence to interpret and respond to reality. Gurus and cult leaders define for them what life means, what actions are right,

and how they should behave, think, and feel. Cult adherents abdi-
cate their right and obligation to perceive, feel, judge, and plan for
themselves. They have lost their basic self-trust – if, indeed, they
ever had it.

Ironically, people who exhibit no self-trust in relation to a cult
leader and who have often been dominated in life prior to entering
the cult can sometimes show tremendous strength in resisting outsiders who try to dissuade them of their religious beliefs. They argue
vehemently against objections to cult doctrines, refute any suggestion
that they are victims of thought control, and systematically resist alle-
gation of theological or moral flaws in the cult system. They *know*
what they believe, where the world is going, and what they should
do, and when outsiders bring criticism, they can be phenomenally
resistant to it. This capacity is typically based on the teachings and
personality of a leader, not on their own individual resources.

To generate the will to leave such a cult requires relying upon one's
own interpretations and judgments and valuing one's own independent needs and interests. One has to detect something wrong – some
inconsistency or flaw in the religious system, some immorality,
hypocrisy, or act of betrayal by its leaders, or some failure of fit between one's personal needs and what the culture requires. To do so
requires independent judgment taken after autonomous thought. One
needs a sense of one's own worth, some inner conviction that one's
own beliefs and logic, interests, feelings, and needs count for something. And one needs a sense of one's own competence – the secure
belief that one has the ability to understand reality, that one's judgment could be correct, even when it conflicts with the decrees of cult
leaders. That is to say, one needs just the self-trust that is likely to be
absent in a cult adherent. A certain lack of self-trust makes cult membership attractive and domination of the adherent by leaders possible.
Then the power structure of the cult and its belief system, exalting the
leader over the member, aggravates this lack.

A disciple of the Rajneesh movement who spent thirteen years in
tutelage, Satya Bharti Franklin came to understand and describe this
dynamic. During the last several years of her involvement with the
movement, she worked twelve harsh hours a day on a ranch in Oregon, withstanding considerable denigration and manipulation from
cult leaders. Bharti Franklin later reflected: "Everything had a meaning. It had to. We were living in a Buddhafield, building a utopia,
growing, changing, learning things about ourselves that we'd never
seen before. For those of us who had been with Bhagwan [Rajneesh]
in India, the commune in Oregon, like the ashram in Poona, was
a mystery school. Trusting Bhagwan, we 'pointed the fingers at our-

selves' whenever we disagreed with anything, looking at our own motivations and conditionings and finally saying yes to whatever Sheela [an associate leader] and her coordinates said. To surrender to Sheela was to surrender to Bhagwan."[19]

Finally, when exploitation grew to include violence and evidence of poisoning and when life on the ranch became fearfully harsh and insecure, disenchantment began to set in. "When I was finally invited to attend one of Bhagwan's lectures, I spent the whole evening wishing it were over. The magic was gone, but I didn't blame Bhagwan; I blamed myself. I was unsurrendered, a lousy disciple; not even a disciple any more."[20] Even when the spell was over, old habits of thought were hard to change. If she could not be fascinated and surrender, the fault was hers.

The dynamic of trust in the cult phenomenon is fascinating; what seems to be characteristic is a curious combination of under-trust and over-trust. Both occur in two dimensions: self-trust and trust in others. With regard to self-trust and autonomy, cult adherents generally function poorly; in entering the cult, they have abandoned their former beliefs and values and accepted a leader as the final authoritative source on values, spirituality, destiny, and the meaning of life. In another sect, the Church Universal and Triumphant, members often wear audio cassettes broadcasting sermons with a message about doctrine and dedication. If a cult adherent begins to doubt, he can "cure" himself of sceptical inclinations by listening to the tape as he goes about his daily routine. Chanting, ritual, and sleeplessness contribute to a lack of intellectual autonomy. Almost by definition, the cult member is not a person who shows moral or personal autonomy; he has entered into a way of life in which life's central decisions are made for him by others – though he can show a kind of intellectual autonomy and self-trust when friends and relatives try to dissuade him of the new "truths" he has learned, preserving self-trust at least in those contexts where he is called upon to defend his own participation in the cult. There is a lack of basic self-trust, but a capacity for enormous self-trust in the face of objections to cult doctrine.

An analogous duality appears in cult members' attitudes to others. Here too we find both extreme distrust and extreme trust. It is often people who are pessimistic and suspicious about mainstream society and traditional religions who are attracted to cults in the first place. Disenchanted, looking for meaning and a sense of purpose not easily found in mainstream life, they turn to a leader and a system for answers that are definite, comprehensive, and satisfying. From a background of considerable distrust directed against society at large and most of its establishment representatives, they enter a situation of very deep trust in a cult leader and great dependence and vulnerability. Pulled from their moorings in the outside world, they focus their entire lives on the cult system. Doctors, the mainstream media, teachers, lawyers, governments, the United Nations, friends and neighbours – these cannot be trusted, in the judgment of the cult members. They are nearly always are suspicious of professionals, seeing them as having ill-founded pseudo-expertise, as bureaucratized, unreliable, and lacking in deep values and spiritual understanding. The cult leader, on the other hand, is perceived as absolutely different. He or she is regarded by members as one who does have deep spiritual values, who has insight into the meaning and purpose of human existence at this time in human history, who is altruistic and dedicated to the group, who can lead in the right path and knows how life should be led.

Once a person is in a cult, this kind of trust polarity (tremendous distrust of the "establishment" combined with deep trust in the leader) will only be reinforced. Cults characteristically distrust and fear Outsiders, who do not share the privileged doctrines, show disrespect and lack of understanding by questioning them, and attempt to kidnap members and "de-program" them. Critics of cults say that members have been kidnapped and brainwashed and are serving as slave labour. Members see themselves as radically misunderstood by Outsiders and as suffering for the truth in a way analogous to that in which Jesus and many other religious leaders have suffered in the past. They argue that they really do believe what they say they believe and they really have chosen to live their lives this way. Members would claim that there is no insidious mind control, and accusations that it exists are based on fear, ignorance, and bigotry. There is no slavish obedience, only enlightened obedience. Critics see leaders as tricksters and abusers, out to exert power and make money from gullible and vulnerable followers.

An attitude of heightened suspicion towards Outsiders may be manifested physically by a collection of weapons or a bomb shelter. In Paradise Valley, Montana, the Church Universal and Triumphant built bomb shelters as long as three football fields and capable of holding 750 people. A bomb shelter is really something concrete (*sic*) to believe in and a massive symbol of distancing from the outside world and the Inside/Outside split. When the catastrophe comes, some will literally be in; others will be out. Elizabeth Clare Prophet, the "Guru Ma" or leader of the group, defends the bomb shelters, which she argues are an affirmation of the value of life.[21] Church leaders were convinced in the late eighties that the Soviet Union was going to launch a nuclear attack on the United States and that bomb shelters were needed for protection; now they foresee some indefinable sort of world disaster. The late eighties were the time of Gorbachev, glasnost, and perestroika; it was a period of rapprochement when even former cold warrior Ronald Reagan was feeling hopeful about the relationship between the Soviet Union and the United States. But the Church Universal and Triumphant had its own analysis. Characteristically, leaders and members did not trust mainstream media or academic scholars to offer an accurate account of developments in the Soviet Union or of Soviet intentions towards the West. On their interpretation, those on the Outside did not understand the risk because they did not analyse Soviet affairs properly (that is to say, as the church did), and they had no insight into the sinister intentions of the Soviets. Cult supporters defended the bomb shelters as an affirmation of the value of life. They contended that Outsiders and those who argued against the usefulness of bomb shelters were defeatist because they were tacitly accepting death as inevitable.

Both in their self-trust and in their trust of others, cult members seem to exhibit extremes, imbalance, and double standards. A critique of cult attitudes could be developed, based on members' implicit recourse to double standards concerning both self-trust and trust in others. They trust themselves not at all in many contexts (those of determining a life path and lifestyle), yet they trust themselves completely in others (when arguing to support cult doctrine.) They are entirely open to ideas from cult leaders, yet wholly closed to ideas from its critics. They trust completely in some other people (on the Inside), yet show radical distrust of others (on the Outside.) Perhaps these dualities contain a key to more balanced attitudes: members are clearly capable both of self-trust and of trust in others. What is needed for more balanced and consistent attitudes is to develop more realistic and specific grounds for trust and distrust in each case.[22]

So far as self-trust is concerned, a still crueller syndrome can exist in individual relationships. An example is that of the dominated wife controlled by a husband who has taken the power to define events, motivations, capacities, and standards of behaviour. Physical force may be used to exert this control: the relation is one of physical battering, where the abused partner complies from fear of physical harm or even death. To resist, to leave the situation, a woman must see herself as valuable and her goals, needs, and interests as worthwhile. She must have, and use, her own standards for judging the partner's behaviour. To escape a relationship of battering or domination, she must be capable, and regard herself as capable, of understanding what is going on around her and running her own life without constant intervention from another.

Tessa Dahl's recent novel *Working for Love* provides a clear illustration of this syndrome.

"Why are you doing that Molly?"
"For fun Jack."
"No you're not, you're doing it to impress Paul."
"I'm not, darling."
"Yes, you are."

You have to tell me why and how and what my every move was for. And the more I started to become independent, the more you'd sit me down and tell me exactly what I was really doing and why, and even what I was going to do next.[23]

In this case, the husband predicates a role in which he is the authority on his wife's emotions and responses. In this superior role he has presumed that he knows better than she what she is doing and why. To escape from him, the woman will have to assume this authority herself. She cannot let him explain her to herself. To emerge from a situation of domination or battering, a victim has to be able to value herself and her needs and take for herself the power to define her motivations and activities.

The need for self-trust can emerge from external events, from our own feelings, or from what is said and done by others. We need self-trust in order to lead authentic, autonomous lives. We do not *in general* trust ourselves *instead of* trusting others, or trust others instead of trusting ourselves. Rather, trust in others can support and enhance trust in ourselves, and trust in ourselves can support and enhance trust in others.

CHAPTER SEVEN

Reasons for Trust
and Distrust

In her recent book *Falling Backwards*, Doris Brothers lists four characteristics for evaluating the "maturity" of grounds for trust. She says
that such criteria count as mature insofar as they are realistic,
abstract, complex, and differentiated. By *realistic* Brothers means that
the criteria for judging trust are not perfectionistic or "phantasmago-
rical." They recognize that a person who is trustworthy on the whole
is not necessarily perfect, infallible, all-knowing, or all-powerful.
Whether we are judging ourselves or other people for trustworthiness, to be reasonable we have to acknowledge, realistically, that a
person can be basically trustworthy without being perfect or trustworthy in every minute respect. By the *abstractness* of trust criteria,
Brothers is referring to their incorporation of such morally salient
general characteristics such as truthfulness, integrity, or adherence to
valued principles. To judge trustworthiness on the basis of size,
attractiveness, or material possessions is to employ more "concrete"
or particularistic criteria, which are less mature than abstract ones
incorporating morally relevant aspects. In alluding to *complexity* as a
feature of trust criteria, Brothers wants the "multifaceted nature of
the human personality" to be recognized; when we judge trustworthiness in a mature way, we recognize that the reliability of people
varies when circumstances vary, and we acknowledge that sometimes scepticism, doubt, and mistrust are appropriate. By *differentia-
tion* she refers to the ability to discriminate between characteristics
and between people so as to avoid oversimplifications, such as
sweeping generalizations about the significance of minor traits or
the stereotyping of people on the basis of religious, racial, or ethnic
group.[1]

The interest of Brothers's discussion is enhanced by the fact that
her criteria emerge from clinical practice, and it provides a helpful

introduction to the question of grounds, or reasons, for trust and distrust. Clearly, though, there is more to be said. Consider an example. Mrs Olsen, a frail, elderly woman, is waiting for the bus. Suddenly rain starts coming down in torrents. She moves into a shopping mall to take shelter, where she encounters a middle-aged woman packing up a few grocery purchases. Making conversation, Mrs Olsen remarks that she is going to get soaked when she has to walk home from the bus stop. The woman, who has a respectable and honest sort of appearance, expresses concern and offers to drive her home. Mrs Olsen gratefully accepts the ride.

Should she have trusted this unknown person to drive her home? One suggested answer is that Mrs Olsen took a chance, but not too unreasonably, since middle-aged women are generally not of criminal intent and there was nothing to suggest that the woman's offer of help was anything but sincere.

Here is another case. Joe and Mary, a young couple who have been happily married for two years, quit smoking three months ago. They did it together because they hope to have children. They are entertaining another young couple, Don and Angela. Don works at the same company as Mary. Halfway through the evening, he offers her a cigarette. Joe is really surprised and says so; does Don not know that Mary quit smoking three months ago? When he asks about it, she seems embarrassed. On being pressed, she admits that she smokes sometimes at the office, especially when there are tough deadlines to meet. Joe thought she had quit completely – as they had both promised each other to do and as he has done, with considerable difficulty. He acts hurt. Mary says, "Trust me, Joe, it's not much really." When Joe hears "trust me," alarm bells start to ring in his head. Don tries to stand up for Mary, saying how tense things are at the office sometimes and how nearly everybody there smokes at least once in a while.

At that point, to Joe, Don and Mary seem too close. He begins to wonder whether they are having an affair. Mary really let him down on the smoking thing. Should Joe be more trusting of his wife? A suggested answer is that he is entitled to feel let down and distrustful of his wife with regard to the smoking in particular, but that to suspect her of having an affair goes too far. That suspicion is not warranted by the episode.

How much trust is "enough"? How much is too much? We could be realistic, abstract, complex, and differentiated, and nevertheless come out with several different responses to these stories. Friends and critics who heard that I was studying trust and distrust wanted to know what *values* I would appeal to, how I would explain when, why, and to what extent trust or distrust was reasonable and right. To respond to this query, I needed help. Working with an assistant, I devised a series of mini-stories, including the two just considered. We interviewed twenty people, asking them whether, why, in what respects, and how much the person in a particular story should trust or distrust the other. In compiling our results, we found a fair degree of consistency. As a separate task, we worked out a more a priori set of principles describing circumstances in which we thought complete, moderate, or slight trust or distrust would be warranted. We checked these abstract principles against the "considered judgments" compiled from the interviews. This process was the basis for a tentative exploration of grounds for trust.[2]

Trust and distrust are contraries, not contradictories. To say that it is not the case that one trusts another person is not always to say that one distrusts him. We may neither trust nor distrust another, either because we lack relevant knowledge or because the evidence and feelings we have are mixed. Both trust and distrust are susceptible to degrees: we may trust or distrust another slightly, moderately, or completely. Both attitudes are often relative to context: we might, without hesitation, trust a person to deliver a parcel and yet feel ambivalent about trusting him to repair a computer.

In reflecting on the reasons that a person, Alex, may have for trusting or distrusting another individual, Brenda, we may consider:

1 Information: the sources of Alex's information about Brenda and what she has done. How reliable is this information?
2 Actions and statements: the sorts of things that Brenda has done and said. How relevant are particular actions and statements to Alex's estimation of her trustworthiness or untrustworthiness?
3 Exceptions clause or "unless" clause: interpretation of actions, statements, and information. Is there a significant likelihood that Alex or his sources of information have misunderstood what Brenda was doing or saying? What he thinks she did suggests trustworthiness (or untrustworthiness) *unless* it means something other than what it appears on the surface to mean.
4 Character: based on information, actions and statements, and a due consideration of interpretations, what is Brenda like?
5 Circumstances: relevance of circumstances to vulnerability and risks. In just what context does the question of whether Alex should trust Brenda arise? What is at stake for him?
6 Judgment: decision by Alex as to how much he is warranted in trusting Brenda, in the light of all these considerations.

By exploring these factors we can take a closer, more detailed look at reasons for trust and distrust.

INFORMATION ABOUT TRUSTWORTHINESS

There are several relevantly different sources of information bearing upon interpersonal trust:

a direct personal knowledge (personal experience, as in the case where Alex encounters Brenda);
b indirect personal knowledge (personal experience wherein Alex encounters Chris, who tells him about Brenda);
c book knowledge (Alex has read in books or journals, by Brenda or others, about what she has said and done);
d knowledge acquired from the mass media (Alex has read in the newspaper or heard on radio or television about Brenda); and
e knowledge based on social role (Alex knows, for instance, that Brenda is a public health nurse, and he makes assumptions about what she is like on this basis).

Information from these sources is interpreted and evaluated on the basis of *general social knowledge* – a person's overall sense of how society works and how people of various types (in various contexts and social roles) are likely to act towards him or her.[3] Knowledge from personal experience and books should be self-explanatory, but media-based knowledge and social role require some comment.

Through television, radio, and the daily press, we may have a sense of whether and how much we would be inclined to trust or distrust such public figures as Helmut Kohl, Bill Clinton, Jean Chrétien, Boris Yeltsin, or Mikhail Gorbachev. Our information and impressions of such figures are nearly always gleaned from newspapers, radio, and television. Certain unique organizational and presentational features of the media, especially television, justify setting out a separate category and distinguishing media-based knowledge from second-hand knowledge.

A person's social role is often significant when we make decisions as to whether, how much, and in what respects to trust him or her. We have beliefs about how people come to occupy such social roles as dentist, doctor, car mechanic, lifeguard, policeman, or professor; what qualifications in terms of character and competence are required for those roles; how people occupying them are likely to act. A person's social role is one factor giving us reasons to trust or distrust him or her, to judge whether he or she is likely to be trustworthy in various respects.[4] Information from all these sources is evaluated on the basis of the individual's general social knowledge. For each person such knowledge depends on personal experience as well as theoretical knowledge and beliefs; thus general social knowledge varies from one person to another, although there are substantial common elements within groups and cultures. Such knowledge, incorporating both background information and personal experience, is clearly involved in our own sense of what significance a particular social role has for the trustworthiness or untrustworthiness of another person. For instance, middle-class persons in most Western industrial countries tend to have fairly positive expectations about what the police will do in an emergency and will, in many contexts, take the fact that someone is in the role of policeman as evidence that he is likely to be honest and helpful. Disadvantaged and minority groups, on the other hand, are less likely to see the police role in this way. Gender, race, and social position also affect a person's experience of the world and hence his or her general social knowledge. We ultimately interpret and evaluate information according to our own sense of how the social world works.

Interesting distinctions and connections can be made between these information sources. There are many relevantly different kinds of direct personal encounters: a brief meeting in a crowd, a prolonged tête-à-tête, a conversation over the telephone, an acquaintance restricted entirely to the other's functioning in one particular social role (doctor or teacher, for instance), or a prolonged intimate relationship.

Even short personal encounters over the telephone can provide a basis of moderate trust, as, for example, in cases when troubled persons confide in and accept advice from apparently concerned and sympathetic persons at the end of the line in a crisis or suicide counselling service. Tacit trust, in this kind of case, is based both on general confidence in the social institutions that set up such a telephone service and on a sense of the person at the other end of the phone line. One tends to assume that anyone who would answer the phone at, say, a drug or suicide counselling centre or office of the Good Samaritans is a helpful sympathetic person – in all likelihood a dedicated and altruistic volunteer. However, the institutional and role basis in such a context only serves to create a *presumption* of trustworthiness: the telephone counsellor is likely to be trusted unless he or she does something to upset that presumption. If, for instance, she sounds angry or hostile or in some other way unsympathetic, or says the "wrong thing," the trust required for the telephone encounter to serve its purpose could easily be displaced by distrust. At that point, the caller would probably just hang up.[5]

An encounter that is one-on-one but requires a translator blends direct personal and indirect personal sources of information. If I were to meet Helmut Kohl in person, I would have a new sense of what sort of person he is, being able to see him, hear his voice, and observe his gestures and responses to me, and this would be first-hand personal knowledge. Yet my understanding of what Kohl had to say would depend entirely on the competence, reliability, and honesty of his translator.

We sometimes feel as though we are personally acquainted with those we have never met, as when we seem to encounter authors whose work we are reading. Walter Kaufmann offered a beautiful description of this sort of experience: "We must learn to feel addressed by a book, by the human being behind it, as if a person spoke directly to us. A good book or essay or poem is not primarily an object to be put to use, or an object of experience: it is the voice of you speaking to me, requiring a response."[6] We might think of Dickens or Kant or Plato as persons behind the text and experience their words as though they were personally speaking to us. No doubt, many reading experiences would be enhanced were we to adopt this attitude. But this is reading *as though* the person is behind the text; it is not a real personal encounter, and it does not give us direct personal knowledge of the author. We have no access to expression and body language and, in reading alone, no opportunity for exchange.

The category of indirect personal knowledge also admits of many relevant qualifications and distinctions. Someone may be known to us as the close friend of a close friend, and in fact such connections often provide the basis of considerable trust – enough for us to sleep in the home of someone who is otherwise a virtual stranger. On the other hand, letters of recommendation, also a source of indirect personal knowledge, often come from those whom we know only slightly.[7]

The issue of media-based knowledge raises especially interesting questions of secondary trust: a judgment about the trustworthiness of someone we know through the media is predicated on a tacit judgment of the trustworthiness of the media themselves. When Bill Clinton appears on television or is quoted in a newspaper, journalists, cameramen, and editors are involved in innumerable decisions that affect how he appears to us. They have selected which events and statements to portray and which aspects of those are represented. Media-based knowledge, especially from television, should inspire some scepticism because it is rather deceptive in its form. We see facial expressions, body language, and sometimes style of responding to questions in apparently personal interchanges, a sense enhanced by the fact that interviewers and notable public figures often seem to interact on a casual, first-name basis. We can easily neglect to reflect that what seems to us to be our own visual and auditory experience is shaped by many others operating in complex institutional contexts under various influences, many of which may work against accuracy. Not only do the media themselves influence us, but we may also sometimes suspect certain figures of influencing the media in their own favour; media institutions provide them with an opportunity to give us the impression they want us to have.

These distinctions and subcategories within direct personal, indirect personal, book-derived, and media-based knowledge are interesting and important; however, to explore all the relevant distinctions and ramifications would be unrealistic here. Instead, I propose two generalizations about the reliability of information bearing on judgments of trustworthiness and untrustworthiness. Other things being equal, direct personal knowledge is preferable to the other sources. And other things being equal, indirect personal knowledge and book knowledge are preferable to media-based knowledge. I propose, then, an ordering: direct personal knowledge, indirect personal knowledge, book knowledge, media-based knowledge.

There are a number of reasons for the higher status of direct personal knowledge. It is based on multidimensional experience; we do not just see a person's face or read or hear a description of him or her, but instead have an impression of a whole person. We may be able to make eye contact; we hear the voice and see and sense gestures, movements, and responses. Body language is significant for trust: with direct personal experience, we have an opportunity to see eye motion, facial expression, posture, and other features of self and personal style that indicate such key qualities as sincerity, ease, naturalness, commitment, and concern. These aspects of our personal experience mean that typically we gain a fuller impression of the person from an encounter than from reading, testimony, or television. We have more to tell us what sort of person this is. In addition, in many encounters we can interact, providing further information and a sense of how the other person responds to us.

Another factor that contributes to the general dominance of direct personal knowledge is our sense that in general we have more confidence in our own observation, interpretation, and common sense than in those of others.[8] Other things being equal, we tend to regard our own observations as more reliable, our interpretations as more sensitive, and our own judgments as more relevant to our situation than those of other people. This is not to say that direct personal knowledge is infallible. After meeting Joseph Stalin in person, H.G. Wells said: "I have never met a man more candid, fair and honest ... No one is afraid of him and everybody trusts him." Stalin must have been a brilliant dissimulator because an American ambassador,

Joseph E. Davis, reached a similar conclusion: "His brown eye is exceedingly wise and gentle. A child would like to sit on his lap and a dog would sidle up to him."[9] In these cases, it seems certain that reading speeches or historical records or studying testimony from aides would have given more accurate ideas. Wells and Davis apparently trusted themselves to be good judges of character, and in this case they were wrong. Evidently Hitler was similarly capable of making an excellent impression on foreign visitors.

To say that in issues of trust, indirect personal knowledge and book knowledge are generally more reliable than media-based knowledge is more controversial, but I think that this judgment can be defended.[10] Key reasons are the complexity of media-based institutions and the many pressures that adversely affect the accuracy or balance of their representations and reports: time constraints and economic constraints, for instance. In addition some powerful figures – most notably politicians in power – may manipulate and control the image they present, especially on television.

WHAT ACTIONS INDICATE TRUSTWORTHINESS?

When we are deciding whether to trust or to distrust someone, we want to know what sort of person that individual is. We try to determine this by reflecting on things that he or she has said and done. Especially significant for trustworthiness are honesty (truth-telling, respect for property); sincerity (as opposed to hypocrisy); promise-keeping; keeping confidences and other forms of loyalty; reliability (performing expected tasks, keeping appointments, promptness); dependability (disposition to do what is needed in a situation); competence (as pertinent to context role); and concern for others (non-manipulativeness, protectiveness, and a capacity for empathy and sympathy). In addition to dishonesty, unreliability, and manipulativeness, characteristics giving reasons for distrust include defensiveness, inability to admit to making a mistake, and evasiveness or failure to accept responsibility.

In deciding whether to trust someone, we try to get an overall sense of the person's character. In a particular context, we focus on those aspects of character especially relevant to our well-being in the circumstances at hand – those that may affect us, insofar as we are vulnerable to the actions of the other person. A sense of the whole person, derived from information about a limited range of actions and statements, is then projected onto circumstances of concern to us. Consider, for instance, the following example.

Juan is working for a cooperative supermarket. His sister is in hospital in labour. When Juan left home to come to work, things were not going well: the latest word from the hospital was that the birth was difficult and there was a chance that the baby would die. Juan feels awful about going to work in these circumstances, but his family needs the money and there is not much he can do at the hospital. So he is at work instead. His sister's husband is with her, and his mother and brother are waiting together at home. Juan tells the manager at the store that there is a critical medical situation in the family and it is really important for him to be called if there are any telephone messages from the hospital. He works his shift. When he returns home, he finds that the baby has died. His brother-in-law had tried to contact him at work; he talked to the manager, who said she would give Juan the message that something was wrong and he should call home. But she failed to find him and he was not given the message. Upset about the baby's death, Juan is angry and hurt to find that the manager cares so little for him in such a situation. He feels exploited; he is just a tool in their machine and they do not care about him at all.

Is Juan overreacting, or is his distrust well founded?

The prevailing judgment by people interviewed for their response to this story was that his reaction to the manager in particular was justified; most said that they would distrust this manager to a moderate degree. However, they qualified their reaction, saying that they would distrust only this specific manager, not the administration in general.[11]

Here the manager is someone with whom Juan had previous contact and knowledge; he did not have to form all his impressions of her from this one occasion. But because the situation was so critical and he felt so strongly about his sister and the baby, Juan based his judgment of the manager mainly on what she did in these highly significant circumstances. Her failure to call him for this kind of family emergency has given him a picture of her in her managerial role: he sees her as unreliable, callous, uncaring, untrustworthy. The broken promise, in this context, is the basis for a general picture of her as a callous, uncaring, and unreliable woman. That picture of her character, in turn, is one that he has focused on her attitude towards him.

Actions that are exploitative, manipulative, or uncaring give grounds for distrust. A person who would deceive, trick, or exploit us – who would try to manipulate our actions and responses in order to reach a goal of his own – indicates in doing so that he has little or no concern for us as persons. He is ready to use us for his own ends. On the other hand, if someone has an opportunity to manipulate, exploit, or harm us and refrains from doing so, that is an important ground for trust because it suggests that he does consider us to be persons in our own right and does not seek merely to use us for his own ends.

An especially blatant example of manipulativeness and distrust can be found in recent Canadian political history. Provincial premiers and much of the public enraged distrust felt when they discovered that Brian Mulroney had deliberately put final decisions about a proposed constitutional accord into a time-frame of extremely high pressure (where provincial premiers participated in closed, intensive meetings for a full week), thinking that, with a deadline facing them and a threat of the province of Quebec leaving Confederation if its demands were not met, the premiers would unanimously support the accord. Discovering that the time-frame had been contrived in an effort to induce agreement, the participating premiers and many Canadian citizens felt manipulated and deceived. They lost all trust in Mulroney, and polls in the following months indicated little recovery. In this case, a perception of manipulation on a crucially important matter led to a reaction of extreme distrust.

If we have information about many different actions of substantial significance for trustworthiness, we have a broad base for judgment. What counts, generally, are the number of actions and statements known to us, the variety of such actions and statements, and the degree to which they are significant for trust. How much is at stake for affected persons, and how far did what was done deviate, positively or negatively, from what is normal or expected? If someone cares for my child in a sudden emergency, that counts positively towards my sense that she is a good and trustworthy person, one who is well intentioned, helpful, and reliable. If she teaches a class for me when I have to be out of town, that counts too. Both actions give me grounds to trust this person, signifying as they seem to do that she is concerned, dependable, and competent. But the first action is more significant for trust than the second, since so much more is at stake. The first case would warrant moderate trust and the second slight trust, in the judgment of people interviewed about these cases.

Sometimes, rather than the actions and statements of another person, we seem to use "intuition" or "insight" as a basis for judgment. We see a person and, from his or her demeanour and facial expression (eyes especially), somehow gain a sense of what sort of person this is. We may feel that he or she is especially trustworthy, honest, and reliable; that just how this person strikes us – as open, friendly, respectable, caring. A slight encounter may give the basis for this kind of intuitive judgment of character. Sometimes we have only to hear a person's voice to gain such an impression: on the telephone, someone we have never met may sound especially caring, honest, open, forthcoming, and competent (or the reverse). Because these sorts of impressions are hard to articulate or make precise and because they are sometimes based on limited experience, we may think of them as quite superficial and feel as though our judgments about the other pop right out of nowhere. "I just knew it was going to be all right," we might say. Or, "I could tell right away there was something fishy about that man." The term "intuition" is used at this point because we do not, and perhaps even could not, articulate the tacit knowledge that underlies the judgment. This is not to say that we have no evidence, but only that we do not put our evidence into words. Such judgments are based on evidence of demeanour, physiognomy, personal style, body and eye language, voice, and so on – cues we use as a basis for overall character judgments. In the absence of reliable information about specific relevant actions and statements, such cues may provide all the evidence we have for judging trustworthiness.

EXCEPTIONS AND "UNLESS"

The matter of interpretation of what others say and do leads us to the exceptions or "unless" clause; our information is that what he is doing is such-and-such, and such-and-such is an indication of untrustworthiness *unless* ... A person's behaviour may not indicate what it appears to indicate; we may misunderstand because we do not fully grasp the motive or the circumstances. What people say and do is nearly always open to several different interpretations. The possibility is illustrated in the following example. Fred, a store employee, sees a manager who has preached long and hard against dishonesty and theft removing an expensive mountain bike from the store where they both work. This manager is certainly a hypocrite! After all that he has been saying to the staff, now Fred sees him stealing a bike himself. Fred concludes that the manager is dishonest, hypocritical, and downright untrustworthy.

If the manager is really stealing the bike, distrust in him is warranted. But *is* he stealing the bike? Fred has first-hand knowledge in the sense that he sees the manager removing the bike, and he concludes that the manager is stealing the bike. If so, he would have grounds for distrust. But is the manager stealing the bike, or is he removing it from the store for some other purpose? Strictly speaking, stealing cannot be *seen* in such a case. Fred saw the manager *removing* the bicycle from the store, but what he sees does not tell him that the manager is stealing the bike, as opposed to taking it out for repair.

We may imagine Fred's reasoning as follows: what I see suggests that he is stealing a bike, which certainly indicates that he is hypocritical and untrustworthy; that is, it suggests this unless I am misled by what I see, unless something else is going on. The "unless" clause allows for the possibility that the interpretations which we (in cases of personal experience) or others (in indirect, book, or media-based cases) have initially placed upon actions or statements is not correct. We may have interpreted correctly or incorrectly, too charitably or too uncharitably. There is a wide range of possibilities here. We may misinterpret what is said and done: our information may, on a corrected interpretation, not be significant for trust and distrust; or it may be significant in some way other than what we first assumed.

The "unless" clause plays the important role of reminding us that in order to make reliable judgments about trustworthiness, we need to consider the possibility that the person's actions and statements do not mean what they seem to us initially, or prima facie, to mean. Keeping ourselves alert to the possibility that there has been a misunderstanding is both a matter of being fair to other people – giving them the benefit of the doubt at least some of the time – and protecting ourselves from presumption. Perhaps we have misjudged the other's actions and motivation. A supervisor who appears to be stealing a bike may be removing it; a critic who seems to lashing out with insults may be trying in his own brash way to motivate improvements in a work. On the other hand, a stranger who appears to be offering help may be trying to sell or steal something. What people strike us as doing, how they seem to us to be motivated, is open to correction. We have to reflect on our initial interpretations and ask ourselves whether there are other possibilities that seem more apt.

Openness to alternative interpretations has to be balanced against confidence in our own feelings, our own sense of what is going on. In programs about sexual abuse, children are urged to trust their own judgment and their own feelings. The kindly uncle who puts his hand between a girl's legs to "see if she is wearing underwear" is not to be believed. Children are taught in such programs to place their confidence in their own sense that something wrong is done, that he is not just "checking underwear" or being friendly, that in such cases their personal space is being invaded by someone who is not what he pretends to be and is not doing what he says he is doing.[12] If it feels wrong, it almost certainly is, and the adult who tries to make it out as something else should not be believed.

In understanding what people do and say, we need to achieve a balance between trusting ourselves in the interpretations we are naturally inclined to make and being open to the possibility that we have misunderstood what others are doing or trying to do. A charitable, well-intentioned person, one determined to preserve a relationship, may go too far in attributing benevolent and caring motives to another, whose behaviour will, to the dispassionate observer, seem callous and uncaring. This attitude could lead to her being deceived and exploited by one not worthy of her trust. That is too much trust. A negatively oriented, suspicious person may reinterpret his experience in the opposite way, systematically explaining what is prima facie positive behaviour as selfishly motivated and manipulative. Such a priori bleakness amounts to too much distrust, and when taken to extremes, to generalized cynicism. The resulting too bleak picture of the social world can be a serious handicap in life.[13] Differences between those who tend to be extremely trusting and others who are so distrusting as to be virtually paranoid greatly affect their natural interpretation of what others do, its reinterpretation, and the resulting picture of the social world.

CHARACTER AND MOTIVATION

When we think about whether to trust someone, we try to get a sense of what sort of person he or she is, on the basis of partial information about some actions and statements. There is always a gap – an interpretive and inductive gap – between our information about the other's behaviour and our overall sense of his or her motivation and character. Not even with intimates do we have complete knowledge of another person's actions, thoughts, motivations, and attitudes. And seldom does someone's behaviour point in an unambiguous and straightforward way to a single, categorical judgment of character. Inconsistencies and ambiguities are bound to appear. No one is going to be honest, sincere, and reliable all the time; nor is anyone likely to be deceitful, manipulative, hypocritical, or incompetent in all circumstances. In an intimate relationship or deep friendship, our knowledge of what another person has said and done is considerable, including many encounters and events and countless conversations. Some of what we know points one way, some another. In deciding whether to trust or distrust, we try to synthesize this information to reach a sense of what sort of person this is. We may decide that the person is dishonest, lacking in integrity, or manipulative. Or we may decide that he or she is honest, has integrity, and is well intentioned towards people in general and us in particular. Inconsistencies in behaviour have to be blurred over or interpreted in order to reach such overall judgments. We decide to take some things seriously while discounting others, to see changes as indications of deterioration or reform, to see inconsistencies between what is said and done as indicative of bad luck or weakness of will, on the one hand, or hypocrisy, on the other.

Is there an excuse for dishonest, harmful, or incompetent actions? Is there a purely self-interested explanation for what appeared to be benevolent actions? Is there a pattern to the way in which the person's actions are changing over time? Does this person seem to be becoming more honest and dependable or less so? What we know about what a person has said and done gives us an indication – a partial one, admittedly – of what that person has been. But what is he or she *becoming*? To trust or distrust is to have expectations about how a person is likely to behave *in the future*. Are some instances of behaviour insignificant or less significant now for our sense of who this person is because they are too long past? Which actions are most significant for our judgments of trustworthiness?

THE RELEVANCE OF CIRCUMSTANCES

Different circumstances require different degrees of trust and distrust. There are several dimensions here. First of all, there is the matter of our own vulnerability. To accept a man's help carrying packages across a busy street, a woman needs to trust him, but slight trust will be sufficient unless the packages contain valuable items. Slight trust is enough in such a case because her vulnerability is relatively limited; the worst this man can do is to run off with the packages instead of handing them back to her. On the other hand, for her to accept a ride from a strange man with whom she will be alone in a car, especially at night, a great degree of trust is needed because she is vulnerable to sexual attack or even murder.

In some cases we may feel we have a kind of duty to trust or to distrust, a duty arising from special moral or epistemic considerations, as is illustrated in the following example. Barb and Mike have been married for six years and have long wanted children, but they do not have any. Mike has been told that he has a low sperm count. Apart from feeling sorry about not having children, they have a good and happy relationship, and each feels secure with the other. Mike has been off on a two-and-a-half-month research trip. When he returns, Barb says that she might be pregnant. Mike is excited about this prospect and wants to come along with her to the doctor, but Barb says she would rather go alone since she feels a little shy about it. Mike finds this rather odd because he has accompanied her to doctors for some truly embarrassing and painful fertility tests. However, he does not push the matter. Barb tells Mike that the doctor estimated that she is about eleven weeks pregnant. As it happens, the baby arrives six weeks early by this estimate, but in very good health. Mike's friend Dave hints to him that the baby might not be his, and the thought has crossed Mike's mind. Perhaps there should be a blood test. However, Mike rejects the idea. Barb has always been a loyal wife, and they want very much to love and care for this baby and each other.

Is Mike right to turn his mind away from such suspicious thoughts? People interviewed found this case a tough one. They tended to think that suspicions and in fact moderate distrust were warranted by the evidence. However, in the context of Mike's basically good relationship with his wife, they were inclined to believe that he should try to trust her, even in the face of adverse evidence. Mike feels that he has a duty to trust his wife, but there is some evidence that would seem to constitute reason for disbelieving her on the details of the pregnancy. To continue to trust her his wife is something that he wants to do because he loves her, wants to be loyal, and wants to continue in the marriage. And yet relevant information suggests that Barb is deceiving him about her pregnancy; it suggests that she has either been unfaithful or had artificial insemination. But Mike puts such thoughts aside, trying to believe his wife. He wants to preserve his sense of her as a loving wife because their relationship is important to him.

It is not evidence or the epistemic reasonableness of trust that should in all cases finally determine how much another person "should" be trusted or distrusted. Considerations of love, loyalty, and role can intersect with those of evidence. A therapist may feel that deliberately placing her trust in a client will help him to develop; thus the helping role in which she finds herself may seem to indicate going one step further in trust than a straightforward assessment of evidence would warrant.[14] Trust can be recommended as a practical and ethical approach to constructively influencing behaviour. Other roles and circumstances may imply an obligation to distrust. Parents seeking to protect their children from harm naturally feel that it is their duty to take seriously even small hints of unreliability on the part of a babysitter, teacher, or other person charged with the care of their child. Yet they may feel that they should err on the side of trust when it comes to the children themselves. Military planners may feel that, in their roles as persons responsible for ensuring the defence of a country, they have a duty to look sceptically at treaties indicating friendly relations, assurances of benign intentions, or arms-control arrangements. Their role is to plan as if the worst case were a significant possibility.

In these ways, ethical or prudential considerations can be superimposed upon the information and interpretation made of another person's character. It may be in a broad sense reasonable and right to trust to a greater or lesser degree than evidence, information, and an interpretation of actions and character would warrant, prima facie. An issue that arises here is, of course, whether it ever makes sense to *require* trust or distrust. It does not. Trust and distrust are complex attitudes involving emotions, beliefs, behaviour, and dispositions, and they cannot simply be created by acts of mental fiat. One cannot simply *trust* another person on command. We cannot simply decide to trust, or decide to distrust, and do so.

In this way, trust and distrust are like belief – which is not surprising, since when we trust or distrust someone, we have beliefs about what he is likely or unlikely to do. We cannot simply decide to believe something, or decide that we ought to believe something, and then believe it, just like that. To believe something is to accept it as true and that we do so because we have evidence or reason, because we have in some way been led to believe this claim. In some contexts where we have only slight evidence for believing a claim, there are moral or practical reasons indicating that it would be useful, or in some other sense good, to believe that claim anyhow. The most famous case, of course, is belief that God exists. Some, like Pascal in his famous Wager discussion, have argued that, although there is no conclusive evidence for God's existence, it is so potentially advantageous (in the afterlife we have an eternity of heaven as a possible gain) to believe this that we *should* believe it. In such reasoning, non-epistemic reasons, prudential ones, are given the status of reasons for belief. According to Pascal, we should try to come to believe in God even though we cannot *simply* will ourselves to do so. We cannot believe by mental fiat, but we can deliberate, direct our attention, and select our activities so as to favour one belief rather than another.[15]

Much the same may be said of trust. To say that we "should" trust, because of a special position or role in which we find ourselves, is to say that, so far as it is feasible, we should reflect and deliberate in such as way as to cultivate trust rather than distrust. This may mean trusting more, or less, than the evidence would warrant, depending on the case.

OVERALL JUDGMENT

Eventually, we reach a kind of judgment, or estimation, of a person's character and motivation, based on our interpreted information about relevant statements and actions and on our own sense of how vulnerable we are in the circumstances. How reliable is our information? What does it suggest about trustworthiness? Could we have misunderstood? What is our overall sense of the person's character? What are our circumstances? How vulnerable are we in these circumstances? Obviously, whether and to what extent trust or distrust is warranted will depend on whether what we know is on the whole positive (indicating honesty, sincerity, integrity, dependability, competence, concern, and sympathy) or negative (indicating dishonesty, lack of integrity, unreliability, incompetence, and manipulativeness). What degree of trust or distrust is warranted will be based on how reliable our information is, how many and how many sorts of actions and statements we know about, the significance of those actions and statements for trustworthiness, our overall assesssment of the other's character, and our own vulnerability and feelings of loyalty or prudence in the circumstances.

Clearly, if attitudes of extreme distrust or complete trust are to be warranted, a solid evidential base is needed. Such attitudes require strongly negative or strongly positive pictures of what the other is like. If we distrust someone extremely, we have the greatest suspicion of that person's actions and intentions – in general and with regard to us. We think he or she is more likely than not to be dishonest, manipulative, or downright malevolent, and we are likely to interpret just about anything that person says and does in the light of this basically negative view of his or her character and motivation. If, on the other hand, we trust someone completely, we are perfectly confident as to what he or she will do; we feel no doubt at all that the person has integrity, is concerned for us, and could be depended upon in virtually any circumstances.

Attitudes of extreme distrust or complete trust require well-founded, unambiguous pictures of the other. For such attitudes to be warranted, these pictures have to be founded on reliable information about actions and statements that are consistent in their implications about the other's character. There is little or no play of the "unless" clause in such cases. If evidence points in inconsistent directions, compelling reasons should exist for ignoring or downplaying the evidence that counts against one's character picture. Either the amount and variety of actions and statements known should be substantial, or they should be highly significant for trust and distrust. With moderate distrust or moderate trust, the information may be somewhat less reliable and the amount, variety, or significance of the behaviour less. The "unless" clause should be considered, where appropriate. But after it is taken into account, interpretive judgments about what the person said and did must be confident and relatively unqualified. We should still have good information about some trust-relevant actions and statements, know what these mean for our judgment of the character of the person, and have reasonably good grounds for our decision to trust or distrust him or her.

For slight distrust or slight trust, the information can be little in quantity or of somewhat questionable reliability, or the actions and statements can be few or very limited in their variety or significance. If these conditions were combined though – a slight amount of questionably reliable information about a small number of relatively insignificant actions – we would have only the most tenuous grounds slight distrust or slight trust. There would be no reasonable grounds for the attitudes. If we add to such paltriness of evidence the recognition of the "unless" clause, the case would be diminished further. One can ask whether we need any evidence at all to be warranted in having an attitude of slight trust. Some would say that, in the absence of any specific grounds or reason to distrust, slight trust is clearly the attitude to be adopted.[16] If evidence is called for, then a slight amount of it will provide whatever warrant is needed for slight trust.

In most cases, it would not make sense to ask whether there are grounds for neutrality. We might criticize neutrality as unwarranted if there were good reason for some other attitude. For instance, it could imply gullibility if a person were neutral towards someone known to have committed exploitative, manipulative, or criminal acts or thought to be a compulsive liar.

FURTHER REFLECTIONS

Interesting asymmetries appear when these matters are worked out. For extreme distrust, indirect personal evidence or information from books and media is acceptable as the only type of evidence. But for complete trust, direct personal knowledge seems to be required. Some people do place complete trust in others (charismatic political leaders or television evangelists, for example) of whom they have only indirect knowledge. But on reflection, it would seem that complete trust in such circumstances is not warranted. There are too many ways in which presentations and appearances could be manipulated to mislead us, and we are too vulnerable if we trust completely. To be warranted in completely trusting a person, we would need some first-hand knowledge of him or her. On the other hand, if I feel extreme distrust for Saddam Hussein on the basis of information gained from books and television, that response does seem to be warranted. I have read, in the *New York Review of Books*, documented statements to the effect that Hussein arranged purges in which some members of his cabinet were compelled to execute others; I have even seen a videotape of the meeting at which the disloyal ones were identified. I have seen on national television pictures of Hussein pretending affection for children of Western hostages; I have seen film footage of centres where Kurdish Iraqis were interrogated, brutally tortured, and killed. On the basis of all this – exclusively knowledge from books and media – I have an attitude of extreme distrust towards this man.[17]

In many contexts, slight trust seems to require virtually no warrant at all. Often the basis for such an attitude seems to be merely that we have no particular reason to distrust the person in question. For instance, if a stranger approaches me on the street asking for directions, and there is no evidence that he is trying to make a sexual approach, sell something, lead me into a religious cult, or exploit me in some way, I naturally take his query at face value and answer it politely. Doing so can be regarded as indicating an attitude of slight trust on my part, and it appears to need no special warrant.

This case raises the issue as to whether slight trust, slight distrust, or neutrality is the most reasonable standing attitude, the one that would be our natural basis for moving towards greater or lesser trust. If we were to have no relevant information at all about another person, would neutrality as regards trust and distrust be the most reasonable attitude to adopt? Slight trust? Slight distrust? People, cultures, and societies appear to differ in their approaches. In a fascinating study of rural southern Italy in the 1950s, Edward C. Banfield described attitudes in the town of Montegrano as so suspicious and cynical as to preclude even the simplest voluntary cooperative endeavour. The standing attitude in this particular peasant society seems to have been one of slight, or even moderate, distrust. There are strong arguments for a standing attitude of slight trust, but how prudent and viable that attitude is depends on background social circumstances.[18]

A recent account of moral legitimacy and power in the People's Republic of China claims that the Chinese approach each other on a basic assumption of distrust.

A further problem in a society in which self-interest must be masked and people pretend to selflessness is that people never feel they know where others really stand. Everybody knows of course that people have hidden interests. There exists, therefore, considerable suspicion about hidden agendas and real motives. From ordinary social relations to international politics, inordinate attention is given to determining the real position of others. Are they potentially friends or foes? Stratagems abound, but they have to be followed with the greatest care because of the danger of causing the other party to "lose face," which is the grievous pain people experience when their masks are stripped away.[19]

Lucian Pye, who wrote this passage, adds that for Chinese leaders, public and published statements are more reliable than first-hand encounters since "They believe face-to-face meetings are where hypocrisy prevails. That is where it is obligatory to tell others what they want to hear." In this culture, Pye says, to discern where another person stands, one reasons interpretively from his or her *public statements*, attaching special importance to symbols and code words. This difference, he argues, has not been understood by American public leaders, leaving some personal American initiatives to China open to serious misinterpretation. An impression of lack of openness and suspicion in China consistent with that described by Pye is offered in several other accounts of Chinese society.[20]

Trust and distrust work two ways. We can think of them, as I have here, from the point of view of the one who trusts or of the one who is to be trusted – from a subject or an object point of view. Looking at trust from the other end of the relationship, we can learn a modest lesson from these reflections on grounds for trust and distrust. If we want to be worthy of trust, we must indicate in our actions, statements, and body language that we are honest, sincere, reliable, dependable, competent persons – persons genuinely concerned for the welfare of others. To deserve trust, we must be, and seem to be, persons of integrity.

CHAPTER EIGHT

Distrust and Its Discomforts

In 1991 approximately 85,000 American women sought private detectives to check out the dependability of men they were dating, according to an article in the magazine *New Woman*.[1] Ed Pankan, an investigator quoted in the piece, reported that his firm did twenty premarital investigations a week. Although most questions about boyfriends and fiancés were resolvable by background checks, matters of sexual fidelity could be addressed only by surveillance. According to Pankan, about one-third of the men he investigated were fully legitimate: their business and sexual lives were as they had said. Another third had been shading over some unpleasant facts. The remainder – a full third of the men investigated – Pankan regarded as outright con artists.

DISTRUST

We would like to think that our friends, relatives, and sexual partners were trustworthy and dependable. Often we do so, and for good reason. But distrust exists even among intimates. Even when the surface of a relationship seems all right, we may feel inklings of suspicion – doubts that we cannot set aside. We are conscious of our vulnerability. We may be fearful – unable to be open, relaxed, and intimate. Seeking a private detective to allay one's fears about a spouse, child, loved one, or friend is relatively rare. But many people who could never resort to such measures would understand the impetus behind them. Sometimes distrust is based on feelings or instincts, a kind of inchoate sense that something is not right and things are not as they seem. Often we have specific evidence, based on things that other people have said and done, which seems to justify our distrust. A lover or friend may lie to us outright or seem to lie. He may tell stories that are inconsistent, seem implausible, or do not ring true. He may have misled us, apparently deliberately, or may have failed to reveal crucial information which we needed and which, we feel sure, he knew we needed.

A friend may have failed to live up to an agreement or broken a promise without any valid reason for doing so. She may be manipulating us, either by deceit or by playing on emotions and vulnerabilities. We may come to think that she does not really care and is using us in some way, enjoying not our company but our social connections, library, or summer cottage. If we sense that a friend or lover is using us, we suspect lack of affection and insincerity. We begin to distrust and are unable to take the other person at face value.

Thoughtless or apparently callous behaviour can make us think that a friend or lover does not care for us anymore, that he is insensitive to our feelings and concerns. Unreliability can signify lack of concern. We expect a person whom we trust to care for us, to feel affection, to appreciate us for what we are, and not to seek to deceive, manipulate, or exploit us. Not only do we want to see our friends and family as loving and caring for us, as acting well towards us, but we want to see them as worthy and lovable people who find us worthy and lovable. Even when they remain kind and loving to wards us, if we gain evidence that our friends and relations are engaging in immoral behaviour, we find it hard to continue trusting them and begin to feel uneasy in the relationship.

Well-established trust may continue even in the face of considerable negative evidence. If a person trusts her best friend and bases this trust on years of experience, she is unlikely to conclude right away that the friend has betrayed her, should she be told of wrongdoing. She is more likely to regard the story as false. Should those acts turn out to be real, she will tend to excuse them or understand them as having only limited implications as to the friend's real character. Only with clear-cut evidence is her trust likely to be shaken.

A poignant illustration of the persistance of trust may be found in the film *Music Box*, which depicts a father-daughter relationship in the context of war crimes. Ann's relationship with her father, Michael, is warm and close. Her mother died when she was young; her father worked in steel mills and raised Ann and her brother. When Michael is charged by the American government with lying in order to gain admission to the United States and committing brutal war crimes during his youth in Hungary, Ann is absolutely convinced that he has been misidentified. Michael admits that he lied about his occupation in Hungary; he claimed to have been a farmer, but (he explains) he had been on a farm only as a boy. During the war he was a policeman, but (he says) he worked only as a clerk. Throughout his years in the United States, Michael has been an outspoken anti-communist, and he tells Ann that he was charged because the government in Hungary plots against people like him. Those communists do all sorts of terrible things. Ann believes him. At first, she trusts her father so completely that she has trouble taking the case seriously.

Ann is a lawyer, and her father wants her to defend him in court. She agrees and begins to go through stacks of documents proffering evidence. Photographs show Michael Lazslo in 1954 and an accused Special Section man in 1944. The pictures and signatures are similar. Ann's assistant finds evidence of some months of unusually high bank withdrawals, cheques to a Timor Zoltan, a Hungarian who later died in a hit-and-run accident. The assistant thinks this information is significant; perhaps Zoltan was blackmailing Michael. But Ann ignores this evidence. During the trial, she energetically cross-examines Hungarian witnesses who describe terrible crimes and identify the photos as depicting one of the perpetrators. A witness describes a cruel torture in which exhausted victims were made to do push-ups to hold themselves above a dagger planted in the ground. (Ann's father liked to do push-ups; they were a favourite form of exercise.) One witness is a woman who describes being brutally tortured and raped at the age of sixteen by "Mishka" and his cohort, who had a long scar on his face. Ann cannot bring herself to cross-examine this woman. The trial is taken to Hungary because a final witness is too ill to travel. Ann is able to discredit this witness, who, it transpires, had previously identified the wartime Mishka with several other people. The judge rejects the testimony of the witness and declares that there is insufficient evidence to convict Michael Laszlo. Against all odds, Ann has won her case.

Then Ann visits Timor Zoltan's widow, who says that Zoltan was a soldier during the war. She has only a few of his effects in a wallet from New York, including a worn ticket from a pawnshop, which she gives to Ann. As Ann is leaving the flat, she sees pictures; Timor Zoltan was the man with the long scar. Yes, his widow said, it had taken many operations to have the scar removed. Ann leaves, disturbed but still not quite convinced that her father was "Mishka," the cohort of this legendary brute. Back in the United States, she takes the ticket to the pawnshop and retrieves a music box. It contains photos of Timor Zoltan and the young Michael Laszlo holding guns, standing proudly over their victims. Her father was guilty.

Ann's trust was deep, and it had led her to dismiss or reinterpret evidence against her father and to accept dubious explanations. She at first believed her father's explanation that he was charged because communists were plotting against him; she accepted his somewhat implausible claim that he had worked only as a clerk, when he was a wartime policeman. She trusted him enough to question photographic evidence and to doubt testimony from witnesses. Her father loved to do push-ups, but she was able to ignore the link between this form of exercise and the terrible stories of torture related by witnesses in court. She dismissed evidence from her assistant which pointed to the possibility that Timor Zoltan was blackmailing her father and might have been killed as a result.

Ann was fighting as a good lawyer, and she won the legal fight. But she was not just playing legal games; she was fighting to protect a father she believed in. Her deep trust in her father led her to question, reinterpret, or ignore considerable evidence and to accept his own somewhat implausible claims about his past and the communist plots against him. Especially after her visit to Zoltan's widow, Ann had some doubts. But not until she saw the photos in the music box did she acknowledge that her cherished and trusted father had committed grotesquely brutal crimes as a young man.

Confronted by Ann, Michael would not admit his guilt. He claimed that the communists in Hungary must have done something to her mind. The film ends with Ann breaking entirely with her father, turning the incriminating photos over to the prosecution, and abandoning her New York life and career for the comparative safety and quiet of the American midwest.

We may think of distrust as a matter of feeling and intuition, of suspicion based on unarticulated worries and fears. Such ideas are sometimes correct: distrust can be largely intuitive. Nevertheless, as the story of *Music Box* so graphically indicates, there is such a thing as evidence warranting distrust. If people do certain sorts of things, we make certain inferences about their character, and to the extent that we infer that they are unreliable or lack integrity, we will not trust them.

Ann's attitudes shifted by degrees, until the end. But attitudes of trust and distrust do not always shift gradually. Sometimes the change may be sudden. A woman who finds her most trusted friend in bed with her cherished husband is likely to reverse her attitudes to both of them in an instant. The fact that trust was deep and complete makes a harmful act all the more shocking, and we are especially hurt and vulnerable if we are betrayed by someone we have trusted deeply. A single aggregious act can result in a sudden shift from complete trust to radical distrust, with nothing in between.

BETRAYAL

In the 1980s Vera Wollenberger was a peace activist in East Germany. Deemed an enemy by the communist regime, she was under heavy surveillance by no less than sixty agents of the Stasi, the East German secret police. After the fall of the Berlin Wall in 1989 and the subsequent reunification of Germany, Stasi files were opened. Vera Wollenberger saw her file in 1991. It was immediately clear that one agent, "Daniel," could only have been Knud Wollenberger, her husband and the father of her two sons. Details of her every headache, backache, telephone call, and personal comment had been passed on to the Stasi. Knud confessed to being Daniel and gave unrepentant interviews. Vera, now divorced, struggles to bring up her two sons, who will have to contend with the fact that their father married their mother in order to spy on her and fathered them in the process.

In a television interview, Vera Wollenberger said the files made it clear that her marriage had been false right from the beginning. Knud Wollenberger had married her under Stasi orders. It was as an infiltrator that he had participated in the East German peace groups where they met, and he married her to get material. Their courtship, sexual love, and home were false to the core, based on a lie. Vera found it unimaginable that a man could marry a woman in order to spy on her, but still more incomprehensible that he would father children in the process. The roles of enemy, friend, lover, and spy were blended together in one person, who, in some bizarre way, was able to fill all of them at once. Knud claimed that he had been trying to improve the GDR by working for the Stasi. He spoke of "going through a mirror and being in a totally different world" when he went from home to work.[2]

It is estimated that 6 million East Germans out of a total population of 17 million were under some form of surveillance by the Stasi. Between 1953 and 1989 some 500,000 people had been recruited by the Stasi as informers. East Germany was a country almost without privacy: virtually all telephone conversations and many personal exchanges were overheard and recorded by agents of the secret police. In a country where buildings bombed in 1945 had been left unrepaired, the Stasi had a billion-dollar annual budget. Anyone not fully supportive of the East German state was regarded as an enemy, anyone over nine years of age as a potential enemy. By the fall of 1992, 600,000 citizens of the former East Germany had applied to see their files. The process will take a long time: the Stasi archives were nearly two hundred kilometres long. But even in this context of widespread surveillance and betrayal, Vera Wollenberger's case was unusual in the way it cut to the very core of her intimate life. Few Germans found that their husbands or wives had betrayed them, although betrayal by friends, trusted pastors, counsellors, teachers, professors – people in virtually every corner of society – was common.[3]

Betrayal is the violation of a deep trust and confidence. A person betrayed is let down by another with whom he or she has experienced a special closeness, intimacy, and history of emotional connection. Such a relationship leads to strong expectations of loyalty and support. Betrayal is worse than unreliability or deception, worse than many acts of harm. It is a special sort of violation, one that jolts against the background of what seemed to be a relationship of deep trust with particular strong expectations of loyalty and intimacy. It is a disturbance of deep and crucial expectations. The trusting person has revealed herself, opened herself, divulged her secrets to the other. Because she has trusted and revealed, because of her deep confidence in the caring and loyalty of the other, she is especially vulnerable. The violation is a shock. Her intimacy has been exploited, her trust destroyed. She feels absolutely vulnerable to the other to whom she has revealed herself, horrified of the dangers to which she is exposed by the betrayal.

In the literal sense, betrayal is a giving over to an enemy, as when Judas betrayed Jesus and placed him in the hands of the Roman authorities. Etymologically, betrayal comes from the Latin *tradere*, which means handing over. This connotation fits the Wollenberger case: Knud exploited Vera's love, exposed her most intimate feelings, concerns, and secrets, and eventually handed her over to the totalitarian state, which arrested and deported her.

There are many expectations in relationships of trust, and not every failure to live up to expectations amounts to an act of betrayal. Friends who fail to keep appointments or respond in a crisis disappoint us, but they do not betray us. Betrayal is a special kind of disturbance of trust, an act of disloyalty in which a basic expectation of alliance and non-harm is violated. It is no mere peccadillo or omission; it violates a profoundly important expectation, exposing a person to serious harm in a context where he would have taken loyalty and protectiveness for granted. Revealing an important secret or undermining a key aspect of the other's life, such as sexual relationships or basic economic security, counts as betrayal, as much as handing the other over to the enemy. After betrayal, an intimate relationship is ruptured, often forever.

THE HARMFUL EFFECTS OF DISTRUST

We cannot assume that distrust is always negative or argue in general that trust is healthier and better than distrust. Some people really are unreliable, even treacherous, and they deserve to be distrusted. By distrusting them, we may protect ourselves from tension, inconvenience, and sometimes serious harm. Whether we should trust or distrust, and to what degree, depends on what evidence and feelings we have and how vulnerable we are. But even allowing that distrust is often warranted and sometimes protective, there are costs to distrust when it affects personal relationships.

Felt distrust is usually accompanied by pretence, because in adult life people as a matter of habit and etiquette play along with professed roles and conventions. When we feel distrust, we seldom express it; it is somehow rude and confrontational to do so. People present a certain face or image to others, conveying their own sense of who they are, where they fit into the social world, and what they are doing; and normally we help each other to preserve a pleasant social face. We create an ordered social reality where we assist others to seem to be what they purport to be. In social encounters, we nearly always try to preserve our self-image and save face. When we distrust someone, when we doubt that he is what he purports to be, social convention almost requires that we disguise our own attitude, hide our doubts, and pretend that all is well. We help each other save face, even when we have good reason to think that something is wrong.[4] Distrust is reconciled with good manners only by pretence. Inhibiting doubts and acting as though things are normal can be stressful, making communication and the conduct of a relationship unnatural. Openness and intimacy become impossible. Falseness, the mutually contrived social life, is the result.

It was no an adult trained in social etiquette who said that the emperor had no clothes; it was an innocent and impolite child. Social convention makes it difficult to express our distrust because that amounts to challenging the other person's conception of himself or herself. But when we feel suspicious and say nothing, we fall into hypocrisy ourselves. Frauds can remain long undetected because people do not directly confront or challenge what they suspect to be a false front. Obviously, such pretence has its negative side. We may sense and believe that another person is not what he seems, have little understanding of him, and feel insecure and unsafe as a result. At the least, such suspicion is stressful, and in some cases it may lead to serious harm. In such relationships no real intimacy can exist, and any attempts at cooperative actions are likely to be stressful at best.

Distrust is harmful to relationships. We feel uneasy and tense, suspicious of the other, uncertain as to what he or she might do. We are not relaxed; we have no way of simplifying our assumptions about the other. If, on the contrary, we trust someone, we simply feel confident that she will do what the situation requires. Trust is simpler than distrust. Insofar as we can trust, we can rule out certain possibilities and complexity is reduced. If we trust someone, we believe that he will do the appropriate thing, and there is a whole range

of inappropriate things that he might do which we need not consider.[5] To coordinate activities and manage even mundane matters
with people whom we do not trust is at best difficult, at worst impossible. Distrust leaves virtually every possibility open, implying anxiety, fear, lack of openness, and poor communication. Where distrust
is warranted by evidence and past behaviour, we cannot sensibly *will*
ourselves to trust in order to establish openness and simplify life.
Distrust is a barrier to many good possibilities between people. It
works to separate us from each other because we cannot act naturally. Distrust prevents people from sharing pleasures and confidences, exchanging help and advice, and working together towards
joint goals.

If distrust is so extreme that we need always consider the possibility
that the other is dissembling, pretending, and hiding things, there is
scarcely a relationship at all. When the other says something, what
does she mean? Probably not what she says. Perhaps – but only perhaps – the direct opposite. Perhaps nothing at all. With so many possibilities to be considered, there is little point in trying to communicate.
Given an attitude of distrust, communication is virtually impossible.
The utterances of the other can scarcely be interpreted as meaningful
statements and serve only to disorient and confuse. We might try to
guess or read his body language, but gestures can be inauthentic too.

Think for a moment of the phenomenon of partnership and the
trust that is required for a genuine partnership to work. A partner is
another person regarded as an equal, with whom one is working col-
laboratively on a common task. If a woman is working with a partner,
she has to be able to communicate with that person – tell him how
she feels, what she has experienced, what she thinks should be done,
how she would go about doing it. She has to feel confident that the
partner will listen, understand, and appreciate what is said, even if he
is not initially disposed to agree with it. Just to talk meaningfully
with someone in a relationship of partnership, she has to believe that
he will not wilfully distort what she says or use it to manipulate,
exploit, or betray her. In these ways she has to trust that person. And
that is just the beginning. When the partner is talking, she has to
credit him with competence, sincerity, honesty, and integrity, even
when there are differences. She cannot assume, believe, or even suspect that he is trying to deceive, lie, or suppress relevant information:
she must think of him as open, sincere, and honest.

Communication between two partners requires trust when speaking and trust when hearing. If they do not trust one another, these people cannot communicate well enough to work together. Partners work
together: they communicate openly and effectively, share goals, coop-

erate, coordinate activities, rely on each other's promises and commitments, and make dependable arrangements that do not presuppose constant surveillance and supervision. Often they like each other; intimate partners love each other. People cannot be partners without a considerable degree of trust. If distrust between them interferes with communication and collaboration, their partnership is doomed.

Distrust may be localized to specific contexts and situations, and as such it need not destroy a relationship. But often it spreads from one context to others, as illustrated in the case of Joe and Mary, described in the last chapter. If Mary tells her husband, Joe, that she has quit smoking and he then finds out from her male colleague that she has continued to smoke at the office, he may begin to suspect that she has been deceiving him about other things too. As a loyal husband who wants to believe in his wife, he could reason that Mary failed *once*, but will keep her commitment on smoking the next time she makes it. That is to say, Joe can limit his distrust. But psychologically and emotionally, distrust tends to spread – not only to further contexts of the same type but to other contexts entirely. Thus Joe may begin to wonder what else Mary could be deceiving him about, given that she has deceived him about this matter, and what other promises she could be breaking, given that she has broken this one. Despite the context dependence of distrust, people very often infer from particular failings that a person lacks integrity and is likely to be unreliable in other contexts.

She lied about quitting smoking.
So,
she is quite capable of lying about important matters.
Perhaps,
she is a liar and an unreliable person.
So,
perhaps she has not made the mortgage payment, even though she said she would.
So,
I do not trust her any more.

Clear cases of lying are especially likely to inspire distrust. Mary must know that she smokes at the office; this is not the kind of thing she could make a mistake about. If she has told Joe that she does not smoke at the office, she has told him something she knows to be false, in order to lead him to believe it is true. In this case, her statement, a simple factual claim, really is false. In lying, Mary has intentionally misled her husband. She made claims that she knows to be false and that are in fact false, and in doing so, she has deprived him of something that he needs to make sound decisions. If Mary wanted to have children, and she and Joe were exploring this possibility, whether she has stopped smoking or not could be an important factor in his response.

Lying indicates a willingness to mislead and manipulate the other person, and the one who is lied to has his autonomy diminished insofar as he has acquired inaccurate information about the world. Even a case of lying in which the liar inadvertently makes a true claim (she tells something that she believes to be false, but it just happens to be true) provides a basis for distrust, because the person who lies has indicated her willingness to manipulate the other person for her own ends. If the claim that the lying person makes just happens to be true, it nevertheless remains the case that she believed it false, wanted to lead the other person to believe something false, and thus was willing to mislead that person, diminishing his capacity for effective action and increasing his manipulability.

From an isolated instance, distrust may spread, its baneful effects extending and tending to become entrenched. One study of trust and distrust in small working groups found that distrust had negative effects on their efficiency. It inhibited the exchange of information, adding to uncertainty and making it more likely that important problems would go unrecognized or unacknowledged. It increased the likelihood of misinterpretation: people did not take remarks at face value. Trying to determine what was "really meant," they often got things wrong. Distrust within the group increased fear and defensive behaviour and made it difficult for people to communicate openly and cooperate effectively. Projects undertaken were less effective than those of more trusting groups.[6]

DOWNWARD SPIRALS AND SELF-FULFILLING PROPHECIES

There is a certain natural dynamic of distrust that often results in a downward spiralling of attitudes: things go from bad to worse. Distrust is communicated, results in hostility and alienation, and is confirmed and spreads, as illustrated in the following example. Peter and Susan are colleagues who work at the same firm. They have been acquaintances for several years. Peter already had a rather negative impression of Susan when she started at the firm: he had heard that she slept around and was once accused of embezzling funds. When he first met her, she seemed to him nervous and shifty, and he immediately thought her untrustworthy. For this reason, Peter never gave

Susan more information than he really had to, even when they were working on projects together. When he was temporarily her supervisor, he tried to control her activities by restricting admission to key areas, making sure she punched the time clock, and having her report frequently about her work. To Susan it is clear that Peter does not trust her. She does not understand why, because she has been a reliable and competent employee in this firm. He appears simply to be prejudiced against her. (She suspects that he does not like working with women.) Peter's barely disguised distrust and attempts to supervise and control her activities make Susan feel resentful and alienated. She does not trust Peter either and feels that her lack of trust in him has a clear justification in his behaviour.

In the beginning Peter felt some distrust for Susan, for no better reason than hearsay and intuition. After several years of uneasy interaction, both Peter and Susan feel a distrust that is entrenched and supported by evidence. Each distrusts the other, and each has some warrant for the attitude; each has found confirmation for suspicions about the other. These co-workers have met many times, and Susan has been evasive and slightly hostile in these encounters. Because of his distrust, Peter is controlling and unfriendly. Their relationship is tense, difficult, and unsatisfying. Without some dramatic confrontation, rupture, or specific effort to become reconciled, their relationship is likely only to worsen. The pattern in such cases is clear. Distrust is self-perpetuating; it grows on itself. Distrustful attitudes generally elicit feelings of alienation, unreliable behaviour, and further distrust. This usually happens to both (or all) parties in a relationship. Characteristically, distrust builds on itself and spreads.

An important factor in the dynamic of increasing distrust is our tendency to function so as to confirm the beliefs we already have. We want to see other persons as stable, predictable creatures, so we tend to construct a picture of them and regard it as definitive, as really indicating what they are like. We may all too readily label and categorize people on the basis of single actions, especially in cases where these actions are negative. ("He told a lie, so he is a liar.") We take an action and turn it into a fixed picture or stereotype.

Involved here are two styles of reasoning documented by social psychologists. One is the correspondence bias: we assume that an action corresponds to a fixed characterization of the person. The other is the attribution fallacy: we falsely assign character attributes on the basis of actions, discounting the possibility that an action may emerge as natural in certain circumstances or because the agent is placed in a particular social role. Such reasoning is deemed by social psychologists to be fallacious; they say that we are too ready to categorize a person, forming a fixed and stable picture of character on too slim a basis of evidence. From even a few inklings of information suggesting that someone is a shady character, we may begin, far too hastily, to see him or her through negative spectacles. It is like looking at the world through green lenses and therefore seeing a green world. With suspecting minds and eyes, we observe suspicious behaviour, and we too readily construct a fixed and negative picture of the other.

Worse yet, the beliefs surrounding such a picture may become true even in cases where they were initially unsupported, as happened in the example of Peter and Susan. Peter's belief that Susan was not to be trusted created evidence for itself. He then had confirmation that his view of her was right; it seemed to be supported by his experience. In terms of her relationship with Peter, Susan seems, and has been, rather untrustworthy. In part, her untrustworthiness is founded in his perceptions; in part, in her own actions in response. His distrust has become a self- fulfilling prophecy. And it will work in the other direction: she has reason to distrust him and will do so.

Self-fulfilling prophecies are common in everyday interactions between sexual partners, dates, friends, and colleagues. We tend to discover what we expect to discover, select evidence that confirms our prior beliefs and stereotypes, and ignore exceptions and counter-evidence. There is a general tendency for expectations to be self-confirming. Distrust will inspire lack of trustworthiness.

The self-fulfilling prophecy phenomenon is supported by our tendency to be biased in favour of our own beliefs. When we believe something, even tentatively, we tend to "investigate" or check out our belief by finding evidence in its favour, rather than by exploring evidence both for and against it, as logic would require. Someone who thinks that physicists are nerds will anticipate and attend to nerdy qualities on the part of physicists. Anecdotes and incidents about nerdy physicists will come to her attention, and she is likely to remember them because they confirm her prejudice. From a logical point of view, cases of non-nerdy physicists are equally relevant to the merits of her belief. But she will tend to ignore them. This is the confirmation bias: we selectively attend to matters that would confirm our beliefs and ignore those that would disconfirm them.

The confirmation bias is another explanation for the fact that trust and distrust tend to build confirmation for themselves. Distrusting Susan initially, Peter ignored evidence that she was a good worker and found nothing to like about her as a person. But he did not ignore evidence of shiftiness, evasiveness, unfriendliness, or unreliability. Whatever happens, attention and memory tend to select in favour of our own hypotheses.

We generally create our own social reality by influencing the behaviour we observe in others. But the problem is that we do not know we have done this; because we do not know, we misinterpret the actions and words of other people. Responses that we ourselves have inspired we mistake to be fixed characteristics of other people.[7] We fail to understand that often, what we assume to be objective features of other people are in part the effect of our own attitudes and actions.

The trustworthiness or untrustworthiness of others is not simply an objective and independent feature of the world; we do not form our beliefs about other people by consistently tallying up their behaviour. Instead, we tend to interpret and assess behaviour on the basis of beliefs we antecedently hold – sometimes on good evidence, sometimes on poor. Unless we take special care, we are selective and cling to our hypotheses and beliefs. When the behaviour of other people fits our beliefs, we attend to it, take it seriously, and think it genuinely reveals their character. When it fails to fit, we attribute it to situational factors. Interpretation is selective; we pick and choose.[8] Our attitudes and expectations tend to evoke confirming responses in other people. In this way, trust and distrust come to be entrenched attitudes, somewhat insensitive to evidence.

The effects of this human psychology can be quite destructive. Applied to the subject of trust, the self-fulfilling prophecy theory offers an important warning: distrust someone and he or she may very well become more untrustworthy. Then we will distrust all the more and find that we have good reason to do so. H.J.N. Horsburgh described the moral hazards of downward spirals of distrust.[9] Reflecting on distrust from the point of view of moral development, he explained that a distrusted person is limited in moral opportunities because she is given no chance to develop into a morally responsible human being. If a person's actions are controlled by others and do not reflect her own judgment, they imply little about her, save that she is capable of obeying orders, and they cannot really be to her credit. Regarded by her parents as untrustworthy, a highly controlled adolescent will be provided with little chance to show that she is trustworthy. It is *morally discouraging* not to be trusted, and that fact is highly significant in bringing up children, in education, and in therapy. A distrusted person feels helpless to overcome the other's attitude that she is untrustworthy and hence unworthy. Distrust withdraws moral support and tends to perpetuate the other's bad traits. It reinforces dishonesty. Why be honest when others will not see one as honest anyway? A person needs trust in order to grow and develop maturity. Moral development presupposes some degree of trust, and distrust is inimical to it.

As Horsburgh argues, a major factor that can work for or against the enlargement of moral capacity is the attitudes of other people. Their actions and attitudes can help or hinder the development of morally responsible behaviour. Because we live together in moral communities, our attitudes, beliefs, characters, and actions are interrelated. As members of a moral community, we are responsible for each other's moral character and development, and distrust limits that development. On these grounds, Horsburgh argues that we have a duty to trust each other at least to some degree, even in cases where past conduct provides some grounds for distrust and seems to indicate that future trustworthiness is unlikely.

We can think of the adverse effects of distrust in various dimensions. Distrust has costs in many areas: to each individual, to the relationship between them, to affected colleagues, friends, or family members, and to society at large. When Peter distrusts Susan, there are adverse effects for him, for her, for their relationship, and for their colleagues. Their work too is almost certainly affected. The effects of distrust – stress, lack of openness, flawed communication, limited cooperation, and entrenching negative attitudes – are usually adverse for all concerned.

When feasible, two people who distrust each other may simply terminate their relationship. But often relationships cannot be severed in this way. People distrust each other, perhaps for good reason, and yet they have to continue in a relationship and must somehow function together. Distrusting, they cannot, in general, function comfortably and efficiently. So they perform badly, with resulting stress, frustration, misunderstanding, conflict, hostility, inefficiency, and even crime and violence. At this point, distrust has become a practical problem that demands some response.

COPING WITH DISTRUST

If we are unwilling or unable to abandon a relationship and apparently cannot establish trust within it, coping with or "managing" distrust appears to be the only alternative. In such situations we have many strategies. None is fully effective, but all are worth examining.

Seeking Reassurance

In intimate relationships a common approach to distrust is to seek assurances from the other. Such an approach is natural for one in a position of lesser power and greater vulnerability. "Do you love me, really love me?" a wife may say to her husband. From the way he acts, she cannot feel sure that he cares about her. Sexually, she is not satisfied; her husband pays little heed to whether she has an orgasm. He is often preoccupied and forgets dates and appointments. She does not feel confident with him, does not know what to make of his gestures and assurances, and suspects that he is not committed to her or to their relationship. She needs more. Both emotionally and sexually, she feels insecure in the relationship. To alleviate this insecurity, and because she does not trust him enough to take his care and affection for granted, she tries to elicit signs. She asks for assurance because she is insecure.

But there is something self-defeating, even slightly paradoxical, in her quest. The problem is that in distrusting her husband, the wife will be unable to take seriously any reassurance he gives. She does not really trust him to say what he means and suspects that he may be using her. Whatever he says or does in response, it is unlikely to satisfy her needs. Under pressure, the husband may say, "I love you. Yes, I want us to stay together." But his wife will suspect that he does not really mean it. He may paint the bedroom, buy flowers, or plan a joint trip; but distrusting him, she will not take these actions as evidence of a firm commitment to their relationship. These, she will suspect, are merely tokens intended to influence her. He is doing these things, she will think, in order to get her to play along with him, to retain for himself a relationship with someone he does not really love, but a relationship that is convenient for him. Or they are ploys of some other sort. Paradoxically, the very distrust that makes this wife need her husband's reassurance makes her unable to believe him.

A recent Australian film offers a vivid illustration of this dynamic. *Proof* depicts Martin, a young blind man living alone in a city apartment. Bitter about being blind, Martin feels hostile towards the world and other people. He has always been extremely distrustful; he distrusts most other people and has done so since his childhood, when he distrusted even his mother. As a child, Martin would hear noises outside and ask her what was there. When she replied, he suspected that she was trying to trick him. Even when his mother died, he doubted that her death was genuine, suspecting that it was part of an elaborate hoax she had contrived so that she could get away from him. At her burial he tapped the casket and thought it sounded hollow.

Martin sought assurance from other people, but he was unable to believe what they told him. When they did offer assurance, it did not really help. Not seeing, he would ask others what they saw. Not believing, he would put his questions again, requesting several descriptions of the same scene. Martin acquired a camera and began to photograph scenes of special interest to him. It was an attempt at a technological solution, but technology could not do the job alone. He depended not only on technology but on other people. And because he did not trust those other people, he could not gain reassurance from them.

As a boy, Martin had distrusted his mother when she said that a gardener was raking leaves, so he had once photographed the garden. After her death, he was dependent on his housekeeper, Celia, whom he suspected of trying to deceive him. Celia resented Martin deeply because she was in love with him and he would not respond to her. She did, indeed, play tricks on him. When Martin went to the park, his seeing-eye dog would sometimes fail to respond to calls, apparently disappearing for short intervals. He suspected Celia of luring the dog away and took photos which he asked his new friend Andy to interpret.

Yet this convoluted search for reassurance did little to resolve Martin's generalized distrust, for the simple reason that he was not willing or able to believe what other people told him. Although some people did try to help him and Andy offered accurate descriptions of his photographs, Martin was too bitter, resentful, and suspicious to be reassured. He tried to manage his generalized distrust by testing others, listening for sincerity, asking trick questions, and comparing the descriptions offered by different people. But radically suspicious, he took nothing as proof; his distrust could not be overcome.

After a crisis with Andy and Celia, Martin opened up to Andy, who told him that he had lied to him several times and was not abolutely trustworthy. Andy had made love to Celia and knew the secret of her love for Martin and her cruel tricks on him, but he did not tell Martin these things. He tried to explain to Martin that people can care and be basically trustworthy even though they lapse once or twice, especially under the pressure of a crisis. (In Doris Brothers's terms, we can say here that Andy tried to give Martin more *realistic* criteria for trustworthiness.) Finally Martin gained a more qualified and reasonable view of what is involved in trusting other people and was able to accept what Andy said. He went to find his mother's tombstone and became convinced that she had really died. He had Andy look at the old photo of the garden, which he took as a child, and realized that his mother had not lied. Martin came to trust Andy and for that reason was able to trust his mother. Painfully, he learned that it is futile to demand absolute proof all the time.

Although *Proof* depicts an extreme case, some aspects of Martin's dilemma are quite general. The paradox of assurance, so vividly and poignantly portrayed, applies to the situation of many people, who, vulnerable and insecure, seek reassurance that they are loved and cared about. The trouble is that in just those cases where we most want assurance, we are least likely to be able to accept it. For this reason, as a strategy for coping with distrust, seeking assurance tends not to be helpful. Firm "proof" of loyalty and dependability will be impossible. Because there is always a need for trust at some level, the person who is suspicious and uneasy can always find a basis for distrust. No partner or friend can prove beyond a doubt that he or she is *absolutely* caring, faithful, honest, dependable, and trustworthy for the indefinite future. If we feel insecure in our relationships with lovers and friends, if we distrust their commitment and feelings for us, our appeals for reassurance are likely only to make us seem more vulnerable and pathetic. We need a grounds for confidence, but those grounds cannot come from the person we distrust because we will be suspicious of what he or she provides.

Rules

Another response to distrust in a relationship is to try to manage some aspects of the relationship by appealing to rules. The relationship between trust and rules is an awkward one. The greater our trust, the less we need rules. The lesser our trust, the more we are inclined to appeal to rules – but the less useful those rules are likely to be. Trying to cope with distrust by imposing rules is unpromising because of the open-ended nature of trust. When we trust another person, we trust him or her to do what is appropriate in the circumstances, whatever those circumstances are and whatever the appropriate action may be. Circumstances are always changing, so trust, if we can maintain it, is more flexible and realistic than relying on rules.

In relationships between people who are roughly equal in status and power, neither is in a position to impose rules on the other. Thus, if two basically equal parties seek to use them to resolve problems in the relationship, they must reach an agreement as to what these rules are going to be. For agreement to be viable, both partners must perceive a need for rules or guidelines, agree on them, and abide by them. Undertaken jointly in this way, a search for rules in response to problems would clearly make sense in some circumstances. But just as clearly, this sort of recourse to rules will not overcome problems of distrust.

The reason is obvious: The problem is that negotiating, agreeing on, and complying with rules *presupposes* trust. People have to trust each other enough to communicate meaningfully and accurately about what those rules are going to be, and they must each feel some confidence that the other will comply with the rules. To the extent that people are able to agree on rules, they trust each other and can work together. To the extent that they do not trust each other and are unable to work together, they are unlikely to be able to agree on rules or follow them to their mutual satisfaction.

We employ rules; they do not run by themselves, and it is people who must make them work.[10] And one of the tricky things about rules is that they do not cover every eventuality. No rule can state within itself just how it is to be applied. Reality is richer than words, a fact that implies significant problems when we apply our verbalized rules to specific situations, as the following example illustrates.

John and Linda found that they quarrelled a lot about housework. Eventually they constructed the rule "If one of us has to attend a meeting in the evening, then the other should do the dishes." They quarrelled about who would do the dishes, so they agreed upon a rule – to avoid the need for quarrelling. This approach seems clear and sensible enough. But suppose that John and Linda both stay home; who is to do the dishes then? Their rule is incomplete; it does not cover this case. If they are in the mood for an argument, John and Linda can always contest the interpretation of their rule. They might, for instance, launch into a dispute about what counts as evening and what constitutes a meeting. If Linda has a meeting from 5 to 7 PM, is that an evening meeting? What about John's meeting that starts at 4 and lasts until 8? If he meets with just one friend, is it a meeting? Having a rule may be useful as a guide to discussion, but it will not solve everything. To make their rule on dishwashing work for them, John and Linda must understand each other and count on each other to interpret and apply the rule fairly, true to its original spirit. Their rule will work only if they can trust each other to understand and follow it, and they want it to work.

Rules do not resolve problems of distrust because their serviceability presupposes that trust exists. The dilemma with trust and rules can be stated in a few words. To the extent that we trust each other, we do not need rules. To the extent that we do not trust each other, we cannot work flexibly with rules. In all likelihood, few would be interested in personal relationships that have to be conducted according to rules. A workable rule, established by agreement, can be helpful in some practical contexts if a relationship is basically running smoothly. But rules are no definitive solution for problems of distrust. Circumstances change, and rules need interpretation and application; therefore they do not avoid the need for trust. In relationships between equals, rules cannot work unless there is cooperation and agreement – which is just to say that there must be some degree of trust.

It is often tempting to resort to rules in relationships with children. They, especially young children, are not our equal partners, and we are in a position to impose rules upon them – or so we may think. We are trying to bring them up; we have limits as to what they can do and not do; we make rules for them and try to have them follow these rules. Some elements of this process are nearly always necessary in child-rearing; though when things go smoothly, the rules may be tacit and not seem to be what they are. Children may learn that certain things are expected and simply do them, without any fuss or difficulty, without our having to state or appeal to a rule. We are more likely to articulate rules for children when an issue or problem arises and things are not going as they should. As more powerful beings, responsible for our children's welfare, we may be tempted by the approach. "No dessert until your vegetables are finished"; "do your piano practising and homework before you go out to play with your friends"; "brush and floss your teeth or you can't watch *The Simpsons*"; and so on. These are low-level rules that can help families function, and with children younger than teenagers, we can often make them work.

But this is routine family life, not territory where there is serious distrust. With rebellious teenagers, who really need guidelines, rules have their perils. Leslie Mahaffey, an Ontario teenager, was given a curfew that she missed. She returned home from a party at 2 AM to find the house locked. Unwilling, apparently, to ring a bell and incur the wrath of her parents, whose rule she had broken, she called a friend for help and then returned to her backyard. From there she was abducted by Paul Bernardo, who brutally raped, tortured, and eventually murdered her. Perhaps for good reason, Leslie's parents did not trust her to use her own judgment about her comings and goings. They imposed a rule that they could not trust her to keep; she broke it and was fearful of the consequences. The results were catastrophic.

Although this tragic case is extreme, it illustrates a more general problem. If we cannot trust our growing children, we are unlikely to be able to trust them to follow rules that we have imposed, and we are going to have to think what we will do when they do not follow the rules. How will we avoid having things get worse? When they are going wrong, wanting to set rules is a natural reaction. And yet imposed rules are a strikingly unpromising solution to problems of trust. If we try to involve our children in arriving at rules and policies, we are more likely to have commitment from them. But that takes us back to the situation of rules between equals, and there, as we have seen, rules can be useful only if there is enough trust to make them workable. Again, we can see that rules are no substitute for trust.

When we trust another person, we can assume that he or she will act as required in a new situation and be flexible and reasonable in working to solve unanticipated problems. When we distrust, we cannot. Distrusting, we will feel the need for some *guarantee* that the other will do *what is required* when a problem arises. And no such guarantee can be contained in rules themselves. For rules to work, we need confidence in the other's good judgment and goodwill. When we have this, it is not really rules that we rely on.

Contracts

Much the same may be said of explicit bargains or contracts. Though helpful on occasion, they do not eliminate the need for trust. Consider, for example, the case of an engaged couple who agree that it is desirable for husband and wife each to do his or her equal share of caring for children after marriage. She is determined not to have to abandon her career if they have children, and she does not want to work the notorious double shift either. So the two sign a marriage contract stipulating that work caring for any children they may have is to be divided equally between them. Obviously, that contract does not eliminate the need for trust and confidence in each other; each must believe in the other's commitment to stay in the marriage and abide by the contract. To anyone who has been married and had children and has dealt with the pressures of children's needs and two careers, the fact that these two people have felt the need for such a contract will probably make them seem less, not more, likely to succeed in their goal of an egalitarian two-career marriage. To make a contract work, they will need flexibility, give and take, and a considerable degree of realism. One suspects that if this couple had these, they would not have written the contract in the first place.

The give and take that is necessary in marriage or any other close partnership will seem all right only if we trust the other and think that inequality and inequities are minor and insignificant in the long run. To do so, we must see our partner as one who cares, as a person committed to our well-being and to basic principles of fairness, who will not try to exploit us. Implementing bargains and contracts in an ongoing relationship requires commitment and goodwill. By themselves, bargains and contracts cannot replace trust and are at best a partial strategy for managing distrust.

Control

Another common response to distrust is to attempt to control the other party. This is a tempting response for parents or others who are in a position to exercise power. Distrusting, we cannot relax and let the other person follow her own instincts and her own judgment. We cannot count on her to do what is right and what is safe. So we try to restrict her, to bind her in.

Attempts to control are especially common in situations of unequal power – relationships between employer and employees, women and children, teacher and student, adults and adolescents, and men and women. When the other has any aspiration for autonomy, attempts at control are unpromising.[11] Efforts to control imply lack of trust or confidence. That distrust breeds untrustworthiness and more distrust, and eventually control leads to resentment and rebellion. Eventually, a woman restricted by her over-jealous husband is likely to resent his domination. His efforts to control her will do little to keep his distrust within bound and, far from contributing to their relationship, are likely to sour it. Even where some degree of control is effective and necessary, as in the case of rather small children, it provides little opportunity for maturation and growth.

An obvious problem about control is that there are practical limits as to how far we can go. Even in the case of our own children, we cannot be with them every minute: sometimes they are in the company of friends, teachers, or other adults; sometimes they are alone. We must rely on them to act sensibly and do what is right when we are not looking over their shoulders and telling them what to do, and that means trusting them. If we do not trust them, we cannot solve the problem of distrust by resorting to control. As noted already, control means that no opportunity is provided for them to become more trustworthy. And furthermore, the moment will inevitably come when we cannot control them and have to trust again. If children have been too strictly controlled, they are likely to strike out in rebellion the moment they can gain their freedom.

When people in a relationship of distrust are equals or near equals, control is even less promising as a response to situations of distrust. In such cases, our potential for exercising control is quite limited, and if we do not understand this, we are apt only to make the distrust even worse and at the same time undermine ourselves.

A case in point is that of Brenda, an elementary school principal, who moved to a new school where she was determined to implement a pedagogical approach involving "multi-aging" and "cooperative learning." Brenda believed that as the school principal she held a position of authority and power to change the school's direction.[12] She was well read and in touch with all the most recent literature about teaching and determined to impose up-to-date pedagogical policies and practices. Brenda brought in "experts" to describe the methods she favoured, distributed supportive literature to teachers and parents, and began to implement changes. She banned spelling tests, forbidding the teachers to give them.

Parents were concerned, and undercurrents of gossip and discontent began to circulate in the school. Most parents and teachers had liked the school the way it was before Brenda's arrival. Her authoritarian decrees and attempts to control parents and staff led them to believe that she had no trust in their competence to evaluate and choose the teaching methods that would work best for the children. Brenda began to fear opposition to her plans to run the most up-to-date elementary school in the city. She tried to use control to solve her problems. Attempting to restrict thought and discussion, she forbade parents to discuss the issues with teachers, insisting that they come to her with their questions and concerns. She contacted parents who raised awkward questions at assemblies, asking them not to speak so much because they were worrying and disturbing other parents and telling them they were "depressing." In short, Brenda made every effort to control discussion in the school. She wanted no expression of dissent or dissatisfaction. She neglected the fact that parents and teachers were capable adult citizens who could and would freely associate and communicate their feelings and ideas outside the school environment, whatever she tried to do about it.

Idealistic and committed to her theories, Brenda nevertheless did not trust herself and her ideas enough to expose those theories to anything like a free debate or to acknowledge responsible criticism. She was adamant and dogmatic, unable to respond to criticisms. Brenda was fearful and suspicious of the parents and teachers who might upset her plans. She did not trust them to make reasonable judgments about educational issues and did not trust herself or her views enough to expose those views to criticism. In her quest for control, Brenda went to amazing lengths. If she overheard parents discussing issues of pedagogy and school organization with teachers or among themselves, she telephoned them later, reminding them not to speak to each other and stating firmly that all enquiries about the new teaching methods should be addressed to her personally.

Not surprisingly, this approach was ineffective; in fact, it was counter-productive. Parents and teachers knew each other in out-of-school contexts, and parent volunteers were independent adults who could not be kept from talking with one another outside the school. Brenda's controlling style produced massive suspicion, alienation, and resentment. She appeared manipulative and domineering. Teachers and parents alike were well aware that, principal or not, she had no right to try to control their conversations. Brenda exercised less control over teachers and parents than she had supposed, and her attempts to stifle them only inspired resistance. Her bid for control did nothing to lessen distrust in the relationship between her and the parents; rather, it vastly increased it.

We could, perhaps, attempt to control people by battering them into submission or keeping them locked up. One newspaper showed a picture of a smiling woman carrying shackles that she had purchased to use with her teenaged daughters. She wanted to prevent them from staying out late at night drinking and sleeping with sailors. Presumably, the purchase was a joke – albeit one in questionable taste. But there are parents who try such desperate things. In Western societes, if they are discovered, they are criminally charged. Few of us will find such pathological approaches tempting. Only rarely can we control other people, and even when this is possible, it does nothing to lessen distrust or cultivate trustworthiness. It undermines the autonomy of others and it alienates us from them. The effort to control is an expression of distrust and not a solution to problems of distrust.

Surveillance

Surveillance is, in effect, an attempt to extend control (or the potential for it) to occasions when one is not present.[13] An extreme measure, it is nearly always symptomatic of a breakdown in the relationship. It is an expression of grave distrust and virtual desperation and will be seen as such by the partner. Surveillance is a violation of privacy that will not be taken lightly. What is sought in surveillance is knowledge of the other's private and free activities – knowledge by which one seeks to control or punish the other. By knowing these activities, one hopes to prove or disprove the other's loyalty and dependability. Presumably that is the hope of the women who hire private detectives to check out their fiancés or boyfriends. If they discover that their man is dishonest, disloyal, or unfaithful, they will decide to end the relationship, perhaps hoping to use the information gained to some advantage in negotiating details of the termination.

The circumstances in which surveillance might serve to resolve issues of distrust are few. If the person watched turns out to be loyal and honest after all (as was the case, apparently, for about one-third of the men checked out by the American detective Ed Pankan); if he never discovers that he has been watched; if the person who arranged the surveillance trusts those watching him and believes their reports – then surveillance might work to overcome distrust. But such a combination of circumstances is surely very rare, and surveillance remains a desperate measure. For most people, such observation of a spouse, former spouse, lover, family member, or friend would seem impractical, too expensive, and fundamentally immoral.

The Law

Other approaches to distrust are scarcely feasible within the context of relationships between family members, intimate friends, colleagues, or partners. Consider, for instance, recourse to the law.[14] If one person does another an injury, and it can be shown that he has been negligent or has broken the law in doing so, the injured party can sue for damages. In the case of harm resulting from seriously immoral actions, such as the sexual assault of a child, a person can take recourse to the criminal law and work to have the other charged, convicted, and punished. Such actions may be appropriate and helpful in giving some relief to victims and in preventing further negligence or crime. But obviously they do not resolve problems of distrust. In fact, it is extremely likely that distrust between the involved parties will be worsened by their appearing in an adversarially defined legal context.[15]

The relationship between law and behaviour can be seen from another angle when we consider the social context in which relationships are conducted. Given the existence of the criminal law specifying minimal norms for decent behaviour between persons, we expect conformity to those norms. The fact that laws prohibit these harmful actions gives us means to seek redress should the actions occur. We can sue for damages or endeavour to have the other party punished. Legal norms are, for the most part, more relevant to social trust than to personal trust. They establish expectations and confidence that most behaviour will conform to basic moral norms. Laws can effect compliance, and compliance – though less so than integrity and trustworthiness – remains important.

The fact that laws do not by themselves change attitudes is critically important in personal relationships. We need to trust our family and friends, and we want more from these relationships than compliance out of fear or respect for the law. We want compliance to emerge from the integrity of the other person and his concern for us. We want and expect to be loved and cherished by our partners, family, and close friends. To think that these intimate others would refrain from robbing or assaulting us only from fear of legal repercussions would be devastating. If their relationship has broken down, a husband may be deterred by a court order from bashing down the door of his wife's house, beating her up, and raping her. In such debased circumstances, the fact that it would be illegal for him to come to her home is highly significant. If there is any chance of its serving this function, such a court order is worth obtaining.

Though it is possibly of fundamental importance in such cases, the legal system obviously does not rectify problems of *distrust*. A woman will not trust her husband or former husband more because she has succeeded in getting a court order against him; rather, the need for such an order is an expression of just how extreme her distrust has become. She may or may not, depending on the enforceability of the order, be less fearful of his behaviour in this case. But even if she is so, it is not because she trusts him more; it is because she has confidence in the law and its enforcement. The law, in such cases, may be an factor in motivating restraint and safety, and it may prevent people from physically terrorizing each other. But legal proceedings and injunctions in themselves do little or nothing to address problems of distrust. On the contrary, recourse to the legal system is an expression of distrust and sometimes a cause of distrust, not an effective method of handling it.

Insurance

Similar comments can be made about insurance. A man about to fly to India at a time of political instability cannot eliminate his fears or dispel his lack of trust in foreign political institutions by taking out insurance. But were he to die on the trip, an insurance settlement would help his family financially. This case illustrates the function of insurance: it reduces *vulnerability* by providing extra resources. Insurance is a device for managing distrust that works by reducing vulnerability and thereby reducing the need for trust. All this, of course, presupposes trust at another level: we have to trust the insurance companies and their agents.

But these themes are not easily applied to personal relationships. We can hardly imagine seeking insurance against the disloyalty of a lover or friend or against divorce. Should we seek contracts with our partners before marriage and then try to insure ourselves against any violation? If a husband turns out to be a physical or psychological abuser, or if he does not do his share of the housework or help care for the children, could his wife obtain get a divorce and then seek compensation from the insurance company? The scenario is more plausible as a satire than an actual sequence of events. Insurance companies would surely be loath to offer such policies. Given the divorce rate, they might well fear that taking on such cases would be tantamount to bankruptcy. Personal relationships are unpredictable in their course; marriages in particular have a failure rate that would make insurance financially untenable. When such relationships go wrong, the "damages" are hard to measure, and it typically makes little sense to think of compensating for them with monetary awards.

In any event, insuring ourselves against damaged interpersonal relationships would be largely futile. In personal contexts, insurance could not perform its usual function of reducing the need to trust.

Within personal relationships, we need to trust because of what those relationships are. Distrust in our personal relationships is going to be uncomfortable because it affects intimacy, communication, and cooperation. That is why it is problematic, and that fact cannot be remedied or diminished by insurance. It may provide for financial or material emergencies, but it can give no protection against emotional damage. In personal relationships, emotional vulnerability is the most important factor.

Of the many strategies for managing distrust, some are partially effective, but none are entirely successful. None overcome the stress, discomfort, and flawed communication that are inevitable in relationships characterized by distrust. In fact, the problems that arise only illustrate again how important and central trust is in human relationships. Instead of trying to manage distrust, we might do better to attempt to overcome it. Difficulties in managing distrust suggest the importance of exploring ways to *restore* trust.

CHAPTER NINE

Restoring Trust

It is a truism that it is easier to destroy trust than to restore it. In many contexts, we indeed try to restore trust, and it is important to do so. Various approaches have been recommended, and it is useful to consider them. But there is no magic recipe.

"TRUST ME"

One who is distrusted in an intimate relationship and wishes to restore the relationship may appeal for trust, asking the other to believe in her loyalty and dependability. She may ask for his trust back, saying in effect, "trust me." In such a case the expression "trust me," though imperative in form, does not express an order. It is more plausibly understood as a request, uttered with undertones of pleading.[1] The request is a strange one because the very fact that it is needed suggests its limitations. If a relationship is affected by distrust, there are some grounds for that distrust. A mere appeal to "trust me" does nothing to overcome those grounds and may even inspire resistance. After all, anyone who could resume trusting on the basis of a mere appeal would not have been very distrustful in the first place. Grounds for distrust will not be dispelled by words, however fervently they might be uttered.

If a man has reason to distrust his wife and she wants to gain back his trust, she needs to offer him some reassurance that she will not let him down in the future, that she will be faithful and loyal, is committed to their relationship, and will keep her promises. The problem with the appeal to "trust me" is that it offers no reinterpretation of the past, no apology, and no specific reassurance regarding the future. And yet it requests a change in attitude. Too little is offered, too much asked. Not reassured, not given so much as a promise, the partner is nonetheless asked to trust. Perhaps for these reasons, the words "trust me" often have a slightly cynical tone. Ironically, the appeal simply to trust is manipulative and risks contributing to *distrust*.

John Updike wrote a story called "Trust Me," about a family in which people tended to appeal for trust to lure others into doing dangerous and unreasonable things.[2] Persuading others to take risks, these people frequently urged, "Trust me, everything will be all right." It hardly ever was. The initial episode in the story features the narrator's near death by drowning at the age of four. His father talked him into jumping into a swimming pool, promising to catch him and holding out his arms. ("Trust me. It'll be all right. Jump right into my hands.") Then, apparently deliberately, he failed to catch the boy, allowing him to sink deep into the chlorinated water. The terrified child nearly drowned and never forgot it.

The request to "trust me" often seems manipulative, as it was in this case. It seeks to exploit the other person's loyalty, innocence, and goodwill, urging him, for no good reason, to ignore fears and doubts that may very well have a reasonable foundation. When urged to "trust me," we are often made to feel unloving or guilty if we do not trust. As used, the expression often implies "you *should* trust me (and if you do not, there is something wrong with *you*)." This is the manipulative element: if we do not trust, we are implicitly accused of having inappropriate attitudes.

A man "should" trust his wife: are they not lovers, life partners, the closest of companions? A woman "should" trust her daughter: does she not think her a worthy person? ("Trust me, Mum, it'll be all right.") We "should" trust our spouse, lover, friend, colleague, or business partner. A kind of tacit trust is the standing norm of any human relationship; when we distrust, it is abnormal and uncomfortable; we are likely to feel uneasy. One who does not trust is likely to sense that trust *should* be a part of this relationship. The request to "trust me" seeks to exploit this sense and the attendant uneasiness. ("A son should be able to trust his father. Right?" "Trust me. If you don't trust me, you should." "Trust me. Just jump right into my arms. You'll be all right.") When others ask us to trust them, we are likely to suspect an attempt at manipulation and feel uneasy, as if we are about to be led somewhere where we do not want to go. Given that trust characterizes good relationships, we are likely to sense that ideally we should trust, that things would be better if there were more trust in this relationship, and that we are being asked to fix the situation ourselves by trusting the other. This makes us feel that we "should" trust; yet there are grounds for distrust, which is what we really feel.

Although these tensions are especially wrenching in close personal relationships, they may also appear in contexts of work and social institutions. Brenda, the school principal who tried so hard to control debate about pedagogy, appealed for trust when she was questioned by Doreen and Phil, parents who were both university professors. She was convinced that routine testing in spelling and arithmetic is harmful to students because it is competitive; she believed that children should work in groups, talk together as they wished during class, and move freely around the classroom. Doreen and Phil had reasons to feel uneasy about this approach. Their son, Alan, seemed to make little progress under this new program. His classroom was noisy and disordered whenever they visited, and there was no drill in math or spelling or practice in handwriting. In addition, the accounts of the new pedagogy that Brenda had provided to them struck them as vague and even incoherent. Insistent that the new approach was valid and the school among the best in town, she responded to their questions by appealing for trust. "Trust us," she said. "We're professionals. Some of us have seven years of university. In my former school, where lots of parents were professors, we never had these problems. Those people were willing to trust us."[3] In other words, "You *should* trust us as other people similar to you have been willing to do. If you do not trust us, then there must be something wrong with *you*."

Brenda's appeal was, in effect, a manipulative attempt to tell Doreen and Phil how they *should* feel and think. Instead of presenting them with evidence and arguments that the new pedagogy would work, she simply appealed for trust and sought to manipulate them by referring to "years of university" and the other parents who had been willing to trust. Predictably, her appeal for trust was self-defeating. Frustrated that they could get no substantive answers to their legitimate critical questions, Doreen and Phil felt that Brenda was trying to manipulate them, blaming them and their lack of trust for the problems that Alan was experiencing, and failing to accept responsibility for the workings of this pedagogy that she so favoured.

Appeals for trust may be effective over the short run. They can work sometimes because people can be led to think that they *should* feel trust, especially in intimate relationships. But their effect is at best short term if nothing is done to affect the causes or grounds for distrust. If the situation does not change, then, because of their manipulative character, these appeals are likely only to increase distrust.

TALKING THINGS OVER

Another approach is to discuss issues of trust directly. There is, again, something rather strange about the attempt. Typically, we take trust for granted and do not like to discuss it. But when we do not trust, we are frequently too insecure to talk about such sensitive matters as distrust. Only in a relationship that is basically good can we hope to raise problematic issues directly. Because it is so difficult to relate to others on a basis of acknowledged distrust, we tend to pretend to a trust that we do not feel, in the interests of etiquette and saving face. To raise an issue of distrust directly and openly, we must break through this convention. This approach is most likely to work when the distrust is contextually quite specific. In a basically good friendship, we may be able to tell the other about our lack of confidence with regard to some particular matter. Consider, for instance, the case of Joan and Beverly, friends who have long been close and who then embark on a political collaboration. Joan finds her old friend Beverly surprisingly unreliable in the new context. Because they are close and have trusted each other for many years, she may be able to raise the matter directly. Good friends or intimate partners may resolve problems of distrust by talking them over – discussing past experiences and working to understand each other's expectations and needs.

But this case is too straightforward to be typical. When distrust is broader in scope, the chances of settling issues by talk and discussion are less. The problem is that distrust in a relationship tends to spread from one context to another. If someone is not reliable about commitments in one area, we begin to fear that she will not be reliable in another. In the worst cases, distrust has become so generalized that we feel that the other person has ceased to care about us at all or to retain any commitment to the relationship. At this point, effective communication about anything – much less the distrust itself – becomes difficult. Communication is possible only if we can assume that the other is basically sincere and is trying to say what he or she means, and thus meaningful communication presupposes some trust. In serious cases, spreading distrust is unlikely to be resolved by talk alone, because those involved will not be prepared to believe each other.

ACTIVE LISTENING

Strategies for active listening, taught in many conflict-resolution and mediation programs, are intended in part to establish trust.[4] The idea here is that we listen attentively to another person, making it clear that we are doing so. We attend closely, maintain eye contact, frequently "affirm" the other, and often "play back" what she has said. Here is a sample dialogue that illustrates the strategy:

SHARON: I'm just overwhelmed since she died. I can't get used to her being not around – we used to take her so many places and phone her every day. And it was so sudden. It was just terrible.

JUNE: Yes, that's awful.

SHARON: I know she was getting old, but we really didn't expect it right then. I mean, she had apparently had a mild heart attack before, but she didn't even know it had happened until the doctor did a test. And she was away on a trip just two weeks before she died, and seemed just fine. It's so hard to get used to it! I just don't know how we're going to cope.

JUNE: So you were really shocked? And you don't know how you're going to cope?

SHARON: Right. We're so upset too. And it's really hard with my daughter right now. She's so depressed, she doesn't want to do anything, and it makes her depressing to be with. When she isn't short-tempered, that is.

JUNE: That must be hard.

SHARON: It sure is. And there's so much extra work with the estate, it's driving us crazy.

The idea behind active listening is to let a person tell her story and to demonstrate our interest and genuine concern by attending closely and expressing our understanding and empathy. Some training programs in conflict resolution give "homework": listen to someone for five straight minutes without interrupting in any way except to reinforce what she is saying. People are instructed not to change the subject or to talk about themselves. For many, such an assignment is difficult.[5] We tend to listen with partial attention, waiting with barely concealed impatience to chime in with news of ourselves and our own projects. As a deviation from this careless norm, active listening will often inspire appreciation and gratitude from the speaker.

This approach serves important purposes. If June shows sustained concern for Sharon and "hears her out," Sharon is likely to feel that June cares about her and wants to be helpful; June is conveying empathy, which will make Sharon feel secure and support her self-trust. Thus active listening tends to elicit trust. Ideally, it will be practised by both parties, who can share their feelings and concerns and how the other views a problem or situation. In cases of distrust or a conflict, active listening can help restore trust. It creates empathy and mutual understanding. Active listening is an indirect appeal for trust; we express in our behaviour and speech a concern and respect for the other. We try hard to understand her feelings, beliefs, needs, and interests, and we show, through our words and attitude, that we are doing so. Not only is this a more subtle approach than saying "trust me," but it is apt to be more convincing. We actually do something (listen and pay attention) to indicate that we care and are trustworthy.[6]

THERAPEUTIC TRUST

H.J.N. Horsburgh defined a notion of therapeutic trust. We rely on a person known to be untrustworthy in certain regards, making our reliance explicit ("I'm really counting on you") in an attempt to affect the other's conduct.[7] Therapeutic trust tries to increase the trustworthiness of the person in whom it is placed. The underlying idea is that we can stir his conscience and inspire him to live up to our belief in him. If such trust is effective, he will become more trustworthy. Therapeutic trust is Gandhian, making an explicit appeal to the potential of a person as a reliable moral agent. Gandhi believed that a basically positive attitude towards human nature was a fundamental moral requirement. We should always look at another human being as potentially good, whatever his role, whatever his past behaviour. A Gandhian axiom, apparently spiritual in origin, is that *every* human being has the capacity to respond to a moral appeal, whatever his or her actions, social role, or apparent character. This is the basis on which we should generally approach other people, even those whom we are inclined to distrust.

Gandhi addressed the problem of trust from the point of view of an activist for Indian independence who had on many occasions interacted with officials charged with upholding the imperial British power in India. He insisted that we respond to other people as human beings and not merely as the occupants of various social roles or functions. For Indian activists, an official in the British colonial regime occupied a highly objectionable position. But it would be an ethical and political mistake to identify the person with his role: such an official is still a *human being* with feelings, interests, and goals of his own, and as such, he merits respect and concern. Every person, whatever his or her history, role, or station in life, is a individual who deserves respect, sympathy, and consideration. As a human being, a colonial official or any other "opponent" merits exactly the degree of concern and respect owing to any other human being – no more, no less. Gandhi made considerable headway by treating colonial officials and other identified "opponents" as human beings.[8] He assumed that they were moral beings capable of a moral response to a moral appeal.

If treated as a morally responsible being, a person is capable of responding as such. If so trusted, he or she may become trustworthy.

In therapeutic trust, we convey to another person our conviction that he or she will be a person of integrity. Gandhi said: "As long as I see the slightest reason for trusting people, I will certainly trust them. It is foolish to continue trusting after one has had definite grounds for not trusting. But to distrust a person on mere suspicion is arrogance and betrays a lack of faith in God."[9] Therapeutic trust is based on conveying to the other person our conviction that he is, or can become, a person of integrity – to encourage him to merit the trust placed in him. Explicitly trusting, we hope to inspire trustworthiness. The approach is often effective, because people are strongly influenced by the conception that other people have of them and are profoundly discouraged when others openly imply that they are untrustworthy.

Horsburgh's interest in therapeutic trust arose from his understanding that distrust tends to be durable, contagious, and reductive of moral opportunities. When a person is honest, someone who distrusts him gives "an invitation to accept a dishonest role, and inveterate distrust is such a pressing invitation that many find it difficult to refuse." "When we distrust a dishonest man, we simply reinforce his dishonesty. Such a man usually develops a debased concept of human nature; for cynicism is a conventional means of combining dishonesty with peace of mind. Other's distrust of him and his own dishonest dealings with them are alike in being self-interested; and therefore is he not on the same moral footing as his partners in the distrustful relationships into which he enters?"[10] The idea behind therapeutic trust is that the previously untrustworthy person will be led by the trust of the other to perceive the moral inequality between himself and the other person, and will thereby be motivated to make moral progress. Every moral agent has a capacity for honourable dealings, and other moral agents can help him to develop or enlarge it by making appropriate moral appeals and challenges. "Trust is one of the most important ways in which one individual can give moral support to another," Horsburgh says.

Having a relationship we need to preserve, we seek to inspire an untrustworthy partner to a state of responsibility. We pointedly put a valued good in his hands, counting on him, allowing ourselves to be vulnerable to his actions, and placing on him the responsibility for our well-being in some matter. This explicit action of placing our trust in another is supposed to evoke trustworthiness. The other (we expect and hope) will feel moved and inspired to live up to our overtly positive expectations. Therapeutic trust assumes a response of some indebtedness or affection towards the other person. A person explicitly trusted in this way will not want to harm us when we have pointedly made ourselves vulnerable. The story of Victor Hugo's *Les Miserables* arises from an instance of therapeutic trust. A kind bishop gives a thief and fugitive, Jean Valjean, some silver that he was about to steal, telling him to use it to go off to build himself an honest life. This single act of trust and generosity inspires heroic honesty and good works by Jean Valjean for the remainder of his life.

But is the strategy of therapeutic trust generally effective? And what are the moral assumptions underlying it? Horsburgh's conception of therapeutic trust can borrow some credibility from psychological studies of self-fulfilling prophecies: people treated as, and assumed to be, trustworthy will tend to become trustworthy. As for Horsburgh and Gandhi, their beliefs about human responses to trust were based on practical experience, which in Gandhi's case was extensive. "I trust you" is likely to be a more promising approach to rectifying a relationship than "trust me." It does not request but *gives* – in patient anticipation of moral reciprocity.[11]

This being said, we can nevertheless feel certain moral doubts about the idea of therapeutic trust. One area of concern is that of sincerity. Ironically, there is a sense in which therapeutic trust seems to involve pretence and manipulation. When we trust another person, we believe that he will do the right thing because he is *competent* and *appropriately motivated* to do so. The beliefs that support trust cannot be put on and taken off like jackets, and the same may be said of the relevant attitudes and dispositions. We cannot simply decide, just like that, to believe that someone is trustworthy in the sense of being well motivated and competent. That is to say, we cannot trust at will. So how do we inspire trust by "trusting" someone who has not been trustworthy? At this point, therapeutic trust begins to seem paradoxical. If the person who "therapeutically trusts" is merely *acting as if she trusts*, or *simulating* or *trying* to trust, then is therapeutic trust based on pretence? If so, is it not insincere? How, then, could it establish a basis for *trust*? We tell the other, "I trust you, I'm counting on you," hoping to inspire him to live up to the image we are projecting and deserve our trust. But in knowing that he needs to *live up* to this positive image, we at the same time know that he does not deserve it *now* – not just as we see him now, when we reflect on what he has done and the ways in which he has been untrustworthy.

The solution to this dilemma is to think of *therapeutic trust*, not as an ongoing attitude, but as a single entrusting *act* in which someone is given a specific responsibility, a responsibility that would normally be assigned on the presumption that she is trustworthy. In acting as though we trust an untrustworthy person, we seem to be trying to influence her, to inspire her to become trustworthy. This is manipulation in a sense, but only in the limited sense that we hope by many of our actions and attitudes to have a positive effect on others. "I'm trusting you to look after him" and "I'm counting on you to take in the cheque" do not express ongoing attitudes of trust, but rather, accompany acts of entrusting. Giving a cheque to an employee, saying, "I'm counting on you to deposit it before four o'clock," one *entrusts* him with this task and with these funds. Giving the silver to Jean Valjean, the bishop entrusted him with wealth as a resource for a new life. We can entrust someone with the care of a particular item or the performance of a particular task, even though we may doubt his trustworthiness overall.

To recommend therapeutic trust is to suggest that a single act of entrusting be inserted into what may be primarily a relationship of distrust, with the goal of inspiring trustworthy behaviour. There are obviously limitations. In some contexts, therapeutic trust would inappropriate because the risks imposed on third parties would be simply too great. A probation officer should not allow a serial rapist out for a weekend leave saying, "Now I'm trusting you to behave yourself and be back here by Sunday at nine." Risks to third parties in such a case would be intolerable.

Therapeutic trust is based on the assumption that people who are explicitly entrusted with certain tasks or goods will feel an obligation to live up to the expectations of others, and guilt if they do not do so.[12] It is based on the human desire to reciprocate goodness and to live up to what others expect. Understood as an act of entrusting, therapeutic trust is unobjectionable when we consider cases where people are developing or reforming (children, ex-criminals, petty offenders, lapsing partners, students, employees learning new tasks) – unobjectionable, that is, provided we assume that the expectations they are encouraged to live up to are reasonable and right, and the risks to third parties are kept at an acceptable level. Telling a ten-year-old that she is being trusted with the care of an infant for an afternoon may inspire trustworthy behaviour. But far from qualifying as "therapeutic," such trust is dangerous and sets the scene for exploitation. These expectations are not reasonable ones; the girl is given a responsibility too heavy for her years. As Horsburgh acknowledges, therapeutic trust is not a "sovereign remedy." It is not feasible or appropriate in all circumstances, and it is to some extent manipulative.

In her book *Caring*, Nel Noddings offers an account similar in important ways to that of Horsburgh. In describing how someone who is caring for another may nurture him and seek to guide his development, she describes the importance of conveying a positive idea of what the other is and can become. Noddings believes that people who take on caring roles (parents, teachers, and counsellors being prime examples) should convey in their words and actions a commitment to the positive potentialities of the person cared for. This commitment emerges not only in such specific acts as pointedly relying on him or saying, "I'm trusting you," "I'm counting on you," and so on, but also in *dispositions* to interpret positively the actions and motives of the one cared for. Noddings emphasizes the importance of conveying a positive image of the other person and in interpreting what he says and does in a positive light.

Nothing is more important in nurturing the ethical ideal than attribution and explication of the best possible motive. The one-caring holds out to the child a vision of this lovely self actualized or nearly actualized. Thus the child is led to explore his ethical self with wonder and appreciation. He does not have to reject and castigate himself but is encouraged to move towards an ideal that is, in an important sense, already real in the eyes of a significant other. It is vital that the one caring not create a fantasy. She must see things – acts, words, consequences – as they are; she must not be a fool. But seeing all this, she reaches out with the assurance that this – this-which-was-a-mistake – might still have occurred with a decent motive. "I can see what you were trying to do," she says, "or what you were feeling, or how this could have happened." The caring person's function is always to raise the appraisal, never to lower it. Thus, the caring person both accepts and confirms the child.[13]

By regarding the other as a worthy and potentially trustworthy being, by approaching him in this light and responding to mistakes with a forgiving attitude, we can encourage him to develop in positive directions. In these ways, placing our trust in another person can help to overcome distrust.

CONSISTENT TRUSTWORTHINESS

The problem of distrust in relationships is explored by Roger Fisher and Scott Brown, of the Harvard Negotiation Project, in their recent book *Getting Together*. They use personal, international, and labour-management conflicts in their examples. A central assumption in their account of relationships is that the same practical devices for managing and resolving conflict can apply at the interpersonal, small group, larger group, and international levels.

Fisher and Brown note that there are many contexts in which we have to interact with individuals and groups of whose conduct we disapprove and whom we may distrust. Although such relationships necessarily include two or more parties, it may take only one party to change their quality. In such cases, Fisher and Brown recommend what they call unconditionally constructive attitudes and actions – attitudes and actions that will be beneficial whatever the actions of the other party. These include trying to understand the other side's interests, attitudes, and beliefs, adopting an attitude of acceptance towards the other side, working to establish good communication, being meticulously reliable, and using persuasion rather than coercion.

Like Gandhi and Horsburgh, Fisher and Brown recommend that we try to adopt a positive attitude towards other people, even those of whose conduct we disapprove. They urge that we have a far better chance of understanding others if we assume that they understand themselves favourably rather than as "bad people pursuing immoral ends through illegitimate means." Yet Fisher and Brown do not recommend trust in general. Instead, they advise unconditional complete trustworthiness. Their reasoning is as follows: in a relationship we do not merely want trust; we want well-founded trust. By and large, we want to place our trust in those whose behaviour and attitudes show that they deserve it. But where there are grounds for distrust, we cannot establish trust unless we do something to alter the situation. We cannot control the other party's actions and attitudes, but we can control our own. Attempts at controlling the other party are more likely to increase distrust than to diminish it. The practical problem of distrust becomes the question of how to act so that a relationship will improve and the other party will become more trustworthy.

What we can most easily modify is our own conduct. According to Fisher and Brown, we should not fully trust, but we should be completely trustworthy. We should be as predictable as possible, speak carefully, especially when making commitments, treat promises seriously, and never be deceptive. They urge a sort of golden mean in trusting others, advising that trust can be overloaded (as when one trusts a ten-year-old girl to care for an infant for several hours) or too stingy (as when one will not trust a ten-year-old to cross a quiet street alone.) They echo Horsburgh's concern that too little trust in another can cause her to become resentful and less trustworthy.[14]

Fisher and Brown suggest that in conflict situations people tend to be too distrustful. Far too readily, we assume that those with whom we experience conflict disagree with us because they are against us or are in some other sense "bad." We have a bias in favour of ourselves, tending to overestimate our own moral uprightness and underestimate that of others. And we are too often facile in lumping all trust issues into one pot – failing to distinguish between lies and disagreement about the facts or between unreliability and cultural difference, for instance. In addition, we often fail to appreciate pressures of social structures that can discourage trustworthy behaviour. What people do may reflect the roles and situations they are in, more than their human and personal characteristics. We can make progress by appealing to them as individuals, trying to get through to the person behind the role.

The Fisher-Brown approach is quite different from the tit-for-tat strategy recommended by some students of game theory for Prisoner's Dilemma situations. In the Prisoner's Dilemma, two prisoners have been arrested and are unable to communicate with each other. The district attorney is quite certain that they are guilty, but he does not have adequate evidence to convict them at a trial. He advises each prisoner that he can choose whether to confess or not. If neither confesses, the district attorney can book them on a minor charge and both will get a light punishment. If both confess, they will both be prosecuted and convicted, but will get less than the most severe sentence. But if one confesses whereas the other does not, the one who confesses will be treated lightly, and the other will incur a heavy penalty. In this scenario, cooperating with the other party is defined as not telling; defecting is defined as telling. The prisoners stand to gain or lose together. If they cooperate with each other and neither confesses, they get a short term. Pursuing their self-interest independently, they do worse than they would if they cooperated. If both defect, both will confess and get a longer sentence. Not trusting the other to cooperate, fearing a harsh sentence if he cooperates and the other defects, each prisoner confesses (defects). In such a situation, the solitary pursuit of one's own self-interest works against that self-interest.

For formalized games involving repeated Prisoner's Dilemmas, *tit for tat* (if you cooperate, I'll cooperate; if you defect, I'll defect) turns out to be a good strategy.[15] One begins by acting cooperatively and then responds in kind to what the other person does. Since Prisoner's Dilemma games are highly intriguing and seem to mirror features of many real-life situations, the fact that tit for tat has been shown effective for them has made the strategy seem plausible elsewhere.

But for personal relationships, tit for tat is rarely sensible. Imagine the wife who suspects that her husband might be having an affair and does not believe his denials. Suppose he has been late for supper every night for a week and has become too distracted and tired to be interested in making love. On the tit-for-tat theory, his wife should adopt a strategy of "defection," being late for a few appointments herself and expressing no sexual interest in her husband. Whatever the results of this response, improving their relationship and lessening the distrust between them would not likely be among them. If the wife begins to act as though she does not care about her husband, that might make him stop and think, but an equally likely effect is that her inattention will worsen their relationship. Responding reciprocally to a lack of concern is a poor way of maintaining a relationship or restoring trust.

Tit for tat is not appropriate for personal relationships for many good reasons, prominent among these being the fact that these relationships lack key features of the Prisoner's Dilemma. Unlike the prisoners in the dilemma, people in relationships can communicate. And unlike the situation faced by those prisoners, what counts as cooperation, as defection, and as pay-off is unclear. In a Prisoner's Dilemma, if one prisoner cooperates while the other defects, the cooperating party has lost out. But cooperative practices do not always, or even typically, have these consequences in relationships. If one partner cooperates when another defects (say, for example, one carefully practises active listening while the other virtually ignores what his partner is saying), the cooperative partner has not lost anything as a result. She may very well have gained; in the case of active listening, for example, she will have acquired knowledge and understanding that could be valuable.

Fisher and Brown argue directly against expectations and responses of close, episode-to-episode reciprocity in relationships. They advise that people who expect close reciprocity in their relationships are almost certain to be disappointed. One problem is our powerful tendency to see our own behaviour through rose-coloured glasses. We tend to evaluate our own behaviour more favourably than someone else's. In a relationship each party is likely to see his or her own behaviour more favourably than that of the other person. Each will tend to exaggerate his or her own generosity and morality while underestimating those of the other. For this reason, expectations of close reciprocity are likely to lead to a downward spiralling in the relationship.

What Fisher and Brown urge is consistently trustworthy and responsible action on the part of the one who is working to lessen the distrust in a relationship. As with therapeutic trust, we anticipate some degree of reciprocity. We hope that by being prompt, reliable, honest, kind, generous, friendly, and concerned, we will inspire that sort of behaviour in our partner. If the desired responses are not forthcoming, we do not immediately give up, walk out of the relationship, or resort to dishonesty and unreliability ourselves. We persist in our efforts to be, and be seen as, completely trustworthy partners. In all of this, emotion is to be balanced with reason in a quest for understanding, acceptance, communication, and reliability. We can implement this strategy ourselves by unfailingly displaying trustworthy behaviour towards the other person. And, Fisher and Brown submit, this strategy for restoring trust can be pursued without risk. Not only is there no Prisoner's Dilemma; there is no dilemma at all.

This approach has much to recommend it. Indeed, trustworthy behaviour is good in any event, because it is morally correct behaviour, expressive of conscientiousness and integrity. But is the strategy of consistent trustworthiness truly without risk? One problem is that there is a danger of the trustworthy partner becoming a dupe of the other, open to exploitation because of his honourable and upright behaviour. The less honourable partner may learn to take for granted the cooperative behaviour of the other and simply continue to be unreliable, while counting on the unfailingly good and reliable behaviour of his trustworthy partner. He may be encouraged to continue his unreasonable demands, having learned that the trustworthy partner is easily exploited. To adopt this approach is to anticipate that consistent trustworthiness will inspire more positive behaviour. In other words, it is to anticipate reciprocation. Do we have already to trust in others to respond well, in order to use this strategy for restoring trust?

Those who are unfailingly trustworthy and virtuous can be sorely exploited by others who feel little need to respond accordingly. Far from making others *more trustworthy*, the person whose behaviour is consistently kind and generous can, in effect, collude in her own exploitation. Consider the case of a couple who have been married for twenty years. Though the husband may not be aware of it, he has been exploiting and manipulating his wife for much of this time. He benefits hugely, both personally and in terms of his career, from her conscientious assumption of most household and family responsibilites and her loyalty to him and their children. Eventually his wife begins to feel resentful. She takes an initiative to try to change the relationship; they see a counsellor. She no longer believes her husband when he says that he loves and cares about her because he has for years exploited her. She feels as though she is just a baby maker, runner of errands, and all-purpose housewife. If he values her at all, she has come to feel, it is only for her usefulness. She now distrusts her husband's assurances that everything is all right between them; she feels that she cannot count on him to do his share in making their relationship work.

In this case, the wife's trustworthy behaviour in the home is the problem, not the solution. It is her very trustworthiness that has set her up to be exploited, and her awareness of that fact is a major reason for her unhappiness. Trustworthiness can and should evoke trust, but it can also faciliatate exploitation. People who are unfailingly trustworthy and virtuous can be sorely exploited by others, who may feel little need to respond accordingly.

In advising general trustworthiness for all relationships, Fisher and Brown have at some level assumed a kind of *reciprocity*. In effect, the assumption is that if a person is trustworthy in her relationship with another, then that other will be, or gradually become, trustworthy in his relationship with her. Often that approach does work: the assumption of reciprocity is grounded both in common experience and in social psychology.[16] People tend to feel under an obligation to respond in kind, and they may be uneasy when they have not discharged such an obligation and have no opportunity to discharge it. For instance, if a street person asks for money, it is, for many people, relatively easy to say no. If, on the other hand, a street person gives them a newspaper and then asks for money *in return*, it is more difficult to refuse. Given that most people want to reciprocate, behaving in a consistently trustworthy way is often a way of appealing for trustworthy behaviour in the partner. But as with other approaches to distrust, the strategy is not infallible. There are people who feel little or no need to reciprocate. And even those who want to reciprocate in some contexts may not do so in the intimate relationships where they have learned over many years to take trustworthiness for granted.

SELF-REFLECTION

We may seek to overcome distrust by a kind of self-questioning. We can begin by reflecting on our own reasons for distrust, attempting, in a kind of self-examination, to determine whether it is warranted and how we ourselves might have contributed to the flawed nature of the relationship. To see an outline of the self-questioning strategy, consider the following case of two parties whom we will call Susan and Elizabeth, whose friendship has become unstable. Suppose that Susan begins to reflect on their relationship and the distrust that has come to characterize it. She may ask herself:

1 What is my idea of Elizabeth? (How do I see her; what sort of person do I think she is?)
2 How did I come to have this conception of Elizabeth? On which of her actions and statements am I basing this conception?
3 To what extent do I distrust Elizabeth? Why?
4 What is the basis (ground or warrant) for my distrusting her? What has she said and done to make me distrustful?
5 Do I have good reasons for distrusting her? Is my distrust based on relevant evidence? Does it warrant the degree of distrust I feel?

6 What has been the history of our relationship? Have the actions that trouble me been typical, or are they exceptional?

7 Could I be misinterpreting or misunderstanding what Elizabeth is doing? Are there plausible alternative interpretations that would put her in a better light?

8 How does Elizabeth see me? Have I given her any reason to distrust me? Have I encouraged her untrustworthy behaviour by expecting the worst or by conveying an attitude of suspicion and hostility?

9 Should this relationship continue? Could I avoid Elizabeth most of the time? Do I want to?

10 If my relationship with Elizabeth is to continue, how can I improve it?

We need this sort of self-questioning because of the selective way we seek and react to evidence, because of our tendency to attend to evidence that confirms what we already believe and ignore or discount evidence that would count against our beliefs.[17] We will express our beliefs in what we do and what we say; thus we convey our beliefs to other people, who will tend to respond to us as we respond to them. To add to the effect, we generally turn actions into attributes, labelling someone who lies once *a liar* rather than treating her as a basically honest person who may lapse occasionally. Self-reflection is an attempt to forestall our harmful psychological drifts in these areas.[18] The assumption underlying it is that we can pause, reflect, and revise our attitudes in the light of evidence, reasons, and self-knowledge, and that we can use these intellectual processes to amend our own attitudes and improve a relationship.

Suppose that Susan has come to feel uneasy about her old friend Elizabeth and has lost her confidence that Elizabeth really cares for her. She may find on reflection that until the last few months Elizabeth always seemed affectionate and enthusiastic about what they did together. She used to be a terrific listener, but things seem to have changed. Asking herself why she now feels uneasy and insecure with this friend, Susan realizes that it is mostly the result of her feelings about two occasions when she discovered that Elizabeth was lying to her. Once she said that she could not go out for lunch because she had house guests, and it turned out that there were none. On another occasion, she said that she was not especially interested in a new man in her life; then she wound up living with him only two weeks later.

Thinking about it, Susan realizes that she is feeling quite hostile and suspicious of Elizabeth these days. She does not want to call her, but senses that without some initiative, their relationship could lapse. Do the two lies provide good grounds for this attitude, against the background of their previously enjoyable relationship? To call what Elizabeth did "lying" puts it in strong terms. In the case of the house guests, perhaps what she said was a mistake and not a lie; perhaps she was honestly expecting them and then they failed to arrive. As to the new man, perhaps Elizabeth did not realize just how serious her feelings were. On reflection, Susan may decide that her feelings of alienation towards Elizabeth are out of all proportion to her evidence and that she has misinterpreted her friend. Asking herself about her own role in the deterioration of their relationship and how Elizabeth may see that, Susan may come to understand that she has communicated this discomfort to her friend. If Elizabeth has not called lately, it could be because she has sensed Susan's suspicion and discomfort. Thinking about the relationship, Susan realizes that she wants their friendship to continue. She is fond of Elizabeth. They have shared many good times together, and they have supported each other through troubles and crises in the past. With a new man in her life, Elizabeth will probably have less time for Susan and other women friends, and the relationship may change. But Susan cares about Elizabeth and their friendship, which she does not want to lose. It would be worthwhile to try to work things out.

Ideally, in such a case we could approach the other person with the results of our self-questioning and discuss the issues threatening our relationship. Though there are some pitfalls when we attempt openly to discuss issues of distrust, having reflected seriously on our own attitudes and beliefs should make it easier to initiate talk with the other person. We may be able to acknowledge our own responsibility, which will put us in a good position to begin the discussion. If Susan can express her own doubts and worries and assume some responsibility for what is going wrong, Elizabeth will more easily explore her own actions, attitudes, and feelings. Rethinking how both partners have contributed to the joys and pains of a relationship is a promising basis for re-establishing it and overcoming distrust. The partners can sort things out together, see the extent to which their growing distrust has been based on exaggeration and misunderstanding, renew their commitment to their relationship, and develop strategies for improving it.

Is such an approach too rational and thus inappropriate for sensitive issues in intimate relationships? Does it demand too much self-scrutiny and self-awareness, too much intellectual talk? When we consider the importance of lovers, family, friends, and colleagues for our personal happiness in life and compare this approach with other strategies that we sometimes adopt to improve our lives (years of expensive therapy, for instance), its demands seem modest. Interpersonal relationships are a key element of life and are worth thinking about. People are capable of considering them seriously, and many do it. To apply thought and reflection to relationships does not require that we be rational calculators instead of affectionate friends and partners. It does not demand that we be intellectualizers who ignore our instincts and feelings. On the contrary: part of what is involved is the examination, precisely, of our own intuitions and feelings to try to determine the basis for them. Emotions are crucial in intimate relationships, and they have an important role in trust and distrust. Fear and anxiety are constitutive elements of distrust; anger and resentment often accompany it.

Emotions, though, are not just *there*, permanently, regardless of how we think about them. Far from it: emotion and belief are closely interrelated. In fact, emotions are typically based on beliefs. Re-examining our beliefs is one way of appraising and (if appropriate) amending our emotions. If Elizabeth, angry *because* Susan lied to her, comes to believe that her friend did not lie after all, she will cease to be angry, will be less angry, or will come to realize that she is actually angry about something else. Thus self-reflection can provide a basis for the restoration of trust. When the rift in a relationship has been severe, leading to alienation and distrust, more than self-reflection may be necessary, however. In a case where one has really wronged another, reconciliation may depend on forgiveness and the acknowledgement of wrongdoing.

CHAPTER TEN

Forgiveness and Reconciliation

When one person has wronged another, that wrong may result in powerful emotions of resentment, including anger, sorrow, and even hatred at having been harmed. When the two have been friends or intimate partners, such resentment undermines or destroys their previous relationship: affection and warmth, confidence and trust, may cease to exist. Such a situation is the background to the dynamic of forgiveness. A wronged person may forgive the other his offence, overcome feelings of resentment, and restore the relationship. If he indicates to the other person, in gestures, actions, or words, that he has relinquished his feelings of bitterness, he forgives the wrongdoer and accepts him. In this way forgiveness can be a route to reconciliation and the restoration of trust. To forgive is to overcome the resentment that is an obstacle to equal moral relations among persons.

Consider this case: Ned borrowed Juan's car without asking his permission because he wanted to go a to party at the other side of town. While driving the car, he got into a serious accident in which it was damaged beyond repair. Juan had to buy a new car, which meant borrowing a considerable sum of money because the insurance was not enough to cover the replacement value. Although Ned has apologized and admits that he was in the wrong, Juan is going to be seriously inconvenienced, even if Ned helps him to pay for the new car. He feels hurt and mad. No one should borrow someone else's car without asking. Why, Juan asks himself, did Ned have to do such a stupid thing? Surely he could have taken a taxi or gotten a ride from a friend. For that matter, Juan cannot understand why Ned had to go to the party in the first place.

After this episode, things are tense between these men, who had been friends for many years before this happened. Juan is angry, and Ned feels terrible and does not know how to make amends. Juan is going to find it hard to trust Ned again; their relationship is in trouble. If he were to forgive Ned, they could be reconciled and resume their friendship as before. If Ned apologizes and vows never to take the car again, Juan may forgive him and come to trust him once more, as he did before the accident. If he were to forgive Ned, he would accept his apology and overcome his feelings of anger and resentment about the car. This does not mean mean that Juan will forget that the misfortune ever happened. Forgiving, he will remember it, but will cease to bear a grudge. He may say to Ned, "I forgive you" or "It's all right." But saying these words does not suffice for forgiveness; it requires a change of attitude. To forgive, Juan has to relinquish or overcome his resentment and anger towards Ned. It was wrong to take the car. But if he forgives him, he goes forward with their friendship instead of dwelling on this wrong.

In a classic case of forgiveness, one person has been wronged by another, the wrongdoer acknowledges that he did something wrong, and the victim accepts the wrongdoer's apology, believing that he is sincere and intends not to do it again. Both people understand what happened in the same moral framework, as illustrated in the case of Juan and Ned. That agreement is presupposed by the bilateral frame-work of apology and forgiveness: the parties agree about what was wrong; the one who did wrong acknowledges that it was wrong and that the other was hurt as a result.[1] On such a basis, two parties may be reconciled. The one who has been wronged forgives the wrong-doer, and their relationship can move ahead with a restoration of trust.

A person who forgives ceases to resent the person who harmed him. Although he knows and remembers that he has been harmed and has been the victim of wrongdoing, he changes his attitude towards the offender and does not dwell on the fact or harbour a grudge against the wrongdoer. In forgiving, he accepts the wrong-doer as a person capable of repentance and change, as a free human being capable of responsible behaviour in the future, seeing him as a moral equal and not merely as a wrongdoer. In this way, forgive-ness is a route to reconciliation in relationships and thereby to the restoration of trust.[2] When we forgive each other, we can overcome the wrongs of the past so that our relationship can move ahead on the basis of a renewed trust and commitment.

Forgiveness is related to trust in interesting ways. Most significant here is its link with reconciliation, which involves the restoration of trust after something has gone wrong. But that route is not simple. A highly significant complicating factor is that forgiveness itself requires a degree of trust. In the case of Juan and Ned, Juan forgives

Ned partly because his friend apologized, was sorry for what he did, and vowed not to do it again. When Juan forgives Ned, he thinks that Ned is sincere in apologizing; he believes that he really meant it when he said he was sorry. Juan also believes Ned to be committed to his promise not to take the car again without permission. In regarding Ned as *sincerely* apologizing and *committed* not to do wrong again, Juan is, in effect, trusting him. It is only because he *trusts* in the sincerity of the apology and Ned's commitment not to take the car again that he is able forgive and be reconciled with him and go ahead with the relationship. Forgiveness can help to rebuild trust, but at the same time it presupposes trust. A foundation of forgiveness is the belief that the wrongdoer not only accepts that what he did was wrong but sincerely regrets it and is committed not to do it again.

Forgiving a wrong is not the same thing as excusing it.[3] If Juan forgives Ned, that does not mean that he ceases to believe that Ned was wrong to take the car without permission and had no good reason to do so. For Juan to forgive does not imply that he ceases to believe that what Ned did was careless and self-indulgent and that he should not have done it. To forgive is not to excuse, not to conclude that what was done was not wrong after all. Ned might be excused if he had borrowed the car without permission because of a medical emergency, but this is not the circumstance here; he only wanted to go to a party. For Juan to forgive Ned for taking the car is not for him to to think that taking the car was all right under the circumstances. To forgive something, then, does not mean coming to believe that what was done was excusable or not really wrong. It is not to excuse; nor is it to condone. Nor is forgiving the same thing as pardoning or offering amnesty. Those are official acts that cannot be performed by ordinary people who occupy no special office. When someone is pardoned or given amnesty, he is permitted to escape punishment for an offence. Only state or church authorities can pardon or offer amnesty in the wake of an offence, thereby releasing a person from the normal punishment.

Forgiving a wrong does not imply a denial that real and serious harm was done. To forgive is not to diminish the seriousness of what happened. In forgiving, we overcome our feelings of resentment and anger; we do not revise our conviction that an offence was wrong. If a woman has been abused and forgives her abuser, she does not thereby deny or forget that she was ever abused or rationalize or excuse the abuse in the way she thinks about it. Forgiving, she takes a different attitude to the abuser, to herself, and to these deeds, but that does not mean she ceases to remember them. The common expression "forgive and forget" is rather misleading in this respect. Forgiving does not necessarily, or even typically, involve forgetting. An action may be forgiven and yet remembered; what changes is the way in which that action is remembered, the attitude towards the wrongdoer that accompanies that memory.[4]

If Juan forgives Ned, he will remember what happened to the car, but with a different emotional tone, without resentment, anger, and hatred, and without allowing this event to mark the end of his friendship with Ned. He may still regret the loss of his car, and he still believes that Ned was wrong to take it without permission. But his recognition of that fact will be accompanied by a sense that the person who did this harmful thing is still one who will continue to be a friend, still a person capable of acting well and likely to act well in the future. The car was taken; the accident occurred; the car was damaged beyond repair; there were costs and inconvenience; and it was Ned's wrong action that led to all this. These things Juan knows. These are facts that are not obliterated because he has forgiven Ned, reconstituted their relationship, become reconciled with him, and begun to trust him again. What is changed after forgiveness is not the facts or the memory of the facts, but the emotional tone of the memory, which no longer arouses anger, hatred, resentment, or a desire for revenge.

What has happened has happened; the past is there and it is remembered. What changes with forgiveness is neither the past nor the fact that we remember that past, but rather the emotional quality of our memories and our attitude towards those who wronged us. After forgiveness, the past and its injuries remain, but we do not feel about them in the same way; we are no longer angry and resentful and have lost any inclination to cultivate hatred or seek out revenge. When we forgive, we feel differently about the person who did wrong and about ourselves, and we are ready to reconstitute a relationship.

SMALL MATTERS

If we never forgave each other, life would be difficult and intimate relationships impossible.[5] There are so many ways we can hurt and offend each other, and we so often do. Ned did something that was clearly wrong, and Juan forgave him, accepting Ned's apology and making him feel better. He stopped carrying a grudge and let their friendship continue. But many of the hurts and disappointments of relationships are not so clear-cut as in this straightforward example. It is easy to *feel* wronged when slight things have happened, things that are not clearly wrong or not even wrong at all. A friend fails to

return telephone messages or is repeatedly late for lunch apoint-
ments. Are these "wrongs" that need to be forgiven?

An example of a small wrong may be found in the case of Alison
and Judy. Alison was the girlfriend of Judy's son Don and the mother
of her small granddaughter Katie. Alison, Don, and Katie had moved
recently and lived about one hundred miles from Judy. Judy, who
had not seen Katie and Alison for four months, made a date to visit
them and rearranged some of her own work so that she could do so.
She was busy and the arrangements were not entirely convenient,
but she wanted to see Katie and Alison. As Judy was preparing to
leave, Don called to say that Alison suddenly had to go out of town;
she and Katie would not be around for Judy's visit. Judy was crushed
and felt really hurt. Alison had cancelled several previously planned
visits, and Judy was beginning to feel that it was abnormally difficult
to arrange to see Katie. She began to feel annoyed and suspicious:
perhaps Alison just did not like her very much. Was she trying to
avoid her, to keep her away from the baby? What was going on?

To speak of Judy forgiving Alison in such a case seems ponderous
and not quite correct. The terminology is altogether too heavy.
Though she felt hurt, Judy was not exactly a "victim" of "wrongdoing." Nor was Alison an "offender" who needed to "repent." What,
after all, had she done wrong that she might need to be forgiven? She
had broken appointments, but always with a warning in advance,
never simply by failing to show up. By breaking appointments and
seeking rearrangements, she had caused some disappointment and
inconvenience for Judy, a highly organized woman who built her life
around careful planning and kept close track of her time. There was
always a reason when Alison cancelled. In this case she was to leave
to be with her sister, who was alone awaiting the imminent arrival of
her first child.

Alison and Judy may never discuss the matter of broken appointments, and even if they do, Alison may not actually apologize,
because she may feel that she did nothing wrong. After all, promises
can be broken and appointments rearranged; she had good reasons
in every case. In her family, people are relaxed about the way they
use their time and do not take appointments as seriously as Judy
does. Judy should try to see the matter in a positive light. But even if
she does consider Alison to have wronged her, she should take a flexible and understanding attitude and not resent what happened.

One might say that this is a kind of forgiveness, but forgiveness in
the classic sense is not involved because there was no clear wrongdoing and no apology.[6] As long as Alison stays with Don – and perhaps
forever, since Alison is the mother of her granddaughter – Judy will

to have some kind of relationship with her. If she can be relaxed and "forgiving" about small matters, her relationship with Alison will go more smoothly than it otherwise would. Finding wrongs in small matters and continuing to resent them, carrying grudges, and dwelling on small "insults" will be unhelpful.

Most of the time, broken dates are small matters. In long-term friendships, even such things as a borrowed and smashed car may be relatively small affairs. Problems, wrongs, and perceived wrongs are features of any relationship. Forgiveness in the full-blown sense may not be an issue in such cases, but a certain non-resentment of perceived small wrongs, an attitude bordering on forgiveness, certainly is. We often feel wronged in cases where others do not think that they have wronged us. Our tendency to see our own interests as paramount and our own values and beliefs as best can easily lead us to believe that we have been wronged by others. We often, and easily, feel hurt and offended where others see no offence.

Alison does not think that she has done anything wrong, and it would be inappropriate to call her a "wrongdoer." Nor can we really say that Judy has been the "victim" of an "offence." Alison has been a little careless and negligent, and Judy is hurt and inconvenienced as a result. Yet it makes sense to think of a kind of forgiveness, in such a case. Judy may experience a shift in attitude similar to that involved in forgiveness if she is able to overcome the slight anger and resentment that she feels towards Alison. Such maturity and emotional adaptability are necessary and important if we are to ride over the bumps and hollows on the road of relationships. About such things, we have choices to make. We can cling to our feelings of resentment, hurt, and anger or we can relinquish them; we can "carry a grudge" or not. We and our relationships will surely fare better if we adopt a flexible and non-resentful attitude and refrain from dwelling on what we see as wrongs. If we do not in this sense forgive our colleagues, friends, and lovers, we are likely to find ourselves in a continual state of resentment and suspicion. Where small matters are concerned, relationships need flexibility and a "forgiving" attitude on both sides.

IN FAVOUR OF FORGIVENESS

For the wrongdoer, to be forgiven is to be acknowledged as a moral being worthy of respect and capable of reform. Yes, he did something wrong, something he should not have done, but he is not only or merely a wrongdoer. He should not be reduced in status to one who is solely "the offender" or "that person who did wrong." As one who is forgiven, he is regarded as a human being sincere in his repentance and commitment not to do the same thing again, a moral being capable of reform and trusting relationships. Forgiven, the wrongdoer is accepted back into his relationship with the victim. Their friendship or partnership is restored, they are reconciled, and he is given a chance to be a loyal partner, friend, or colleague again.

In significant respects, forgiveness can also benefit the victim: it is good for her mental health.[7] She relinquishes her feelings of anger, resentment, and hatred towards the offender, accepting that a wrong occured, not diminishing that wrong, but being willing to move forward instead of dwelling on the past. In doing so she frees herself from a preoccupation with the past and the negative emotions that accompany her sense that she is a hurt and wounded person. She can move forward in life as a happier, more cheerful, and more competent human being. She can understand what happened to her and how it affected her, and without forgetting the wrong, she can go ahead to be a non-victim in a constructive life.

In many cases where forgiveness is an issue, the two people had a relationship of considerable importance. Forgiveness presents an opportunity for recommencing that relationship on a basis of renewed trust and concern. Often such a restoration benefits people other than the two original parties because relationships have an effect on more than two people. If Judy becomes alienated from Alison because of broken dates and her difficulty in seeing the baby, her husband and son, her granddaughter, and possibly the whole family will be adversely affected; whereas if the two have a good relationship, family life will run more smoothly.

The past is what it is and cannot be altered. We can study and reflect on the past, and it is useful to do so. We cannot change the past as such, although we can change our interpretation of it, our sense of what it means to us, and our feelings towards it.[8] There is little point in dwelling on the negative aspects of the past if that means concentrating on how we were wronged and unfairly treated, feeling anger and resentment, sensing ourselves as victims, and cultivating sentiments of vindictiveness and revenge. In leading our lives, we cannot literally go backward; there is no option save to go forward. For this reason, in a fundamental sense, the future is more important than the past. It is in the future that we live our freedom and in the future that we will act and feel and form new relationships.[9] What has happened in the past affects who we are and what we believe; it cannot be ignored. But we distort our thinking and restrict our possibilities for action if we dwell on the past without reflecting on how we are going to move forward from that past. To concentrate on past wrongs and cultivate our feelings of resentment is to distract ourselves from the choices we must make with regard to the future and to ignore the prospects for positive change. Forgiving, we shed our negative emotions and free ourselves for positive relationships and constructive action.

Another consideration in favour of forgiveness stems from the fact of our own fallibility. We all make mistakes, and for some of those mistakes we need to be forgiven. One argument in favour of forgiveness starts from the fact that we are fallible creatures. Others do wrong, make mistakes, or are careless, and they may hurt us, sometimes deeply. But to put this in perspective, we recall that we ourselves are not perfect and we have wronged and hurt other people. When we have done something wrong, we typically feel grateful if people whom we wronged have forgiven us. If we feel this gratitude, we may conclude that we too should forgive those who have wronged us. Being forgiven has preserved our moral dignity and self-respect and our sense that we are free moral beings who can do right as well as wrong. In addition, it has helped to preserve the relationships we need to lead our lives.

The Christian ethic urges us to forgive others because we want them, and ultimately God himself, to forgive us should we commit a sin. "Lord, forgive us our trespasses, as we forgive those who have trespassed against us." A fundamental assumption behind this Christian ethic of forgiveness would appear to be that of original sin and the universal need for salvation. Everyone does wrong sometimes; we are born to do so; thus we will all need God's forgiveness. As creatures whose nature it is to do wrong occasionally, who will ourselves have to plead for God's forgiveness, we should be humble enough to forgive other people who have done wrong. To be unforgiving is, on this view, to blame another as though we ourselves are in a position to pass judgment. "Let him who is without sin cast the first stone." No one is without sin; hence no one is entitled to blame harshly and cast the stone. From our general tendency to sin comes an argument for forgiveness.[10]

This Christian ethic is valuable in reminding us of our own moral fallibility and warning against harsh judgment. But it is likely to perplex the sceptical secular mind for various reasons, not the least being its grounding in egalitarian sinfulness. In the Christian position, it seems that all wrongs, or "sins," are rendered morally equivalent. We are all sinners. Some sin by having lustful thoughts, others by resenting God's power, others by telling minor lies and having sex outside marriage, others by committing tortures and rapes, and still others by commanding troops to commit genocidal acts. Because someone is a "sinner" who may tell minor lies and feel rebellious against God on some occasions, it is argued that she "should" forgive another who has committed heinous crimes against her. Jeffrie Murphy contends that this view makes an "overly ambitious use of the important insight that each one of us is morally flawed," pointing out that a person who is not entirely without flaws may nevertheless be relevantly different, in a moral sense, from a brutal rapist.[11]

The Christian commendation of forgiveness can, however, be supported by quite different arguments which do not depend on the premise that we are all (apparently in some divinely equivalent sense) sinners who will need forgiveness. There are secular arguments for forgiveness based on the interests and intrinsic human worth of the offender; there are also secular arguments for forgiveness based on the interests of the victim. In fact, even in a case in which a wrongdoer does not apologize and is unwilling to acknowledge that what he has done is wrong, there are considerations that point in favour of forgiveness from the victim's point of view. Forgiving a wrongdoer, even one who is dead or who never apologized, can benefit the victim by enabling her to overcome her negative emotions, cease to see herself as a victim, and move forward constructively into the future. Such are the benefits for the victim that one might even argue that repentance is not strictly necessary for forgiveness. Clearly, if a wrongdoer or supposed wrongdoer is dead, he need not repent to be forgiven. People speak of forgiving their parents, often after their parents are dead. There is no notion of apology or repentance and no direct sense of reconciliation in such cases, because the parent is gone. Yet people who have forgiven their parents report that it is a tremendous relief and a great step forward towards a new life as a creative and autonomous person.[12]

As a mother, I always feel a little nervous when people speak of forgiving their parents. I begin to wonder what their parents did to them, or what they think their parents did, that they need to be forgiven. And I wonder what I have done or am doing myself as a mother, for which my children will someday blame me and later forgive me. On a wintry day, I told my son that he had to walk home from school because I was unwilling to cut off my writing in mid-afternoon to come and pick him up. Besides, I argued, he needed the exercise. Will he some day feel a need to forgive me for this? Do I need to be forgiven? The notion of forgiving your parents should be an unsettling one for those actively involved in being parents themselves. Most people who discuss the theme seem, even in middle age, to think of themselves as *children* rather than as *parents*. Have our parents wronged us? Did we have fathers who were too strict, who spanked us when they should not have, who worked too hard outside the home and had little time for their children? Who were grumpy about bathroom stops on holidays? These are small matters, and as adults we should be mature enough to understand that fact.

But there are larger issues about forgiving parents. Some people were neglected, humiliated, insulted, beaten, or sexually abused by their parents. These are not small matters. What about forgiveness, trust, and restored relationships in such cases? If the parent is dead, trust is no longer an issue, not least because reconciliation is not in question. What is important is somehow understanding the past, acknowledging that it was the way it was, and using one's understanding and response to the past in order to go on with life. The case is different when abusive parents are still alive and there are real issues about whether and how to conduct relationships with them. Forgiveness in such cases is difficult, but perhaps more than ever necessary because we cannot build positive adult lives on the feelings of victimhood and resentment that remain from a tragic past.

PROBLEMS AND PITFALLS

In some compelling cases, the moral framework of forgiveness is not clear because the victim and the wrongdoer do not agree on what happened. Both may regard themselves as victims; neither may accept the role of wrongdoer. A "victim" may feel wronged while a "wrongdoer" feels that he has done nothing at all to deserve blame. If a "victim" were to "forgive" or restore relations with a wrongdoer in such a case, he or she would appear to be compromising in accepting an alien moral viewpoint, one that refuses acknowledgment that she or he was ever wronged.

A poignant political example is that of victims of Stasi (secret police) spying in the former East Germany. As we have seen, when the two Germanies were united, Stasi files were opened up, and it became obvious that many people had been spied upon by their friends and colleagues. Every German citizen is entitled to inspect his or her file and may find out the identities of those who were spying on him or her. The result of the opening of files was initially a crisis of personal and social trust in the former East Germany. It was in this context that Rolf Michael Turek, a pastor in the Lutheran church in Leipzig, established a group for reconciliation.[13] His intent was to use frank talk and exchange as a route to understanding and forgiveness among those whom the old system had rendered enemies: victims of Stasi spying, informal agents and employees of the Stasi, and members of the official media. Turek hoped that these people could come together to discuss the past and understand what had happened; his goal was initially one of reconciliation and the restoration of trust between former spies and former victims. In 1990 some forty-five people came to his group in Leipzig. Turek and other members of opposition groups and victims of Stasi activities expected former Stasi agents to feel guilty and sorry for what they had done. They anticipated expressions of responsibility and regret and apologies, and on this basis, they were prepared to forgive and be reconciled.

But there was no possibility of a dynamic of forgiveness in this case because there was no admission of wrongdoing by former Stasi employees and agents. Those who had been spied on thought that they had been grievously wronged; in the changed situation of the new Germany, they sought reconciliation and were willing to forgive those who had hurt them. However, the former Stasi agents refused to acknowledge that they had ever done anything wrong. They had many rationalizations: they had been coerced into spying; they were trying to change the regime from within; they were mere cogs in a system, and what they did was harmless; they were trying to protect possible victims; they were merely doing their jobs ... Their work was compartmentalized, and each person was able to see his own part as a small isolated thing that brought no harm to anyone.[14] Naturally, the victims in the group were angry and frustrated with these responses. They had tried to reach out for dialogue and, by joining the group, had indicated their desire for understanding, reconciliation, and the restoration of some kind of trust. Instead, they came to feel that by talking with these former spies, they were only helping them to rationalize their activities and providing a platform for self-justification.

To forgive seemed inappropriate or impossible in this context because there was no common moral frame of reference for what had happened between those who spied and those who were spied upon. There was no acknowledgment by informers and Stasi employees that they had been wrong and thus, in this context, no possible dynamic of forgiveness. There was no agreement on the status of victim and wrongdoer and hence no consensus that the moral framework of forgiveness applied to the case at all. Within months of starting his group, Turek came to regard as unobtainable his original goal of forgiveness, reconciliation, and the restoration of trust. He began to think of the group in other terms, as one that could provide a setting in which people would articulate their feelings and beliefs and reflect on what they had been doing. By the winter of 1994, the original group of forty-five had only twelve members remaining, and Turek felt little confidence that even his secondary goal was reachable. It seemed as though few people shared his aim of seeking an understanding of the oppressive East German regime and the human tendencies and practices that had made it possible. Some (victims) came to the group in order to express their feelings; others (Stasi) came to justify themselves. Stories became more elaborate, with some former Stasi employees insisting that they had all along been hidden friends of the opponents of the regime, a fact that they had not previously understood because they did not really grasp what the opposition groups were trying to do. Some victims abandoned the discussions, feeling that their participation was only helping former Stasi members to justify their actions to themselves and others.

Similar patterns surfaced elsewhere in the former East Germany. At Checkpoint Charlie, which had been a border point between the eastern and western sectors of Berlin, discussion sessions were organized in 1991 and 1992. These were media events, public in a way that Turek's sessions were not. There was a moderator, and people spoke at a podium. Former victims of Stasi spying confronted former agents.[15] Here public discussion and understanding, rather than reconciliation, were the initial goals. It was at first expected that former Stasi employees and agents would speak openly of what they had done and would publicly and openly atone for it. But here too the former Stasi members were so firm in their insistence on self-justification that victims came to feel that they were providing a platform for rationalizations and excuses. There were many elaborate rationalizations and attempted justifications. Some former agents claimed that they had been attempting to influence and reform the regime. Others alleged that they had done opposition groups a favour when they infiltrated them, because they had on occasion prevented them from undertaking especially risky and provocative actions that would have brought harm to their members. Some agents claimed to have been coerced into collaboration; others insisted that they were merely protecting their families and jobs; still others argued that what they had done was insignificant and harmless. Though the Stasi had been a huge system instrumental in maintaining an oppressive regime, though many lives had been ruined as a result of its activities, no one would acknowledge having chosen to do something that was wrong and had harmed another.[16] Those controlling the agents had told them that they were not betraying their friends, but helping them. Apparently, many agents continued to believe this, even after German reunification.

Gestures and actions of forgiveness can serve as a route to reconciliation and the re-establishment of trust between parties who will have contact again only if the one who is to be forgiven acknowledges that he has done something wrong. If there is no acknowledgment of wrongdoing, a victim may decide to forgive for other reasons, relinquishing feelings of resentment and anger for her own benefit, to improve her own mental health and go ahead with the rest of her life. But reconciliation and the ending of distrust, the restoration of relationships based on forgiveness, cannot be achieved in such a case.[17]

In *Music Box*, Ann was wronged by Michael's deception and manipulation decades after the war. He wronged her by deceiving her through her childhood and early adulthood and during the trial itself. He exploited her love for him and her faith in him. He deceived her and then urged her to defend him against charges of appalling crimes – tortures, killings, and rapes. He manipulated her. Even when confronted with clear evidence, Michael refused to acknowledge that he had committed those crimes or that he had wronged her in his deception and his exploitation of her skills and her love for him. When she found out what he had done, Ann did not forgive him and did not seek to be reconciled or rebuild her trust in him. Rather, she moved far away from Michael, broke off all contact, and supplied the prosecuting attorney with the evidence that would convict Michael of war crimes.

Ann was left with a sense of a whole childhood based on falsehood, of a father she had loved who had a secret past as a cruel rapist, torturer, and murderer. If Michael never acknowledged the wrongs he had committed, Ann could be not reconciled with him. She might, for her own mental health, some day achieve a kind of unilateral forgiveness in which she would overcome her anger and resentment of her father and what he had done. But a genuine reconciliation and the restoration of their relationship would (if possible at all) surely have required acknowledgment by Michael of the enormity of his crimes during the war and repentance for what he had done to her as his daughter. To be reconciled with his daughter, he would have had to admit and renounce his past and become a new being, something that he was not prepared to do.

THE UNFORGIVABLE

What Michael did was appalling; it was, as we say, "unforgivable." When we speak of things being unforgivable, we suggest they *cannot* or *should not* be forgiven. War crimes, terrible rapes and murders, crimes of incest and sexual battery, tortures, the robbing of childhood – these are among the horrible crimes that human beings inflict on one another. What do we mean when we say, as people often do, that such things are unforgivable? It may be a metaphorical way of indicating that the crimes are appalling and terrible. Or does it mean that they *cannot* (psychologically) be forgiven? That they *should not* (morally) be forgiven? Amazingly, it is psychologically possible to forgive people who have done appalling wrongs. Mediator Dave Gustafson described a case in which a woman who was a victim of incest forgave and was reconciled with her father. As the one who (at the daughter's request) had mediated between them and helped to facilitate their reconciliation, Gustafson had initially been extremely uncomfortable with the case. He had agreed to intervene only after the daughter insisted that she wanted to resume a relationship with her father, who was her only living relative. Unlike some abusers, this man did acknowledge that he had seriously wronged his daughter, and his acknowledgment was a fundamental aspect of the basis for forgiveness and reconciliation.[18]

Those who commit appalling crimes are sometimes capable of reform and rehabilitation. Sometimes they do change, repent of their past, and seek to make amends, and reconciliation with victims or families of victims can be part of this process. Thus, from a psychological perspective, even some who have committed deeds that we deem "unforgivable" may turn out not to be literally impossible to forgive. Some such persons – in fact, many of them – have been forgiven. A recent book, *Forgiving the Unforgivable*, is based on interviews with hundreds of people who have forgiven brutal assaults and deep betrayals, mostly by family members.[19] But what about the moral perspective? Are some deeds are so appalling, so horrendous, that it would be morally wrong ever to forgive the people who committed them? It is people whom we forgive or do not forgive; yet we speak of deeds as being unforgivable. To say that they are unforgivable is a way of indicating that they are appalling and atrocious, of pointing to the horrific nature of the offence. But this does not quite say that the persons who committed such deeds should themselves never be forgiven, because there is a distinction between the action and the agent, as expressed in the Christian saying that we should love the sinner but not the sin.

Paul Bernardo and Karla Homolka abducted, sexually molested and tortured, and then killed two teenage girls, Kristin French and Leslie Mahaffey. They made video tapes of the brutal rapes of these girls, with soundtracks of their pain and agony. Homolka was sentenced to twelve years in jail. Bernardo, who confessed to additional rapes, was locked away permanently as a danger to the public. The parents of Kristin French and Leslie Mahaffey live on, with agonizing images of their daughters' humiliation and torture fixed in their minds, probably forever. Should these parents forgive Bernardo and

Homolka? Should they even try to forgive them, even if these offenders should some day appear, repentant and reformed, and apparently ready to make a contribution to society? Debbie Mahaffey, Leslie's mother, stated to the press that she does not believe in capital punishment and thinks Homolka may be capable of rehabilitation and of making a contribution to society some day.

One reason it might be morally wrong to forgive those who have committed appalling acts is that to do so would somehow imply that those acts are not so horrendous after all, that they have been excused or condoned, or that in some other way the moral seriousness of the defence has been diminished. A related idea is that forgiving appalling deads would be wrong because it would be disloyal and disrespectful to the memory of the primary victims. If Bernardo and Homolka were some day to be rehabilitated, accepted into mainstream society, and forgiven by the Frenches and the Mahaffeys, they would be rehabilitated people who might lead constructive and meaningful lives. But after living through agonizing and brutal sexual tortures, Kristen and Leslie died miserably. They can never be brought back to life. A powerful emotional reason against forgiveness in such horrendous cases is that it seems to diminish, or not fully acknowledge and respect, the suffering of the victims.

Traditional Jewish theology maintained that forgiveness was obligatory, provided that a wrongdoer had repented of his action. But this position was amended for Holocaust crimes, which are deemed unforgivable. No matter how many years go by, no matter how much the perpetrators repent of their wrongdoing, no matter how much they reform themselves as persons or how many good deeds they do, those responsible for genocide during the Second World War remain guilty of appalling crimes against humanity and against the Jewish people. According to Jewish theology, there is no obligation to forgive war criminals, and there is, on the contrary, an obligation *not* to do so. Why? These deeds were *unforgivable*; they were appalling horrors against a people, a religion, and a culture. To forgive the wrongdoers would itself be wrong because it would implicitly diminish the significance of these crimes and would be disloyal or disrespectful to the victims.[20]

While one can understand and respect such arguments, they are open to question. Forgiving does *not* mean excusing, condoning, ceasing to blame, losing respect for the victims, or forgetting that wrongdoing occurred. What happens in forgiving is that we relinquish our feeling of hatred and resentment and accept that the wrongdoer has repented and reformed. To imagine being a Holocaust survivor, the child of a survivor, or a parent of Kristin French or Leslie Mahaffey is to *feel* unforgivability. How could anyone forgive another who committed appalling atrocities? Yet, unbelievably, some have forgiven in comparable cases. They have sought to comprehend the wrong, to understand the world and their place in it after the wrong, and to move forward in life without concentrating their thoughts and feelings on hatred and revenge. Forgiveness in such a case might be something that a devastated person could attempt some day to do for herself, to build for herself the strength to continue living. Or it might be a necessary basis for the reconstitution of a political community in which victims and criminals somehow have to live together.

FURTHER CONSIDERATIONS

A secular argument in favour of forgiveness, stated by the philosopher R.S. Downie, is that all persons merit respect because they are moral beings who should be valued as such, and forgiveness is a manifestation of respect because it recognizes the possibility of moral reform.[21] As Downie understands the matter, our most general moral obligation is to have a loving concern for the dignity of other persons. Persons are *ends in themselves* and must be valued as such. To refuse ever to forgive another person who has committed an appalling crime is to say, in effect, that he or she can never again become a morally upright human being and can never resume a place in the human moral community. According to Downie, to refuse forgiveness is morally wrong because it closes off a human being from any possibility of rehabilitation and it fails to recognize his dignity and freedom. Downie argues that we should always *try* to forgive if there is repentance. To take a permanently unforgiving stance against wrongdoing, even decades after its commission, is ignore the possibility that the offender has become a different person.

H.J.N. Horsburgh takes a similar stance, arguing that we should *always* try to forgive others who have wronged us because we should strive to maintain an attitude of goodwill towards all other moral agents.[22] The requirement to forgive wrongdoers does not mean that they should not be blamed or punished; nor does it mean that their wrongdoing should be excused, pardoned, condoned, or forgotten. Rather, it expresses a recognition of the desirability of their eventual acceptance into the moral community. Under appropriate circumstances, we have an obligation to try to overcome feelings of anger and resentment that stand in the way of such acceptance, even for those who have committed gross and brutal wrongs. In a case of brutal and appalling offence, it may be psychologically impossible for a victim to forgive a wrongdoer. But according to Horsburgh, we should always try. He argues that, whatever the offence, ultimately forgiveness is best. It respects the moral personhood of the wrong-doer, and it will keep the victim from dwelling on the past in an unhealthy way. Thus, Horsburgh argues, forgiveness also benefits the one who was harmed. The unforgiving person's inner world, he says, is "a private museum of wrongs" in which every item will taunt until "destroyed by some act of vengeance." Thus, according to Horsburgh, we should make an effort to forgive wrongdoers, seeking reconciliation and a renewed relationship.

But it would seem to require moral heroism to apply such prin-ciples to the Holocaust or the Bernardo case. Indeed, the idea that we "should" try to forgive even those who have committed awful offences seems to many to be contrary to common sense and common morality. Alice Miller is one example of a thinker who has criticized a generalized recommendation of forgiveness. She believes that it is too focused on the needs and prospects of the offender and too insensi-tive to those of the victim. In her influential book *The Drama of the Gifted Child*, Miller describes how people are easily damaged by mistreatment or abuse in childhood. Many parents, she maintains, knowingly or unintentionally damage their children by ignoring their feelings and their dignity and manipulating them into conformity with the expectations of an adult world and the needs of their par-ents. People damaged by their parents in this way lose touch with their own emotions and needs, and as a result they are likely to suffer depression and unhappiness in adult life. In the context of such child-hood suffering, Miller argues against forgiveness, saying that the last thing that people damaged by mistreatment in childhood should do is try to forgive their parents. She denies that victims should feel any obligation to forgive those who have hurt them.

Miller may be reacting here against the Christian recommendation of generalized forgiveness, which, as we have seen, is premised on egalitarian and generalized sinfulness. She claims that when dam-aged people are urged to "forgive," they are further harmed because they are put under pressure to suppress or amend their anger. Those who urge forgiveness wrongly put the emphasis on the offender rather than the victim. Victims of childhood mistreatment need to focus attention on themselves, find and feel their own emotions, and build their own strength. When they have been seriously harmed, they need to be encouraged to express and recognize the real feelings that they have so long had to suppress. They need to feel their anger and sadness; in this process, they should not be encouraged to concern themselves with the condition of the people who wronged them. Victims may have a tendency to blame themselves, and that harmful tendency will only be aggravated if they are made to feel guilty because they have not succeeded in forgiving those who wronged them. If victims are made to feel that in some sense they *should* forgive, they will fail to acknowledge their repressed anger, blame themselves, lessen their concern for themselves, and reduce their chances of building autonomous personalities. Concentrating on forgiveness will divert the victims' energy from what Miller sees as the real problem, their inability to feel their own emotions.

Miller's account is useful in forcefully reminding us of the basic sense in which victims have a moral first place. Fundamentally, it is victims who have been wronged and it is victims who need to recover. They should not feel guilt or inadequacy because of what has happened to them, and they should build a strong and positive self before concerning themselves with the state of the offender. Miller argues that a sense that forgiveness is obligatory puts the pressure in the wrong place and can be harmful to victims. But in urging the priority of the victim's position, she seems strangely insensitive to the benefits that forgiveness can bring to a victim. To be sure, those who have been victims should find and feel their own emotions before trying to relinquish them; to be sure, as victims we should rebuild ourselves, respect and trust ourselves, and be confident of our own autonomy.[23] But forgiveness is compatible with these goals if the timing is right. In fact, it may contribute to them.

TRUST, RISKS, AND RECONCILIATION

In the play *Keeley and Du*, Keeley, a young woman who had sought an abortion has been kidnapped by radical anti-abortion activists and is being held captive in a basement room, where an older woman, Du, guards her.[24] After some weeks Keeley and Du develop a kind of friendship. Keeley explains that she was raped by her ex-husband, with whom she had agreed to one last meeting in order to finalize things. This man, who had been a drinker and abusive, held her down brutally, raped her, and bit her when she fought against him, and it is as a result of this attack that she finds herself pregnant. Keeley and Du are visited from time to time by the religious leader of the radical group, who seeks to convert Keeley to his understanding of abortion and the value of family life. Eventually, the leader brings Keeley's ex-husband to visit her. Clad in a respectable-looking suit, he comes to beg her forgiveness and plead for a reconciliation. Keeley has no choice but to listen to him because she is literally a prisoner, guarded by Du and handcuffed to a bed. Her husband says that he is sorry for the terrible things he did to her, and he wants them to get together and live as a family. He appeals to the fact that she is carrying his baby and will be the mother of his child. Keeley looks away, unrelenting. She does not forgive her husband. She spits in his face. Furious, he falls upon her in a vicious attack from which she is saved only because the others pull him off.

Keeley did not forgive, and the sympathies of the audience were certainly with her. She could sense that her ex-husband was not sincere and was being used by the religious leader for propaganda purposes of his own. The violent attack after Keeley refused him showed that she was right not to forgive. Her husband had not fundamentally changed, and she would have been gravely at risk had she gone back to him.[25]

In addition to its comments on the abortion issue, which was its central topic, the play *Keeley and Du* illustrates an important fact about forgiveness. When it leads to reconciliation, forgiveness can be risky precisely because it heals old wounds and enables us to go forward again. Implicit in this healing is our trust that the one we forgive is genuinely sorry for what he has done and genuinely committed not to do it again. When we forgive and become reconciled with someone living, with whom we continue to have contact, we resume a relationship that requires and will be based on some degree of trust. That is risky when we are vulnerable – as Keeley certainly would have been had she gone back to her husband and lived with him as the mother of their child.

Keeley did not trust her husband. Despite his superficial respectability when he came to visit in the company of the religious leader, despite the apparent fervour of his appeal, she believed that he was insincere in his apology and not committed to reforming himself. Not trusting him, she did not forgive him and did not become reconciled with him. His brutal attack showed that she was right. He had not been committed to change, and she would have been gravely at risk had she gone back to him. The play illustrates the fact that reconciliation with someone who has been brutal and abusive is dangerous. The trust that is required for forgiveness may be unwarranted, and if it is, we are at great risk. To forgive and be reconciled is to trust again. But sometimes we should not begin to trust again, and we do so only with grave risk to ourselves. Many women not so cautious as Keeley have come to terrible harm as a result.

What Keeley saved herself from was an appalling pattern in cases of abuse. With apparent sincerity, the abusive partner says that he is sorry and will never do it again. His partner, loving him or thinking that she ought to love him, feels that she should believe him or try to believe him. ("Trust me; after all, I'm your husband; if you don't trust me, there is something wrong with you.") She tells herself that he will reform; this time it is a real commitment. She tries to believe, tries to have faith in him, feeling perhaps that she should believe him because he is her husband and the father of her children. Perhaps she genuinely believes him; perhaps she partially believes him, partially deceives herself. What if she takes him back and continues to live with him in the same home, and he does not change? He beats her again. Notoriously, women in such situations are vulnerable to the point where their lives are at stake.

Does this mean that women should *never* forgive partners who have beaten them? Are women in relationships simply too vulnerable to forgive and be reconciled? To say that would be going too far. But clearly there are terrible risks in such cases. When there is potential for great harm in the resumption of a relationship, we should forgive and become reconciled only with great caution. We should never do it only because someone tells that we "should" because we "should" love or trust or care for the one who has hurt us. Is this person sincerely and genuinely sorry for what he has done? Does he mean it when he says that he will change? Even if committed, is he capable of change? Likely to change? Because the risks are so serious, people in such circumstances have to consider these questions carefully. When the wife and husband in a battering relationship are reconciled, the original context for the battering has not disappeared, and there is real potential for future tragedy. Keeley did not forgive, and Keeley was right.

Writing about forgiveness, Joanna North said: "It is not easy to forgive another ... We are required to accept back into our heart a person who is responsible for having hurt and damaged us. If I am to forgive, I must risk *extending my trust* and affection, with *no guarantee* they will not be flung back in my face, or forfeited in the future. One might even say that forgiveness is an unconditional response to the wrongdoer, for there is something *unforgiving* in the demand for guarantees."[26] North suggests that, if we demand guarantees, there is "something unforgiving." And to be sure, a demand for guarantees would imply a doubt, a sense that the other may not really be reformed and may lapse. Apparently, North thinks that in contexts of forgiveness, we should trust the one we are about to forgive. If we cannot trust him, we are not yet ready to forgive him. To be unwilling to take risks, to seek guarantees, is to imply that the other is not yet ready to come back into the relationship as a moral equal. All this is simply to say that forgiving with a demand for "guarantees" would be too distrustful to count as real forgiveness.

One can admire the generous moral tone of these remarks. But there is a fundamental problem with North's approach: it ignores risk and such things as the notorious battered woman syndrome. People may be exposed to terrible risks in some contexts where they feel they "should" trust and forgive; they may feel compelled to try to be reconciled in contexts where they remain vulnerable to harm from the very people they trust and forgive. What North says cannot be wise advice for Keeley or any other person contemplating reconciliation with an abusive partner. Nor, indeed, would it be wise counsel for anyone considering forgiveness and reconciliation in a relationship that had been grossly harmful, provided that circumstances with the potential for serious damage continued to exist.[27] In such contexts, the ethical and personal factors that would support forgiveness have to be considered along with strategies for realistic self-protection.

There are profound moral complexities in forgiveness and reconciliation. Prominent among them is a dilemma of trust. Like various other strategies for restoring trust in human relationships, forgiveness turns out to presuppose some basis for trust. Without that trust there can be constructive emotional shifts, but not the forgiveness that can support reconciliation and the restoration of relationships. This dilemma of forgiveness points again to the ineradicable centrality of trust in human relationships.

CHAPTER ELEVEN

Dilemmas of Trust

Without trust, personal and social life would be impossible. With the dubious exception of hermits, holding back from trust is not an option for human beings. We must trust; yet we are vulnerable in doing so. Trust is risky. The primary dilemma of trust is that to have a meaningful personal and social life, we have to trust; yet we take risks when we do. The second dilemma is that trust, an essential element in all satisfying relationships, is a fragile thing, easier to break than to build. Although trust is crucial to relationships, it is often easy to undermine and difficult to restore. Trust that has developed gradually can be destroyed with a single lie or act of betrayal. It is an enormous advantage in relationships. Trusting, we can relax. We need not be suspicious and fearful; we can be open and express our true feelings and beliefs. We are not insecure and defensive, and we can communicate and cooperate. In a relationship flawed by distrust, we are uncomfortable and unproductive.

It would be presumptuous and absurd to claim to "solve" the basic dilemmas of trust. These dilemmas and the issues that flow from them constitute central problems in living which confront human beings. Accepting, refusing, risking, fearing, judging, deciding whether to trust or distrust – these are inevitable when we live together as human beings. We trust in some respects, distrust in others. As free agents, we must acknowledge that other people are also free agents who shape their own characters and may not always do what we want or expect. In relationships, we have to judge when, whether, and how much to trust another. We can expect no guidebook telling us how to do this, no formula or magic rule offering infallible advice as to whether to trust the stranger at the doorstep, undertake an ambitious project with a new friend, or be reconciled with an abusive husband.

Our responses to those situations – and, in fact, the situations themselves – are greatly affected by our underlying attitudes and approach to the world. Basic attitudes structure our general approach to people and situations; some are helpful, others less so. A person who has an unforgiving attitude will tend to remain angry and resentful over time. One with a charitable attitude will downplay faults and wrongs, tending to see the best in others. One with an unduly charitable attitude will too readily discount and excuse wrongful actions and overestimate the trustworthiness of others. A pessimistic person will expect the worst and may undermine her own abilities; an optimist is likely to open up opportunities for herself and attract others to work along with her.[1] Also fundamental in responding to issues of interpersonal trust is our own self-trust. If we trust ourselves, we can more easily be flexible and responsive to new people and new situations and make our own decisions. With confidence in our own feelings and judgments, we can remain open-minded and hopeful for the future, sensitive to the new opportunities and possibilities that it may hold. We need not be rigid and rejecting or fixed in our assumptions and attitudes. Optimists generally see what is positive in people and situations, and they maintain positive expectations about the future. To the extent that we are optimists, we will have confidence in our own ability to respond to events, and we will usually expect good from ourselves, from others, and from the turn of events. An optimistic attitude is helpful in many respects, although it should not be taken so far that we become blind to difficulties and limitations.

Related to optimism is another helpful attitude, that of underlying hopefulness. When we hope, we see an open future with positive possibilities. That future holds the prospect of new events, new situations, and new relationships. With an attitude of hope we can preserve our sense that there are promising possibilities ahead, that unexpected things will happen, and that some of these unexpected things we will find good. When we hope, we see the future as holding desired possibilities and our own actions as ways in which those possibilities can become real. In addition to specific hopes, there is an underlying general attitude of hopefulness about ourselves and our lives, that of *latent hope*, a foundation of positive expectation and flexibility that gives us the energy and strength to begin again after we have been disappointed. This underlying attitude permits us to go on hoping again, even when we have been disappointed in specific hopes.

Consider, for example, the case of a woman who spent four years writing an ambitious play and was then unable to have it published or produced. She hoped for a strong production, publicity for her ideas, and personal success. But she could not arranged for the play to be produced at all. Bitterly disappointed, this woman was initially unable to start any new work; she just did not know where to go. But after several months of depression, she began to look at new possibilities and develop ideas for new projects, believing that with these, success would be attainable. What made this possible was an underlying sense of hope – latent hope – and a trust in herself, a sense that she was capable of commitment and good work. If "hope springs eternal in the human heart," it is latent hope that, despite our many disappointments, allows it to do so. We rally our energies, recognize that the future holds many possibilities, and move on to other things. Latent hope allows us respond positively to disappointments and move on to new activities and projects in which we place our hopes. It gives us the sense that the present disappointment is not the end of our story and also the will to keep going.[2]

Hope and hopefulness are not the same as optimism. Optimists expect that good *will* come, whereas hopeful people believe that it *could* come: it is possible; there will be opportunities in the future, and the product of our efforts could be something good. Hope requires trust in ourselves and in others. To despair is to see the future as closed off, as having only negative outcomes. Hope is the opposite of despair, the belief that the future could hold good, and we could do something to bring it about.

Attitudes of self-trust, autonomy, optimism, and hope will help us to make better decisions about trust. They will enhance our flexibility and competence, and support a conviction that we can do something about ourselves and our situation. A victim outlook, on the other hand, is decidedly unhelpful. It makes us see ourselves as helpless and hard-done-by, beleaguered by hostile forces that we cannot control, powerless to respond to new situations or effect change. It leads to generalized suspicion, even paranoia. A victim outlook on the world will render us less competent and active than we could be. Such an attitude is often accompanied by a generalized attitude of resentment, a sense that we have been unfairly harmed and others are responsible. Feeling we are victims, we are often angry and tend to carry a grudge. These attitudes are generally counter-productive and unhelpful, supporting negative feelings and encouraging us to blame others and see the worst in them and regard ourselves as powerless objects of injustice rather than active subjects seeking positive change.

Pessimism and cynicism are also negative attitudes to be combatted. Pessimists believe the worst is to come; then they respond to the world in a way that tends to confirm their own beliefs. Pessimism is discouraging and disempowering; it lets us believe that things usually go wrong and there is little we can do to prevent that outcome. Cynicism is still worse, going so far as to reinterpret even positive events and actions as self-interested and greedy underneath. A pessimistic or cynical outlook on the world works against us personally and socially.

NEEDING TO TRUST

It is absolutely necessary for us as human beings to trust some other human beings, and when we do so, we allow ourselves to be vulnerable to them. We have some autonomy; we are not completely dependent on others; we have our own feelings and beliefs and can make our own judgments. But we have to trust and to accept that we cannot control other people. Our situation and sometimes our very lives depend on others as well as ourselves. The need for trust in relationships explains why we should select lovers and friends carefully. If we cannot trust a lover or friend, the relationship will be seriously flawed; whereas if we can trust that person, things are likely to go well. To conduct a smooth and happy life, we need to select reliable and trustworthy friends and partners, and establish and maintain trusting relationships with them.

Unless circumstances are especially bleak, we do best to approach the world with an initial attitude of slight trust. That means assuming that people are basically well intentioned and unthreatening unless we have a special reason to think otherwise. We should not begin with an attitude of fear and suspicion; we should be open to new people, new ideas, and new experiences. Otherwise we close ourselves off and deny ourselves much of the world. But such openness should be tempered with caution. It should be an alert, attentive openness, not a naive acceptance. We can be open and interested, non-rejecting, without being gullible. When we meet someone new, it is usually best to begin with the assumption that that person is a decent human being, a potential acquaintance, friend, or colleague. But if we notice small signs of unreliability, dishonesty, or falseness, we have grounds for slight suspicion. We should respect these feelings in ourselves and reflect on them. What do they mean? How vulnerable are we? Is there something a little bit odd or wrong about this person? Self-trust enters the picture at this point: we have to respect our own instincts, our own reasoning and reflection about what is going on, and our own judgment. Beginning with trust is good and right, but responding, without jumping to conclusions, to signs that something is not quite right is critically important too. That suspiciousness may protect us; it may even save our lives.

We begin by trusting the world and other people, but when we feel specific doubts, we trust our own feelings enough to explore them further. Specific doubt in a particular situation is quite different from a generalized distrust or cynicism, which paints for us a bleak picture of people and the social world. Generalized distrust is a negative, unwise, and counter-productive attitude, but specifically grounded doubts are quite another thing. Being open and beginning from an attitude of alert trust, a trust still sensitive to grounds for distrust, we avoid the mistake of seeing the worst, negatively interpreting our world, and responding to it accordingly. A suspicious outlook will restrict our opportunities, limit our relationships, and diminish the world itself. When we look for the worst, we are all too likely to find it; even more seriously, we sometimes help to create it.

A key factor in avoiding the facile rejection of other people is to refrain from stereotyping and labelling. Everyone has his or her own combination of qualities. No one is "just" a white man, just a young punk, just a floozie, cute guy, little old lady, Jew, pre-teen, housewife, or member of a motorcycle gang. Thousands of years ago, Heraclitus, the philosopher of change, advised his fellow Greeks to "expect the unexpected." In the context of relations with other people, this advice means being open to possibilities that we had not considered before. Heraclitus counselled flexible and open thinking as a road to hopefulness. Stereotyping and labelling are the very opposite of flexibility and openness. When we stereotype, we assume that a person fits a pattern and will act as "people of that type" do. She is "just a housewife" or "an accountant" or "a churchy type." We assume that the label exhausts her and gives us a recipe for relating to her. To stereotype people in these ways is to try to pin them down like biological specimens. Such categorization is hasty from a logical point of view and questionable from an ethical one; it works against good thinking and good relationships.

Being rigid, suspicious, negative, and pessimistic will be damaging to our mental health, our relationships, and our social world. Although we are vulnerable beings, we can still be open to other people, approaching them and the world with an initial attitude of trust. But when there are signs of unreliability and we are faced with difficult decisions about whether to trust another person, we have to think carefully and assess our own vulnerability. What is it that suggests untrustworthiness? Could we have mistaken information, or have we misunderstood? If we go on to trust this person on the basis of mistakes, what are the risks we face? What is the worst that could happen, and how likely is it? What, if anything, could we do to avoid it? We have seen and felt these grounds for distrust in our lives, and we have found them in some of the narratives in this book: unreliability, deceptiveness, lying, cheating, manipulativeness, exploitativeness, insincerity, hypocrisy, immorality, disloyalty, betrayal ... When such things are present, we should not feel guilty or blame ourselves when we do not trust.

Although trust is, in general, a good thing, distrust on occasion is also a good thing, and our failure to trust is not always a fault in us. We should never feel that we have to trust someone who tries to manipulate our attitudes or expects us to discount harmful actions. If we distrust someone we know and have dealt with, there is probably a reason for our attitude. A person who presses us to trust, who tries to persuade us that we "should" trust and to make us feel guilty for not trusting provides grounds for distrust; he is trying to manipulate us into trusting him when we do not. Overcoming distrust in relationships is desirable, but it has to be done properly – by talking, reflecting, cooperating, forgiving, becoming reconciled, not by trying to suppress our feelings and instincts and telling ourselves that things must be all right because this is someone whom we really "should" trust and it is not "nice" to be suspicious. Distrust is sometimes warranted and necessary for our own protection, and that fact deserves to be remembered.

We begin with an initial attitude of trust which we maintain unless there is evidence that something is not quite right. Then we have to think about it. When deciding whether to trust, we start to rely on ourselves and our trust in ourselves. We know ourselves and the risks we are taking; we try to know the other person. If there are grounds for distrust, we hold back, and we do not feel guilty about it.

TRUST AND TRUSTWORTHINESS

The first thing step towards trustworthiness is to trust ourselves and be careful in what we say and do. With a firm sense of ourselves and confidence in our own judgment, we will feel secure enough to hold back from indulging our own interests and biases at the expense of others. Trusting ourselves, we can move outward to be concerned with other people. We need not put up a false front; we need not be self-preoccupied and self-absorbed; we know who we are and what we are. Feeling and showing a genuine concern for others, we are likely to strike them as a fundamentally trustworthy person. When people need to trust us, they want some sign that we care about them as people and are not prepared to harm, exploit, or manipulate them. The best way to seem trustworthy is to appear to be caring and morally responsible persons – and the best way to do that is really to be such persons. With an awareness of the importance of trust and a firm sense of ourselves, we can seem and be trustworthy.

From a basis of trust in ourselves, we can acknowledge that we might be wrong and sometimes are. We will seem more trustworthy if we are open to criticism and able to admit that we make mistakes. When something we say or do turns out to be wrong, we do not try to cover up or rationalize it; nor do we try to defend ourselves. We pay attention to criticisms, acknowledge them if they are correct, and try to offer a reasonable response. We listen to others and try to understand and appreciate what they have to say, even if it is critical of us. We make every effort to understand and come to terms with what other people say to us, even when their views differ from our own. With a conviction that we are basically competent and sensible people, acknowledging that even competent and sensible people can make mistakes some of the time, we are able to be frank and honest about ourselves and what we have done. The fact that we are open and do not try to cover up makes us seem more trustworthy.

Being trustworthy means being reliable out of a sense of concern and commitment. To be regarded as trustworthy, we must seem dependable; and to seem dependable, we must be dependable. Breaking promises and not living up to commitments is not something that we can keep secret. In relation to trustworthiness, dependability has many dimensions. Central are honesty, non-deceptiveness, non-manipulativeness, keeping promises and other commitments, and respecting basic moral norms so as not to harm others. If we frequently tell small lies or deceive our friends and colleagues about our activities, if we overcommit ourselves and make promises that we cannot keep, we will begin to seem undependable and untrustworthy.

A key to trustworthiness is a firm sense that other people matter, a basic moral conviction that their needs and interests *count* from a moral point of view and must be significant in our lives. With such a conviction, we will not use other people as instruments for our purposes. We will recognize that they are human beings in their own right, not creatures for us to exploit or manipulate. If we want other people to help us with our projects, we must explain what we are doing and ask for their cooperation. Since those others are free agents, we must be willing to take no for an answer; we should not apply pressure to persuade them to do as we wish. If we want them to agree with us, we should honestly and accurately explain what we think, give them our reasons, and seek their consent on the basis of conversation and rational argument. Expecting them to listen to us, we must be willing to listen to them. As people who trust ourselves, we have learned to value our own autonomy. Our lovers, family members, friends, and colleagues may be expected to value their autonomy as much as we value our own. They appreciate our respect for their free and informed consent. The short advice as to how to be trusted by others is to be a trustworthy person. That means being open, honest, and reliable and showing respect for the autonomy of others.

But that is far from the last word on the dilemmas of trust.

Notes

1 Several important works have emerged since I did the bulk of my research. These include Putnam, *Making Democracy Work*; Fukuyama, *Trust*; Shapin, *A Social History of Truth*; and Brothers, *Falling Backwards*. Only the last puts its primary emphasis on personal and interpersonal trust, which is the subject of this book. The first three concentrate primarily on issues of social trust. I make some comments on Brothers's work in chapters 5 and 6.

2 These matters are discussed further in chapter 7.

3 Morgan, "On Trusting."

4 For a discussion of the risks and costs of distrust, see chapter 8. Useful accounts of trust may be found in Baier, "Trust and Antitrust"; Horsburgh, "The Ethics of Trust"; and Luhmann, *Trust and Power*. I have also been influenced by Bok, *Lying* and *A Strategy for Peace*, and Code, *Epistemic Responsibility*. However, the account here is essentially my own.

5 Hardin, in "Trustworthiness," argues that trust is valueless without trustworthiness.

6 This story is based on a real case described to me by a reliable friend. Several details have been altered to protect the identities of the people involved.

7 The point is argued by L. Thomas, in "Trust, Affirmation, and Moral Character," and also in Govier, *Social Trust and Human Communities*.

8 As noted by Hardin in "Trustworthiness." He thinks that the "moralization" of trust is a mistake because in order for trust to be good, the trusted people or institutions must be trustworthy. I agree with Hardin's view that the moralization of trust is a mistake and that trust is generally not good if the people trusted are not trustworthy. However, I do not think that he has described all the reasons why trust may fail to be good.

Even in some cases in which the trusted party is trustworthy from the point of view of the one who trusts him or her, their relationship may be centred around criminal activity or set (as in the case of Auschwitz) in an appallingly flawed context; in these cases, we would want to say, I think, that over all, trust is not good.

9 I am saying, then, that there can be such a thing as trust among thieves. But when there is, it likely bodes ill for the rest of us. I suspect that trust among thieves will be less stable than among more virtuous people. If A and B are both thieves and their relationship is one based on shared criminal behaviour, A knows that B is willing to act wrongly and harm others. Given such knowledge, it is only a small step for A to wonder whether B might be willing some day to harm him.

10 Levi, *The Drowned and the Saved*. This beautiful book was Levi's last and his most pessimistic.

11 "Living with Grizzlies: Research Takes Cochrane Couple Deep into Bear Territory," *Calgary Herald*, 3 November 1996. When I began to work on the topic of trust, I found examples about animals somewhat trivial. I have now begun to think that the subject may be of some significance, both theoretically and in terms of environmental ethics. However, it is not the theme of the present book, and I am unable to say more about it here.

12 Waal, *Peacemaking among Primates*.

13 Harre, conversation with the author; K. Govier, *Angel Walk*. For a discussion of our trust in various people doing jobs behind the scenes and producing objects that we take to be reliable, see chapter 5 of Govier, *Social Trust and Human Communities*, especially the discussion of scatter trust.

14 The notion of trusting an object such as a rope, life jacket, or computer makes sense if we adopt an Aristotelian stance on useful objects. For Aristotle, the good object is the one that serves its purpose: for example, a good knife cuts well. In these terms, a good rope for mountaineering is one that will support a person's weight. A good life jacket will keep someone afloat. To trust a rope or a life jacket is to feel confident that it is good in this sense and to rely on it to serve its function. In both cases, life may be at stake. For a better sense of what would be involved in trusting the people who made the rope or the life jacket, see Govier, *Social Trust and Human Communities*, chapter 5.

15 The question of trusting the dead was raised, and taken very seriously, when I presented an early version of my account of trust at a meeting of the Canadian Philosophical Association at the Learned Societies Conference in Victoria, BC, on 29 May 1990. My own view on the issue of life after death is a resolutely secular one. I believe that when people are dead, they do not exist in any realm and are not capable of speech or action.

16 Based on my personal experience as a volunteer mediator for the Dispute Center at the Better Business Bureau of Calgary, 1992–95.

17 Thanks to Helen Hooker for helping me to understand the tremendous importance that this topic will have for religious believers. As an agnostic, however, I feel no obligation or capacity to theorize further about such matters.

18 I consider social trust, professionals, institutions, and political contexts in *Social Trust and Human Communities*.

CHAPTER TWO

1 Pogrebin, *Among Friends*, chapter 1.

2 Mayeroff, *On Caring*, 20.

3 Quoted in Telfer, "Friendship." See also Friedman, "Friendship and Moral Growth." Friedman emphasizes the centrality of trust in friendship.

4 Buber, *I and Thou*, 78; my emphasis. See also Buber, *The Knowledge of Man*.

5 Aristotle, *Nichomachean Ethics*.

6 L. Thomas, *Living Morally*, chapter 4.

7 Kupfer, "Can Parents and Children Be Friends?"

8 Hutter, *Politics as Friendship*.

9 As common experience and empirical studies such as that of Pogrebin in *Among Friends* both testify.

10 The question as to whether and how preference for friends over strangers can ethically be justified has been a central one in recent moral philosophy. In particular cases, there is always room for argument. I would maintain that the more general question as to whether the kind of valuing needed for intimate friendships is morally permissible is easily answered, because such intimate connection is necessary for our development as moral persons.

11 Relevant accounts of trust include Morgan, "On Trusting"; Rempel et al., "Trust in Close Relationships"; Isaacs et al., "Faith, Trust, and Gullibility"; and Rotter, "Interpersonal Trust, Trustworthiness, and Gullibility."

12 Malone and Malone, *The Art of Intimacy*. See also L. Thomas, "Trust, Affirmation, and Moral Character."

13 Cited in Pogrebin, *Among Friends*, chapter 4.

14 Morgan, "On Trusting." The relation between trustworthiness and genuineness is beautifully emphasized in Haim Gordon's *Dance, Dialogue, and Despair*. Gordon used Buber's theory of interhuman relationships and existentialist literature and philosophy in a project seeking to improve relationships between Arab Israelis and Jews.

15 Kahn and Turiel, "Children's Conceptions of Trust."

16 My discussions with children about trust were conducted with Sue Govier's grade four and five class at Harold W. Riley School on 3 June

1992, with Linda Campayne's grade six class at the same school on
11 June 1992, and with Carol Daffney's grade five and six class at
Glenbrook Elementary School on 23 June 1992.

17 There was perhaps some exaggeration of the significance of trust as a
    result of a bandwagon effect and a desire to play to my expressed interest
    in the issue.

18 Rawlins and Holl, "The Communicative Achievement of Friendship
    during Adolescence."

19 Similar conclusions emerge from various sources. I have been greatly
    influenced by Pogrebin, *Among Friends*, and Tannen, *You Just Don't Under-
    stand*. See also Strickwerda and May, "Male Friendship and Intimacy,"
    and Rubin, *Intimate Strangers*.

20 Tannen, *You Just Don't Understand*, 59.

21 Ibid., 42.

22 McGill, *The McGill Report on Male Intimacy*; cited in Pogrebin, *Among
    Friends*.

23 Pogrebin, *Among Friends*, 263.

24 Ibid., 276. The theme of close relationships in the face of an adversary is
    beautifully treated in Kathleen Hildebrand's "The Mythic Enemy in the
    American Dream."

25 As implied by McGill and Pogrebin.

26 Did Dora betray Laura by telling Jake what Laura said about never
    having an orgasm? The question as to whether this sexual confession
    should have been confidential is never raised in the novel. Laura's use of
    intimate exchange presupposes that Dora would naturally tell her
    husband about it, which was why the manipulation was effective.

27 Baier, "Trusting Ex-Intimates," 230.

CHAPTER THREE

1 *Globe and Mail*, 1 January 1994.

2 See Coontz, *The Way We Never Were*. In preparing this chapter I was also
   assisted by Meyers et al., *Kindred Matters*; Dizard and Gadlin, *The Minimal
   Family*; Thorne and Yalom, *Rethinking the Family*; Orbach and Eichenbaum, *What Do Women Want*; Lerner, *The Dance of Deception*; Poster, *Critical Theory of the Family*; and Tavris, *The Mismeasure of Woman*.

3 This statistic is taken from Thorne, "Feminism and the Family," in Thorne
   and Yalom, *Rethinking the Family*. For strong and influential arguments
   about how calculations of the GNP systematically ignore women's work
   within the home, see Waring, *If Women Counted*.

4 See Brothers, *Falling Backwards*, for documentation and persuasive cases.

5 Clark, "Meaningful Social Bonding as a Universal Human Need."

6 Ibid.

7 Poster, *Critical Theory of the Family*.
8 Collier, Rosaldo, and Yanagisko, "Is There a Family? New Anthropological Views," in Thorne and Yalom, *Rethinking the Family*.
9 Wittgenstein, *Philosophical Investigations*, 67.
10 Barrie Thorne, "Feminism and the Family: Two Decades of Thought," in Thorne and Yalom, *Rethinking the Family*, 3–30. The Statistics Canada figures were cited in the *Globe and Mail* for 10 June 1996.
11 An actual case; names are altered to protect identities.
12 Interview, Victims Assistance Unit, City of Calgary Police, September 1989.
13 Poster, *Critical Theory of the Family*.
14 See Clark, "Meaningful Social Bonding as a Universal Human Need."
15 The Milan Approach to Family Therapy, as presented in workshops offered by the University of Calgary Family Therapy Unit in the period 1982–85.
16 Poster, *Critical Theory of the Family*.
17 Bradshaw, *Bradshaw On: The Family*.
18 Kaminer, *I'm Dysfunctional, You're Dysfunctional*.
19 Coontz, *The Way We Never Were*, 210.
20 Lerner, *The Dance of Deception*.
21 These points are extremely well argued in N. Chodorow and B. Contratto, "The Fantasy of the Perfect Mother," in Thorne and Yalom, *Rethinking the Family*.
22 Based on real cases; details are changed slightly.
23 This point is developed in detail by Okin in *Justice, Gender, and the Family*.
24 There are, of course, unusual cases, such as those in which people are sexually aroused by danger or pain.
25 There is a great deal of anecdotal evidence for unwillingness, on the part of people in their twenties and thirties, to commit themselves to relationships. Doubts about commitment emerged with painful clarity on the CBC's phone-in show *Cross Country Check up* for 14 February (Valentine's Day) 1993 and in Dennis, *Hot and Bothered*.
26 Bonnelle Strickling (philosopher and therapist), interview, May 1993. See also Brothers, *Falling Backwards*.
27 Erikson, *Childhood and Society*.
28 Winnicott, *The Family and Individual Development*.
29 Coontz, *The Way We Never Were*, chapter 11.
30 Winnicott, *The Family and Individual Development*, 90.

CHAPTER FOUR

1 Tannen, *You Just Don't Understand*.
2 Based on a real case; names are altered.

3 Brothers, *Falling Backwards*. Brothers notes that there has been a tendency
   to assume that trust is diminished after assault and other traumas. She
   argues plausibly that another kind of disturbance is possible: trust in the
   self or in a family member may be *exaggerated* as a method of making
   sense of the world after a traumatic event.

4 Havel, "New Year's Address 1990."

5 This seems to have happened in eastern Europe. See Govier, *Social Trust
   and Human Communities*, chapter 7.

6 Lerner, *Dance of Deception*.

7 Pittman, *Private Lies*.

8 Ibid., 108, 130.

9 For a discussion of Freud's rejection of the "seduction theory," see
   Masson, *The Assault on Truth*. For a still more radical, and more recent, critique of Freud, see Crews, *The Memory Wars*. The matter is also discussed
   in Brothers, *Falling Backwards*.

10 The Carleton study was described and criticized in the *Globe and Mail* in
   December 1993.

11 Quoted in the *Washington Spectator*, 1 May 1991; cited by Stephanie
   Coontz in *The Way We Never Were*.

12 Annalies Acorn, Law Reform Commission, Edmonton, Alberta, interview,
   October 1993. Acorn is a researcher on law and domestic violence.

13 Just one example: my sister Katherine Govier came across a high proportion of such cases in 1975 while interviewing a number of young Canadian women for a government project associated with International
   Women's Year. This aspect of her work was never made public. The
   project was intended to be cheerful and to offer a positive account of the
   aspirations of young women. When K. Govier tried to interest various
   media outlets in the problem of incest (which her interviews suggested
   was more common than people supposed), she was told that it was "too
   depressing."

14 Forgiveness and reconciliation are explored in chapter 10.

CHAPTER FIVE

1 The case of Ellen West is described in Rogers, *A Way of Being*.

2 Brothers, "Trust Disturbances in Rape and Incest Victims." This account
   of self-trust strikes me as slightly flawed in the way that it makes expectations of future success integral to self-trust. For instance, in a time of war
   or social turmoil, one might believe that one had few opportunities to
   develop one's talents and that one's prospects for success were limited,
   but one might quite reasonably attribute these poor prospects to problems
   in the larger world rather than to one's own shortcomings. Brothers later,
   in *Falling Backwards*, 35, defines what I would call four dimensions of

trust, but she calls four dimensions of *self-trust*. These are (a) trust-in-others, (b) trust-in-self, (c) self-as-trustworthy, and (d) others as self-trusting. I would include only one's sense of (b) and (c) as *self-trust;* (a) concerns our sense of whether other people are trustworthy (as regards us), and (d) concerns our sense of whether others trust themselves. Thus my terminology is quite different from that of Brothers in this later work.

3 Women do not always blame themselves, and it is not only women who blame themselves. Various trust disturbances follow upon assaults, including, sometimes, exaggerated trust in others. See Brothers, *Falling Backwards*, 59, for instance. "A person whose trust-in-others is traumatically betrayed may become suspicious, hyper-vigilant, secretive, and withdrawn or so unswervingly trustful that even blatant signs of another person's untrusworthiness are overlooked. Disturbed trust-in-self may be expressed either as insecurity, indecisiveness, and self-doubt or as blind self-confidence." A description of a man who was traumatized and responded by taking blame upon himself is summarized on page 69.

4 In emphasizing the importance of autonomy, I do not mean to suggest that people are totally self-sufficient, or that being autonomous is incompatible with dialogue or cooperation. Compare chapter 3 of my *Social Trust and Human Communities*. For relevant accounts of autonomy, see Kymlicka, *Liberalism, Community, and Culture*, and Meyers, *Self, Society, and Personal Choice*. Quoted passages from Meyers are from pages 76, 83, and 84. Obviously, no one has complete autonomy. We acquire our concepts, ideas, and skills from others; we must interact and cooperate with others; we must make decisions and choices with some respect for the needs of others, especially vulnerable friends and family members, to whom we may have special obligations.

5 Self-trust requires the ability to reflect on what others do and say and to make independent judgments about their actions. It also requires the ability to reflect on what we ourselves do and say and to make independent judgments about that.

6 It strikes me as plausible that self-trust is more of a problem for women than for men; however, I have no good empirical evidence for this claim and will not defend it here.

7 Cases in Brothers, *Falling Backwards*, also suggest that absolute self-trust is dangerous. Brothers claims (47) that mature criteria for trustworthiness, whether of the self or of others, should be *realistic, abstract, complex*, and *differentiated*. Criteria used by people who have been repeatedly traumatized are usually immature by this definition. Compare chapter 7 below.

8 Brothers argues in *Falling Backwards* that self-trust should be central in therapy and psychoanalytic theory. She says (145) that all her patients have had their self-trust "scarred by past betrayals" and in response have

"disturbed" patterns of trust. (In interpreting this statement, it is important to remember that on her definitions, as described in note 2, *self-trust* is understood to include trust in others.) The trust disturbance is represented either by remote, suspicious, and formal behaviour or by the patients indiscriminately revealing their most intimate thoughts, feelings, and pain-shrouded memories at the first meeting. If Brothers's work should gain influence, we may come to think about self-trust far more than we presently do.

9 Compare Austin, *Sense and Sensibilia*. Austin speaks of contrastive terms and asks which "wears the trousers" *(sic)*. He is in effect asking which term is the one by means of which the other is defined. Interestingly, for some contrastives, it is the negative form that is primary. Austin argues that this is the case for "real" and "unreal." (I owe this reference to Bela Szabados.) If we ask this question for "trust" and "distrust," we find, I think, that "distrust" wears the trousers. Trust tends to be assumed, to be taken for granted; it is frequently not noticed. Often we notice that we did, or should, trust only when there begins to be some reason to distrust. And this relationship seems to hold for all the various forms of trust, including self-trust.

10 Ludwig Wittgenstein argues this point in *On Certainty*.

11 This does not mean dogmatism or ignoring the views and interpretations of others. What it does mean is that we reflect on what others tell us; that we make judgments about it after reflection; that we do not simply accept their values and beliefs as correct because we assume that other people know, whereas we do not. My account here owes much to Meyers, *Self, Society, and Personal Choice*.

12 Self-respect is discussed in chapter 6.

13 Compare chapter 4 of Govier, *Social Trust and Human Communities*.

14 The same view is taken in Brothers, *Falling Backwards*.

15 A person may trust herself as someone who is especially trustworthy for others. Compare Brothers, *Falling Backwards*.

16 This clearly raises the tricky problem of just what the inductive evidence *does* indicate. Ultimately, one comes to the whole philosophical problem of inductive and interpretive knowledge of people and social affairs, a problem that I obviously cannot solve here. In this discussion I rely on commonsensical judgments without defending them, as to do so would require (at least) another book.

17 I suspect that this phenomenon is more common in women than in men.

18 Bias in favour of oneself is well described in Greenwald, "The Totalitarian Ego." Compare also Seligman, *Learned Optimism*. I make no pretence of being able to specify exactly and exhaustively what would constitute too little self-trust and what would constitute too much. The standards would come from three sources: first of all, logical and epistemological standards

of inductive reasoning; secondly, ethical tenability and consistency of standards for judging the self and others; and thirdly, psychological and ethical standards of sound personal functioning. Compare chapter 7 below.

CHAPTER SIX

1 In *A Theory of Justice* John Rawls has much to say about self-esteem and why it is a basic good. The expression "plagued with self-doubt" is taken from this work. Interestingly, however, Rawls does not mention self-trust.
2 Michalos, in "The Impact of Trust on Business, International Security, and the Quality of Life," cites a number of studies showing that most people think they are in various significant respects above average. The paradox involved is briefly discusssed in chapter 2 of Govier, *Social Trust and Human Communities*.
3 Brothers, *Falling Backwards*; see especially chapters 2 and 6.
4 Buber, *I and Thou*, *The Knowledge of Man*, and *The Way of Response*.
5 Carl Rogers, "The Characteristics of a Helping Relationship," in Rogers, *On Becoming a Person*; see especially 42–3.
6 Gordon, *Dance, Dialogue, and Despair*, 38–9.
7 Brothers, *Falling Backwards*. Brothers makes claims – which seem fairly plausible in the light of case studies she cites, but are not clearly explained – that empathy from one person, A, may support self-trust in another person, B. From Buber and Rogers, we find support for the claim that, in order for A to support B's self-trust by empathizing with him or her, it is necessary for A to trust himself or herself.
8 Snyder, "When Belief Creates Reality." Compare also Govier, *Social Trust and Human Communities*, chapter 2.
9 Social psychologists sometimes refer to this strategy as "self-handicapping." Clearly, it can be taken too far, as, for instance, when a person does not accept responsibility for failings and errors, but always conjures up a reason to explain these by appealing to external circumstances.
10 Seligman, *Learned Optimism*.
11 Ibid.
12 As argued in chapter 5, self-trust can go too far. That it is advantageous when kept within reasonable bounds is apparent from arguments in Seligman, *Learned Optimism*, and Brothers, *Falling Backwards*.
13 Belinda Cooper, interview, Berlin, Germany, 18 March 1994.
14 Cooper, "Women and the Stasi."
15 The link between betrayal and self-doubt was confirmed also by Fritz Arendt, Berndt Joop, and Wolhard Prehl in an interview, Dresden, Germany, 22 March 1994.
16 Schmookler, *Out of Weakness*.

17 Ibid. It would obviously be an exaggeration to say that the lack of self-
    esteem and self-trust among these men was the *sole cause* of their rising to
    power and being able to impose brutality on others. Obviously, political,
    social, and economic circumstances need to be conducive to the operation
    of tyranny.
18 Brothers, *Falling Backwards*.
19 Franklin, *The Promise of Paradise*, 262.
20 Ibid., 263. The use by leaders of the idea that a devotee is shown by his or
    her rebellious or critical thoughts to be at fault because he or she is *unsur-
    rendered* (so-called) is also documented in Hudner and Gruson, *Monkey on
    a Stick*. Franklin describes herself, before entering the Rajneesh cult,
    as having been dominated by her husband and, after her divorce, as still
    affected by his demands as to how she should handle herself and take
    care of their children.
21 CBC *Journal* documentary on the Church Universal and Triumphant in
    Paradise Valley, Montana, broadcast in February 1990. The *Calgary Herald*
    for 2 and 3 March 1997 contains several lengthy articles with further infor-
    mation about this movement. The analysis of cult membership and trust
    is my own. It coheres with other sources cited here and has been corrobo-
    rated in interviews by John Guy, who has worked extensively with former
    cult members.
22 I do not wish to imply that affiliation or disaffiliation with a cult is wholly
    a matter of correct and consistent reasoning about issues of trust. Obvi-
    ously, far more is at stake. However, the double standard on self-trust and
    trust in others is noteworthy and could provide the basis for constructive
    discussion.
23 Dahl, *Working for Love*, 35.

CHAPTER SEVEN

 1 Brothers, *Falling Backwards*, 47–9. Despite the obvious importance of this
    subject, Brothers does not devote much space to it.
 2 The conception of balancing principles against judgments about particular
    cases is derived from John Rawls, who developed the idea of reflective
    equilibrium in *A Theory of Justice*. Interviews were intended, not as part of
    a rigorous empirical survey of beliefs, but rather as a format to explore
    reasoning about particular cases. In Rawlsian terms, this could be con-
    strued as provided a better-than-armchair basis for "our considered judg-
    ments." Donald Conrad's help in developing cases and conducting
    interviews was indispensable. So too was the assistance of those who
    participated in interviews, especially Helen Colijn. Conclusions similar to
    those reached here are stated by Russell Hardin in "The Streetwise Episte-
    mology of Trust." For other discussions of evidence and trust, see K. Jones,

"Trust as an Affective Attitude," Hardin, "Trustworthiness," and Becker, "Trust as Noncognitive Security about Motives." Several of these papers contrast cognitive or "evidentialist" and non-cognitive accounts of trust. I see trust as an attitude founded on beliefs; those beliefs may be more or less warranted. In this chapter I discuss reasons and evidence for the beliefs and expectations underlying interpersonal trust. But I do not want to imply by doing so that trust is *solely* a matter of beliefs based on evidence.

3 One might wish to speak of general social beliefs instead of general social knowledge, in deference to the fact that many of the claims accepted may not be true. I have no objection to this approach; the word "knowledge" is used loosely here.

4 Harre, *Varieties of Realism*. See also Govier, *Social Trust and Human Communities*, chapter 4.

5 This is clearly a case where institutional and individual factors intersect.

6 Walter Kaufmann, translator and editor, in Buber, *I and Thou*, 39.

7 We do trust, to varying degrees, in letters of reference. Ideally, they should be used only in conjunction with other sources of information, preferably interviews. A discussion of the lessening of confidence that is likely to result from the practice of inflated letters of reference may be found in Bok, *Lying*, chapter 5.

8 Presuming, of course, that we trust ourselves.

9 Johnson, *Modern Times*, 276.

10 It seems to me that the Internet should be rated lower in reliability than the media because of ease of misrepresentation and the lack of institutional restraints. Notoriously, on the Internet people have deceived others about even such basic matters as their gender.

11 A real-life example supplied by Donald Conrad. Reactions to this case support Brothers's idea that more mature criteria for trust are more differentiated. One should make a distinction between the manager and the administration in general.

12 This case obviously brings us back to the subject of self-trust and why it is important.

13 Compare chapter 11 of Govier, *Social Trust and Human Communities*.

14 The same themes emerge in the discussion of therapeutic trust in chapter 8.

15 Compare Govier, "Belief, Values, and the Will." The fact that we cannot just trust or distrust by fiat, but can nevertheless affect our attitudes of trust and distrust, is noted by Russell Hardin in "Trustworthiness."

16 Arguments that slight trust as a standing attitude has advantages in most contexts may be found in Govier, *Social Trust and Human Communities*. People who tend to be "high trust" approach others with an attitude of slight trust and are inclined to give them the benefit of the doubt or to see things in a positive light. Those who are "low trust" begin with an

attitude of slight distrust and are inclined to see things in a negative light. See Rotter, "Generalized Expectations for Interpersonal Trust" and "Interpersonal Trust, Trustworthiness, and Gullibility." For a description of an ethical system premised on basic generalized trust, see Logstrup, *The Ethical Demand*.

17 One might object that the question of whether I trust or distrust Saddam Hussein does not arise because I am extremely unlikely ever to have any personal dealings with him; I do not have to decide whether to dine with him or accept a ride in his car. However, I think that that objection is based on an oversimplificaton. In an indirect way I "deal with" Hussein when I support or dissent from foreign policy concerning his country, Iraq.

18 Banfield, *The Moral Basis of a Backward Society.* See also Putnam, *Making Democracy Work*, and Govier, *Social Trust and Human Communities*, chapter 6.

19 Pye, "China."

20 See Lord, *Legacies*, and Trevor-Roper, *The Hermit of Peking*.

CHAPTER EIGHT

1 Brown, "Dating: The Trust Principle."

2 Translated from the German on an interview played by the CBC program *Fifth Estate* on 9 November 1992. See also Ash, *The File*.

3 Elon, "East Germany"; Jackson, "Germany"; and Kramer, "Letter from Europe." An excellent discussion may also be found in Rosenberg, *The Haunted Land*, and Ash, *The File*. The latter became availabe only as this book was going to press.

4 The notion of face work is taken from Erving Goffman. See his *The Presentation of Self in Everyday Life* and *Relations in Public*.

5 To the extent that one does trust, complexity is reduced. This theme is emphasized in Luhmann, *Trust and Power*.

6 Zand, "Trust and Managerial Problem Solving."

7 E.E. Jones, "Interpreting Interpersonal Behavior." Jones reports on his own work and summarizes that of a number of others.

8 Kulik, "Confirmatory Attribution and the Perpetuation of Social Beliefs."

9 Horsburgh, "The Ethics of Trust."

10 The classic discussion of the relationship between rules and public practice is that of Wittgenstein in *Philosophical Investigations*, 185–210. I have been influenced by Kripke, *Wittgenstein on Rules and Private Language*.

11 There are some contexts in which control over a short term or in a specific regard may assist in development. But in general, it works against the development of the autonomy and critical thinking that are necessary to support maturity and growth.

12 Based on a real example at a Calgary elementary school in March 1992; the name is altered.

13 In the fall of 1996 there were several items on television news broadcasts about the growing popularity of surveillance devices among women who hired nannies or babysitters. One showed a film obtained from such a device; a nanny was striking a small child very hard. The installing of such a device is an expression of distrust against the babysitter. Apart from invasion of privacy, the obvious objection to this practice is that if one distrusts a babysitter to that degree, one should not be hiring him or her. Relations with the babysitter will surely worsen if such a device is discovered, because the distrust and invasion of privacy are certain to be resented. The dilemma is, of course, that some parents need to work, require childcare, and cannot find anyone whom they trust deeply enough. Hence they look to technology for a solution.

14 A common criticism of recourse to the law, urged by proponents of "alternate dispute resolution," is that it sets relationships in an adversarial framework from which it is difficult to emerge.

15 In making these comments, I do not wish to imply that law is unimportant. The nature of law, the rule of law, and people's attitude to the law are profoundly important aspects of a culture and society. The point here is that the law has little power to rectify problems in personal and intimate relationships.

CHAPTER NINE

1 Often, "trust me" is said ironically; however, the appeal is also frequently sincere (people really do want us to trust them when they say it).

2 Updike, *Trust Me*.

3 An actual case at a Calgary elementary school in 1992.

4 Active listening has been emphasized in all of the many workshops and lectures on conflict resolution that I have attended since 1989. It has an obvious relation to empathy. Compare chapters 5 and 6.

5 These observations are based on personal experience.

6 The strategy of active listening can, of course, be abused – as in a case when someone uses it deceptively, pretending concern in order to elicit information.

7 Horsburgh, "The Ethics of Trust."

8 Gandhi's view on human nature in the context of his activism are usefully explained by Gene Sharp in *Gandhi as a Political Strategist*. Gandhi's comments on trust and distrust are spread throughout his works. See for instance, *Collected Works of Mahatma Gandhi*, 22: 333, 83, and 282; Gandhi, *Young India*, 2 December 1924, 430; and Gandhi, *The Way to Communal Harmony*, 188 and 246.

9 Gandhi, *Collected Works*, 22: 333.

10 Horsburgh, "The Ethics of Trust," 352.

11 The appeal "trust me" comes from the one who is distrusted and whose behaviour has (typically) provided some warrant for distrust. The expression "I trust you" comes from the other person in the relationship.

12 The tendency of people to want to reciprocate is described and documented in Cialdini, *Influence*, chapter 2.

13 Noddings, *Caring*.

14 Fisher and Brown, *Getting Together*, chapter 7.

15 There is, of course, a vast literature on cooperation and the Prisoner's Dilemma. A good general source is Axelrod, *The Evolution of Cooperation*. Contrary to what was assumed in many early studies, making the cooperative move in a Prisoner's Dilemma situation does not necessarily demonstrate that the player trusts his "opponent." Trust is an attitude too complex to be successfully operationalized in a single discrete act.

16 Cialdini, *Influence*.

17 Mark Snyder, "When Belief Creates Reality." For a more specific application to trust and distrust, see chapter 2 of Govier, *Social Trust and Human Communities*.

18 Psychological studies support the existence both of the confirmation effect and of the attribution effect. It would appear, then, that we naturally think in these ways. At several places in this book, I have emphasized the significance of these results because they help to explain the often-observed tendency for both trust and distrust to be self-buttressing attitudes. But the naturalness of thinking in this way does not imply its inevitability; nor does it imply its correctness. When there is a problem in a relationship, as in the imagined case of Susan and Elizabeth, we can stop and reflect, examine the evidence, and make a conscious effort to avoid selective evidence and the attribution fallacy, and we can change our views if it is our considered judgment that the evidence warrants it.

CHAPTER TEN

1 There are various different accounts of forgiveness, including the belief that only God can forgive, the idea that forgiveness is bilateral to the extent that it is appropriate only if there is repentance from the offender, and the concept that forgiveness may appropriately be unilateral provided that the victim does not forgive out of a lack of self-respect and failure to understand that she was wronged. Forgiveness may be approached through an analysis of the implications of discrete acts of forgiveness or by examining the implications of having a disposition to forgive (here forgiveness may be seen as a virtue).

2 Forgiveness is not always linked tightly to reconciliation. One may forgive and yet not be reconciled – as when the other person is dead or absent or, though forgiven, still seems dangerous to be with. One may be reconciled, in some sense, without forgiving, in a case where there is practical pressure to do so.

3 There is, nevertheless, some relation between excusing and forgiving. We may find some aspects of what a person has done understandable, though wrong, and insofar as we do so, find him or her easier to forgive.

4 Relevant articles on forgiveness include McGary, "Forgiveness"; North, "Wrongdoing and Forgiveness"; Richards, "Forgiveness"; Beatty, "Forgiveness"; Downie, "Forgiveness"; Horsburgh, "Forgiveness"; Murphy, "Forgiveness and Resentment"; Lauritzen, "Forgiveness"; Holmgren, "Forgiveness and the Intrinsic Value of Persons"; Lang, "Forgiveness"; Harvey, "Forgiving as an Obligation of the Moral Life"; Hughes, "Moral Anger, Forgiving, and Condoning"; Benn, "Forgiveness and Loyalty"; and Hampton and Murphy, *Forgiveness and Mercy.*

5 I owe this point to a questioner at a meeting of the Calgary Apeiron Society for Practical Philosophy in November 1995.

6 Harvey, "Forgiving as an Obligation of the Moral Life."

7 Benefits of forgiveness for the victim are emphasized by Holmgren, "Forgiveness and the Intrinsic Value of Persons," and Flanigan, *Forgiving the Unforgivable.*

8 The past, or our interpretation of it, is enormously important both politically and personally. Perhaps it is harder to transcend the negative politically than personally, since for nationalist politicians there will always be the temptation to build power by cultivating a sense of grievance, resentment, and humiliation, the latter needing to be overcome by fresh victories. Obviously I cannot pursue such themes here. But see Scheff, *Bloody Revenge.*

9 This is not meant to diminish the importance of the past or its impact on the present and future. But we live in the present and must make decisions about how to go forward into the future. I am arguing that from the point of view of practical and ethical decision-making, the future has more importance than the past. That is not to deny that we go into the future with our "baggage" from the past.

10 I am aware that there is not only one Christian account of forgiveness; however, the theme treated here has certainly been a prominent one. Compare Shriver, *An Ethic for Enemies.*

11 Murphy's criticism of the Christian account is in "Getting Even: The Role of the Victim," in Murphy, *Punishment and Rehabilitation.*

12 On occasions when I have spoken on the ethics of forgiveness, people have told me that they had managed to forgive their parents, sometimes after their parents were dead, and that they felt great personal relief in doing so.

13 The description here is based on an interview with Pastor Turek in Leipzig in March 1994. Of course, the situation of East Germany is not unique. Issues of reconciliation in the wake of totalitarian regimes are significant elsewhere in eastern Europe and also in South Africa and Latin America. Forgiveness is a political topic as well as a personal one. For their reflections on the situation in East Germany, I am also grateful to Fritz Ahrend, R.M. Turek, Ulrich Seidel, Berndt Joop, and Wolfhard Prehl, with whom I had extremely useful interviews in Dresden in March 1994.

14 Described to me by Belinda Cooper in an interview in Berlin in March 1994.

15 These events and the overall dilemma of political forgiveness in Germany are described in Rosenberg, *The Haunted Land*, and Ash, *The File*.

16 By my brief description of this morally troubled situation, I do not mean to imply that the lines between victims and wrongdoers were always clear. There were Stasi agents who were coerced into reporting, victims who were, in other contexts, wrongdoers, and many other complex and problematic cases. Some such complexities are explored in Rosenberg, *The Haunted Land*, and Ash, *The File*.

17 Holmgren, "Forgiveness and the Intrinsic Value of Persons."

18 Gustafson, "Incest."

19 Flanigan, *Forgiving the Unforgivable*.

20 Reflections on the Jewish theology of forgiveness may be found in McGary, "Forgiveness," and Newman, "The Quality of Mercy."

21 Downie, "Forgiveness." Downie's position is similar to that of Holmgren in "Forgiveness and the Intrinsic Value of Persons." It may be termed broadly Kantian because it relies on a notion of the dignity of the person and of treating people as ends in themselves and not as means to ends. But in light of the fact that Kant argued in favour of capital punishment for murderers, the positions of Downie and Holmgren should be distinguished from his. See also Hampton in Hampton and Murphy, *Forgiveness and Mercy*.

22 Horsburgh, "Forgiveness."

23 The need for victims to reflect on what has occurred, understand that and why it is wrong, and forgive from a position of self-respect is urged by Hampton in Murphy and Hampton, *Forgiveness and Mercy*, and by Holmgren in "Forgiveness and the Intrinsic Value of Persons."

24 *Keeley and Du* was presented by Alberta Theatre Projects in Calgary in October 1995. The playwright was listed as Jane Martin. This is a pseudonym; because of the vicious intensity of the abortion debate, the author did not want his or her name revealed.

25 The play was not primarily about forgiveness; it was about abortion and tried to portray both pro-life and pro-choice stances in a fair way. What it illustrated was a case of non-forgiveness and one in which non-

forgiveness seemed to be the right stance, because of the risks involved should the repentance and commitment to reform not be sincere.

26 North, "Wrongdoing and Forgiveness," 505. My emphasis.

27 In some situations, changes make the likelihood of the same kind of abuse being repeated extremely small and thus lessen the risks of a reconciliation where there is less than complete acknowledgment or repentance on the part of the offender(s). An example would seem to be that of post-apartheid South Africa. Many whites who participated in abuse seem unrepentant; however, given the new political situation, the likelihood of apartheid being resurrected would seem to be extremely slight.

CHAPTER ELEVEN

1 A classic discussion of the benefits and occasional perils of optimism is Seligman, *Learned Optimism*.

2 Dauenhauer, "Hope and Its Ramifications for Politics." Themes of optimism, pessimism, and hope are also explored in the final chapter of Govier, *Social Trust and Human Communities*.

Bibliography

Ash, Timothy Garton. *The File*. London: Harper Collins 1997.

Austin, J.L. *Sense and Sensibilia*. Oxford: Oxford University Press 1962.

Axelrod, Robert. *The Evolution of Cooperation*. New York: Basic Books 1984.

Baier, Annette. "Secular Faith." *Canadian Journal of Philosophy* 9 (1980): 131–48.

– "Trust and Antitrust." *Ethics* 96 (1986): 231–60.

– "Trusting Ex-Intimates." In *Gender Basics: Feminist Perspectives on Women and Men*, ed. Anne C. Minas, 223–31. Belmont, Calif.: Wadsworth 1993.

– "What Do Women Want in Moral Theory?" *Nous* 19 (1986): 53–63.

Banfield, Edward C. *The Moral Basis of a Backward Society*. New York: Free Press 1958.

Barber, Bernard. *The Logic and Limits of Trust*. New Brunswick, NJ: Rutgers University Press 1983.

Beatty, Joseph. "Forgiveness." *American Philosophical Quarterly* 7 (1970): 246–52.

Becker, Lawrence. "Trust as Noncognitive Security about Motives." *Ethics* 107 (1996): 43–61.

Bellah, R., with R. Madsen, W. Sullivan, A. Swidler, and S. Tipton. *Habits of the Heart*. New York: Harper and Row 1985.

Benn, Piers. "Forgiveness and Loyalty." *Philosophy* 71 (1966): 369–84.

Bok, Sissela. *Lying: Moral Choice in Public and Private Life*. New York: Pantheon 1978.

– *A Strategy for Peace*. New York: Pantheon 1989.

Boulding, Elise. *Building a Global Civic Culture*. Syracuse, NY: Syracuse University Press 1990.

Bradshaw, John. *Bradshaw On: The Family*. Deerfield Beach, Fla: Health Communications, Inc. 1988.

Brothers, Doris. *Falling Backwards: An Exploration of Trust and Self-Experience*. New York: W.W. Norton 1995.

– "Trust Disturbances in Rape and Incest Victims." Doctoral thesis, Yeshiva University, New York 1982.

Brown, Sue. "Dating: The Trust Principle." *New Woman*, October 1991, 63–7.

Buber, Martin. *I and Thou*. Trans. Walter Kaufmann. New York: Charles Scribner and Sons 1970.

– *The Knowledge of Man: Selected Essays*. Trans. Maurice Friedman and Ronald Gregor Smith. Atlantic Highlands, NJ: Humanities Press 1965, 1988.

– *The Way of Response. Martin Buber: Selections from His Writings*, edited by N.N. Glatzer. New York: Schocken Books 1966.

Carter, Michele. "Ethical Analysis of Trust in Therapeutic Relationships." Doctoral dissertation, University of Tennessee, Knoxville 1989.

Cialdini, Robert. *Influence: The New Psychology of Modern Persuasion*. New York: Quill 1984.

Clark, Mary. "Meaningful Social Bonding as a Universal Human Need." In *Conflict: Human Needs Theory*, ed. John Burton. New York: St Martin's Press 1990.

Code, Lorraine. *Epistemic Responsibility*. Hanover and London: University Press of New England 1987.

Coontz, Stephanie. *The Way We Never Were*. New York: Basic Books 1992.

Cooper, Belinda. "Women and the Stasi." Unpublished paper, Berlin 1994.

Crews, Frederick. *The Memory Wars: Freud's Legacy in Dispute*. London: Granta Books 1997.

Dahl, Tessa. *Working for Love*. New York: Delacorte Press 1989.

Dauenhauer, B. "Hope and Its Ramifications for Politics." *Man and World* 17 (1984): 453–76.

Dennis, Wendy. *Hot and Bothered: Love and Sex in the Nineties*. Toronto: Seal Books 1992.

Dizard, Jan E., and Howard Gadlin. *The Minimal Family*. Amherst: University of Massachusetts Press 1990.

Downie, R.S. "Forgiveness." *Philosophical Quarterly* 15 (1965): 128–34.

– *Roles and Values*. London: Methuen 1971.

Eisler, Riane. *The Chalice and the Blade: Our History, Our Future*. San Francisco: Harper Collins 1988.

Elon, Amos. "East Germany: Crime and Punishment." *New York Review of Books*, 14 May 1992, 6–11.

Erikson, Erik. *Childhood and Society*. New York: Norton 1950.

Fisher, Roger, and Scott Brown. *Getting Together*. Boston: Houghton Mifflin 1988.

Flanigan, Beverly. *Forgiving the Unforgivable: Overcoming the Bitter Legacy of Intimate Wounds*. New York: Collier Books, Macmillan 1994.

Foster, George. "Peasant Society and the Image of the Limited Good." *American Anthropologist* 67 (1965): 293–315.

Franklin, Satya Bharti. *The Promise of Paradise: A Woman's Intimate Story of the Perils of Life with Rajneesh*. Barrytown, NY: Station Hill Press 1992.

Friedman, Marilyn. "Friendship and Moral Growth." In *What are Friends For?* ed. Marilyn Friedman. Ithaca: Cornell University Press 1993.

Fukuyama, Francis. *Trust: The Social Virtues and the Creation of Prosperity.* London: Hamish Hamilton 1995.

Gandhi, Mahatma. *Collected Works of Mahatma Gandhi.* Vol. 22. New Delhi: Publications Division, Ministry of Information and Broadcasting.

- *The Way to Communal Harmony.* Comp. and ed. U.R. Rao. Ahmedabad: Ahmedabad Navajivan Publishing House 1963.

- *Young India,* 26 December 1924.

Goffman, Erving. *The Presentation of Self in Everyday Life.* New York: Anchor 1959.

- *Relations in Public: Microstudies of the Public Order.* New York: Harper and Row 1970.

Gordon, Haim. *Dance, Dialogue, and Despair: Existential Philosophy and Education for Peace in Israel.* Tuscaloosa, Ala.: University of Alabama Press 1986.

Govier, Katherine. *Angel Walk.* Toronto: Little Brown 1996.

Govier, Trudy. "Belief, Values, and the Will," *Dialogue.* 1976.

- "Distrust as a Practical Problem." *Journal of Social Philosophy* 23 (1992): 52–63.

- "How We Trust Ourselves and What Happens When We Don't." *Cogito* 1991: 145–53.

- "Self-Trust, Autonomy and Self-Esteem." *Hypatia* 8 (1993): 99–120.

- *Social Trust and Human Communities.* Kingston and Montreal: McGill-Queen's University Press 1997.

- "Trust, Distrust, and Feminist Theory." *Hypatia* 7 (1992): 16–32.

- "When Logic Meets Politics: Prejudice, Distrust, and Rhetorical Credibility." *Informal Logic* 15 (1993): 93–104.

Grant, Rebecca, and Kathleen Newland. *Gender and International Relations.* Bloomington, Ind.: Indiana University Press 1991.

Gratton, Mary Carolyn. "A Theoretical-Empirical Study of the Lived Experience of Interpersonal Trust." Doctoral dissertation, Duquesne University 1975.

Greenwald, Anthony C. "The Totalitarian Ego: Fabrication and Revision of Personal History." *American Psychologist* 35 (1980): 603–13.

Gustafson, Dave. "Incest: The Theft of Childhood." *Interaction* 3 (1991): 12–13.

Hanen, Marsha, and Kai Nielsen, eds. *Science, Morality and Feminist Theory. Canadian Journal of Philosophy,* supplementary volume 13. Calgary, Alta: University of Calgary Press 1987.

Hardin, Russell. "The Street Level Epistemology of Trust." *Analyse und Kritik* 14 (1992): 152–76.

- "Trustworthiness." *Ethics* 107 (1996): 26–42.

Harre, Rom. *Varieties of Realism.* Oxford: Basil Blackwell 1986.

Harvey, Jean. "Forgiveness as an Obligation of the Moral Life." *International Journal of Moral and Social Studies* 8 (1993): 211–21.

Havel, Vaclav. "New Year's Address 1990." *Globe and Mail,* 24 January 1990.

Held, Virginia. "On the Meaning of Trust." *Ethics* 78 (1968): 156–9.

Hertzberg, Lars. "On the Attitude of Trust." *Inquiry* 31 (1988): 307–22.

Hildebrand, Kathleen. "The Mythic Enemy in the American Dream." Master's thesis, University of Calgary 1991.

Holmes, John G., with John K. Rempel and Mark P. Zanna. "Trust in Close Relationships." *Journal of Personality and Social Psychology* 49 (1985): 95–112.

Holmgren, Margaret. "Forgiveness and the Intrinsic Value of Persons." *American Philosophical Quarterly* 30 (1993): 341–51.

Horsburgh, H.J.N. "The Ethics of Trust." *Philosophical Quarterly* 10 (1960): 343–54.

– "Forgiveness." *Canadian Journal of Philosophy* 4 (1974): 269–82.

Hudner, John, and Lindsey Gruson. *Monkey on a Stick: Murder, Madness, and the Hare Krishnas.* New York: Penguin 1988.

Hughes, Paul M. "Moral Anger, Forgiving, and Condoning." *Journal of Social Philosophy* 25 (1995): 103–18.

Hutter, Horst. *Politics as Friendship: The Origins of Classical Notions of Politics in the Theory and Practice of Friendship.* Waterloo, Ont.: Wilfrid Laurier University Press 1978.

Isaacs, K.S., with James M. Alexander and Ernest A. Haggard. "Faith, Trust, and Gullibility." *International Journal of Psychoanalysis* 44 (1967): 461–9.

Jackson, James O. "Germany: State of Treachery." *Time*, 3 February 1992, 16–19.

Johnson, Paul. *Modern Times.* New York: Harper and Row 1983.

Jones, Edward E. "Interpreting Interpersonal Behavior: The Effect of Expectancies." *Science* 234 (1985): 41–6.

Jones, Karen. "Trust as an Affective Attitude." *Ethics* 107 (1996): 4–25.

Kahn, Peter H., Jr., and Elliot Turiel. "Children's Conceptions of Trust." American Educational Research Association, San Francisco, 26–30 April 1986. ERIC document no. ED271205.

Kaminer, Wendy. *I'm Dysfunctional, You're Dysfunctional.* Reading, Mass.: Addison Wesley 1992.

Kohn, Alfie. *No Contest: The Case against Competition: Why We Lose in Our Race to Win.* Boston: Houghton Mifflin 1986.

Kramer, Janet. "Letter from Europe." *New Yorker*, 25 May 1992.

Kripke, Saul. *Wittgenstein on Rules and Private Language.* Cambridge, Mass.: Harvard University Press 1982.

Kulik, James A. "Confirmatory Attribution and the Perpetuation of Social Beliefs." *Journal of Personality and Social Psychology* 44 (1983): 1171–81.

Kupfer, Joseph. "Can Parents and Children Be Friends?" *American Philosophical Quarterly* 27 (1990): 15–26.

Kymlicka, Will. *Liberalism, Community, and Culture.* Oxford: Clarendon Press 1989.

Lang, Berel. "Forgiveness." *American Philosophical Quarterly* 31 (1994): 105–15.

Lauritzen, Paul. "Forgiveness: Moral Prerogative or Religious Duty?" *Journal of Religious Ethics* 15 (1987): 151–4.

Le Doeuff, Michelle. *Hipparchia's Choice: An Essay Concerning Women, Philosophy, Etc.* Trans. Trista Selous. Oxford: Basil Blackwell 1991.

Lerner, Harriet Goldor. *The Dance of Deception: Pretending and Truth Telling in Women's Lives.* New York: Harper Collins 1993.

Levi, Primo. *The Drowned and the Saved.* Trans. Raymond Rosenthal. New York: Vintage International 1988.

Lewis, J. David, and Andrew Weigert. "Trust as a Social Reality." *Social Forces* 63 (1985): 967–85.

Logstrup, Knud Ejler. *The Ethical Demand.* Trans. Fru Marie Logstrup. Introd. Hans Fink and Alasdair MacIntyre. Notre Dame: University of Notre Dame Press 1997.

Lord, Bette Bao. *Legacies: A Chinese Mosaic.* New York: Knopf 1990.

Luhmann, Niklas. *Trust and Power.* Trans. H. Davies, J.F. Raffman, and Kathryn Rooney. London: John Wiley and Sons 1979.

McGary, Howard. "Forgiveness." *American Philosophical Quarterly* 26 (1989): 343–51.

Malone, Thomas Patrick, and Patrick Thomas Malone. *The Art of Intimacy.* New York: Prentice Hall 1987.

Masson, Jeffrey Moussaieff. *The Assault on Truth: Freud's Suppression of the Seduction Theory.* New York: Farrar, Straus and Giroux 1984.

Mayeroff, Milton. *On Caring.* New York: Harper and Row 1971.

Meyers, Diana T. *Self, Society, and Personal Choice.* New York: Columbia University Press 1989.

– Kenneth Kipnis, and Cornelius Murphy, eds. *Kindred Matters: Rethinking the Philosophy of the Family.* Ithaca: Cornell University Press 1993.

Michalos, Alex. "The Impact of Trust on Business, International Security, and the Quality of Life." *Journal of Business Ethics* 9 (1990): 619–38.

Miller, Alice. *The Drama of the Gifted Child: The Search for the True Self.* Trans. Ruth Ward. New York: Basic Books, 1994.

Morgan, George W. "On Trusting." *Humanitas* 9 (1973): 237–51.

Murphy, Jeffrie G. "Forgiveness and Resentment." *Midwest Studies in Philosophy* 7 (1982): 503–26.

– ed. *Punishment and Rehabilitation.* 3rd ed. Belmont, Calif.: Wadsworth 1995.

– and Jean Hampton. *Forgiveness and Mercy.* Cambridge: Cambridge University Press 1988.

Newman, Louise. "The Quality of Mercy: On the Duty to Forgive in the Judaic Tradition." *Journal of Religious Ethics* 15 (1987): 155–72.

Noddings, Nel. *Caring: A Feminine Approach to Ethics and Moral Education.* Berkeley and Los Angeles: University of California Press 1984.

North, Joanna. "Wrongdoing and Forgiveness." *Philosophy* 1987: 499–508.

Okin, Susan Moller. *Justice, Gender, and the Family.* New York: Basic Books 1989.

Orbach, Susie, and Luise Eichenbaum. *Bittersweet: Facing Up to Feelings of Love, Envy, and Competition in Women's Friendships*. London: Century 1987.

– *What Do Women Want?* New York: Berkeley Books 1983 .

Pittman, Frank. *Private Lies: Infidelity and the Betrayal of Intimacy*. New York: W.W. Norton 1989.

Pogrebin, Letty Cottin. *Among Friends: Who We Like, Why We Like Them, and What We Do with Them*. New York: McGraw Hill, 1987.

Poster, Mark. *Critical Theory of the Family*. New York: Seabury Press 1978.

Putnam, Robert. *Making Democracy Work: Civic Traditions in Modern Italy*. Princeton: Princeton University Press 1993.

Pye, Lucian. "China: Erratic State, Frustrated Society." *Foreign Affairs* 69: 56–74.

Rawlins, William K., and Melissa Holl. "The Communicative Achievement of Friendship during Adolescence: Predicaments of Trust and Violation." *Western Journal of Speech Communication* 52 (1987): 345–63.

Rawls, John. *A Theory of Justice*. Cambridge, Mass.: Harvard University Press 1971.

Rempel, John, with John Holmes and Mark Zanna. "Trust in Close Relationships." *Journal of Personality and Social Psychology* 49 (1985): 95–112.

Richards, Norwin. "Forgiveness." *Ethics* 99 (1989): 77–97.

Rogers, Carl R. *On Becoming a Person: A Therapist's View of Psychotherapy*. Boston: Houghton Mifflin 1961.

– *A Way of Being*. Boston: Houghton Mifflin 1980.

Rosenberg, Tina. *The Haunted Land: Facing Europe's Ghosts after Communism*. New York: Random House 1995.

Rotter, Julian. "Generalized Expectations for Interpersonal Trust." *Journal of Personality* 35 (1967): 615–54.

– "Interpersonal Trust, Trustworthiness, and Gullibility." *American Psychologist* 35 (1980): 1–17.

Rubin, Lillian. *Intimate Strangers: Men and Women Together*. New York: Harper and Row 1983.

Scheff, Thomas J. *Bloody Revenge: Emotions, Nationalism, and War*. Boulder: Westview Press 1994.

Schmookler, Andrew Bard. *Out of Weakness: Healing the Wounds That Drive Us to War*. Toronto, New York: Bantam Books 1988.

– *The Parable of the Tribes: The Problem of Power in Social Evolution*. Boston: Houghton Mifflin 1984.

Seligman, Martin E. *Learned Optimism*. New York: Alfred A. Knopf 1991.

Sellerberg, Ann-Mari. "On Modern Confidence." *Acta Sociologica* 25 (1982): 39–48.

Shapin, Steven. *A Social History of Truth: Civility and Science in Seventeenth Century England*. Chicago: University of Chicago Press 1994.

Sharp, Gene. *Gandhi as a Political Strategist*. Boston: Porter Sargent Publications 1979.

Shriver, Donald W. *An Ethic for Enemies: Forgiveness in Politics.* New York: Oxford University Press 1995.

Snyder, Mark. "When Belief Creates Reality." *Advances in Experimental Social Psychology* 18 (1984): 2247–305.

– and Seymour W. Uranowitz, "Reconstructing the Past: Some Cognitive Consequences of Person Perception." *Journal of Personality and Social Psychology* 36 (1978): 941–50.

Strickwerda, Robert, and Larry May. "Male Friendship and Intimacy." *Hypatia* 7 (1992): 110–25.

Tannen, Deborah. *You Just Don't Understand: Men and Women in Conversation.* New York: Ballantine 1990.

Tavris, Carol. *The Mismeasure of Woman.* New York: Simon and Schuster 1992.

Telfer, Elizabeth. "Friendship." *Aristotelian Society Proceedings* 71 (1970): 223–41.

Thayer, Nancy. *My Dearest Friend.* New York: Macmillan 1989.

Thomas, D.O. "The Duty to Trust." *Proceedings of the Aristotelian Society* 79 (1978): 89–101.

Thomas, Laurence. *Living Morally: A Psychology of Moral Character.* Philadelphia: Temple University Press 1989.

– "Next Life I'll be White." *Globe and Mail*, 16 August 1990.

– "Statistical Badness." *Journal of Social Philosophy* 23 (1992): 30–41.

– "Trust, Affirmation, and Moral Character: A Critique of Kantian Morality." In *Identity, Character and Morality*, ed. Owen Flanagan and Amelie Oksenberg Rorty, 235–57. Cambridge, Mass.: Bradford Books 1991.

Thorne, Barrie, and Marilyn Yalom, eds. *Rethinking the Family: Some Feminist Questions.* Boston: Northeastern University Press, 1992.

Trevor-Roper, Hugh. *The Hermit of Peking.* Harmondsworth, England: Penguin 1976.

Updike, John. *Trust Me.* New York: Fawcett Crest 1962.

Waal, Francis de. *Peacemaking among Primates.* Cambridge, Mass.: Harvard University Press 1989.

Waring, Marilyn. *If Women Counted: A New Feminist Economics.* San Francisco: Harper San Francisco 1988.

Winnicott, D.W. *The Family and Individual Development.* London: Tavistock Publications 1965.

Wittgenstein, Ludwig. *On Certainty.* Oxford: Basil Blackwell 1969.

– *Philosophical Investigations.* Oxford: Basil Blackwell 1953.

Zand, Dale E. "Trust and Managerial Problem Solving." *Administrative Science Quarterly* 17 (1972): 229–39.

Index